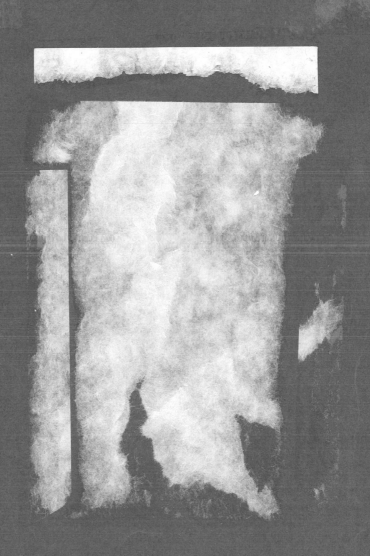

4

The Psychologically Battered Child

*Strategies for Identification,
Assessment, and Intervention*

James Garbarino
Edna Guttmann
Janis Wilson Seeley

The Psychologically
Battered Child

Jossey-Bass Publishers

San Francisco · London · 1986

THE PSYCHOLOGICALLY BATTERED CHILD
Strategies for Identification, Assessment, and Intervention
by James Garbarino, Edna Guttmann, Janis Wilson Seeley

Copyright © 1986 by: Jossey-Bass Inc., Publishers
433 California Street
San Francisco, California 94104

&

Jossey-Bass Limited
28 Banner Street
London EC1Y 8QE

362.7044
G213p

Library of Congress Cataloging-in-Publication Data

Garbarino, James.
   The psychologically battered child.

   (The Jossey-Bass social and behavioral science series)
   Bibliography: p. 249
   Includes index.
   1. Child abuse—United States.   2. Child abuse—
United States—Psychological aspects.   3. Child abuse—
United States—Psychological aspects—Prevention.
4. Parent and child—United States.   I. Guttmann,
Edna.   II. Seeley, Janis Wilson.   III. Title.
IV. Series. [DNLM: 1. Child Abuse.   2. Stress,
Psychological—in infancy & childhood. WA 320 G213p]
HV6626.5.B37   1986   362.7'044   86-10536
ISBN 1-55542-002-8

Manufactured in the United States of America

The paper in this book meets the guidelines for
permanence and durability of the Committee on
Production Guidelines for Book Longevity of the
Council on Library Resources.

JACKET DESIGN BY WILLI BAUM

FIRST EDITION

Code 8631

The Jossey-Bass
Social and Behavioral Science Series

To Irving B. Harris and Muriel F. Smith,
two tireless advocates for children

Preface

When the U.S. Congress enacted the first federal child abuse and neglect treatment and prevention act in the mid 1970s, it was giving voice to a movement that had its roots in the nineteenth century. The impulse to protect children from abuse and exploitation took shape in the 1800s in the efforts of "child savers" who sought to remove children from dangerous environments and depraved caregivers. This movement addressed a host of issues— child labor, primary education, health care, foster care, and adoption. It led to the first White House Conference on Children, held under the auspices of President Theodore Roosevelt, in the first decade of this century. Although the early reformers were concerned with the mind, spirit, and heart of the child, child protective service agencies since then have tended to focus on the physical neglect and abuse and sexual exploitation that is easiest to document.

As American society has come to terms with child abuse and neglect, one after another related issue has come to the forefront. Since the "battered child syndrome" captured public and professional attention in the 1970s, child sexual abuse has emerged as a matter of grave concern. One outcome of the exposure of these problems has been a clear recognition that damage can result from abuse and neglect, even when no physical harm is done. Indeed, psychological harm is now the principal issue in almost all cases requiring intervention. As a result, psychological maltreatment is currently a topic of significant concern among professionals and the public.

Most professionals have long believed that psychological maltreatment is a significant social issue. But the lack of research and theory, which would give clear guidance on the basic threats to development, and the difficulties involved in defining psychological maltreatment have seemed insurmountable problems. Consequently, the consensus among professionals as well as the general public has been that psychological maltreatment must remain a peripheral issue for the day-to-day practice and jurisdiction of protective service intervention. This book is a response to that need for formal delineation of the problem.

The Psychologically Battered Child presents our efforts to define psychological maltreatment and to link that definition to intervention—both prevention and treatment. It is designed to help the professional who is caught in the bind of knowing that psychological maltreatment and harm are the core issues in most child protective work but who feels that the basis for proceeding with action is weak and obscure. The book begins with a look at the issues involved in distinguishing psychological from other forms of child maltreatment. It then offers a definition of psychological maltreatment that comprises five categories: terrorizing, isolating, ignoring, rejecting, and corrupting. The book illuminates these categories through case examples and explains their implications for identification, assessment, and intervention. Our emphasis throughout is on parent-child relations, although we also include material on psychological maltreatment in out-of-home situations and discuss a variety of public policy issues that bear on this topic.

Who Should Read This Book?

We have written this book for professionals and for professionals in training. It is designed to apply to a wide variety of theoretical and therapeutic orientations. Practitioners in child mental health, family therapy, parent counseling, child development, and parent-child relations will find this book useful in defining their professional missions in cases of psychological maltreatment. It will also equip them with tools for carrying out effective intervention.

Because it couples wide-ranging conceptual discussion with practical application (that is, specific techniques for assessment and intervention), the book can serve as a resource in the education and training of professionals in a wide range of disciplines, including psychology, social work, counseling, and nursing. By introducing a set of specific cases early in the text and developing them throughout the volume, the book presents an integrated picture of how theory and practice work hand in hand.

This book will also serve the needs of sophisticated lay volunteers seeking guidance in how to approach the problem of psychological maltreatment of children from the point of view of community-based prevention and family support programs.

Overview of the Contents

Chapter One offers an exploration of the issues involved in defining psychological maltreatment. It dissects the historical impediments to definition and reveals how the field of child abuse and neglect has matured to a point where it can handle the challenges of psychological maltreatment as an "actionable category" in protective services. This first chapter explores the broad developmental and epistemological concerns surrounding the issue of definition. It also presents a five-category definition that includes terrorizing, isolating, ignoring, rejecting, and corrupting as facets of psychological maltreatment.

Chapter Two explicates the operational definition through analysis of twenty case studies. Most important, it places the definition in a developmental perspective, illustrating each type of psychological maltreatment across and within child developmental stages from infancy to adolescence.

Chapters Three and Four discuss the concepts and applications of exploratory identification and assessment. We offer a broad selection of techniques and strategies for identification and assessment that apply to nested systems of interaction within the family as well as to the community and its host culture. The challenge of linking parental behavior to child outcomes is a major theme throughout this discussion.

In Chapters Five, Six, and Seven we focus the "ecological" perspective presented in earlier chapters on the issues of intervention in three areas: the broad social environment; the family, with individual members; and the institutional network of social services. Here we link exploratory assessment to the diversity of resources for family intervention that exist in contrasting communities. Recognizing that resources for assessment and intervention differ markedly from place to place and from case to case, we try to present a range of alternatives, with some guidance on selecting from what is available and on building resources.

Chapters Eight and Nine deal with psychological maltreatment in out-of-home care settings, such as day care centers and residential institutions. Chapter Eight presents our analysis of definition and identification while Chapter Nine addresses assessment and intervention. Throughout these chapters we emphasize "generic" issues—that is, issues common to psychological maltreatment in the family *and* in out-of-home care—while we focus on the special challenges imposed by the out-of-home setting, such as raising children to be fully functioning adults when there is an initial disadvantage to cope with.

In the Afterword, we briefly consider the likely future of attempts to deal with psychological maltreatment. We believe that progress is necessary to society's efforts to improve the quality of life for children and that progress is a realistic expectation, based on what we have accomplished thus far. We recognize that the same process is involved in defining and acting on a concept of psychological maltreatment as has been employed in dealing with physical and sexual maltreatment. Definition is fundamentally a matter of blending active community beliefs about what children deserve out of life (and indeed what it means to be a child) with professional knowledge about how parent-child relationships work (and why they sometimes do not).

This book contains four resources that will be useful to readers who wish to carry their ideas forward into action. The first, following this Preface, is the list of experts who served as our review panel during the writing of this volume. They may be consulted as resource persons by readers who need advice beyond what we offer in this book. At the end of the book, Resource A presents information about the instruments we discuss in Chapter Four and describes some additional ones. Resource B offers names and addresses of a variety of organizations active in the child welfare and child protection field. Resource C lists contact points for the chapters of the National Committee for Prevention of Child Abuse, the leading citizen group concerned with child abuse prevention.

This book reflects a decade of study and discussion on the topic of psychological maltreatment. It also reflects our efforts (funded by grant number of OH DS 90-CJ-0072 from the Department of Health and Human Services, Administration on Children, Youth and Families) to synthesize ideas about the meaning and origins of child development and the threats to development that are posed by harsh, cold, negativistic, or morally inappropriate treatment of children by parents, family members, and others. Having formulated a concept of psychological maltreatment as "assault on the psyche," we have striven to determine the implications of this formulation for intervention. The result is this volume.

In preparing this book we had access to a group of professionals and lay volunteers who are active in the field of child abuse and neglect. Their expertise in clinical, prevention, assessment, and research methodologies is extensive, and we have drawn upon their wide-ranging knowledge. The review panel took on the task of critiquing the outline for this manuscript and the preliminary draft of it. Their comments and suggestions were very useful to us as we attempted to shed some light on this complex and difficult topic. We assume final responsibility for the outcome of our efforts, of course, but we thank the review panel for their help.

We also thank Alice Saxion and Joy Barger, the support staff at Pennsylvania State University's Department of Individual and Family Studies, for helping us complete this manuscript.

July 1986   James Garbarino
                                            Chicago, Illinois

                                            Edna Guttmann
                                            Haifa, Israel

                                            Janis Wilson Seeley
                                            University Park, Pennsylvania

Contents

㋡ ㋡ ㋡ ㋡

The Authors

James Garbarino is president of the Erikson Institute for Advanced
Study in Child Development, in Chicago, Illinois. He received his
B.A. degree (1968) from St. Lawrence University in liberal arts, his
M.A.T. degree (1970) from Cornell University in social studies
education, and his Ph.D. degree (1973) from Cornell University in
human development and families studies.

   Garbarino's main research activities have been in issues of
applied human development and child welfare, particularly child
abuse and neglect. He is the author of more than sixty articles and
chapters dealing with child welfare, social development, and
education. His books include *Understanding Abusive Families*
(1980), *Protecting Children from Abuse and Neglect* (1980),
Children and Families in the Social Environment (1982), *Successful Schools and Competent Students* (1981), *Social Support
Networks* (1983), and *Troubled Youth, Troubled Families* (1986).

   In 1985, he was the first recipient of the National Conference on Child Abuse and Neglect's C. Henry Kempe Award for
outstanding professional contribution to the field of preventing
and treating child maltreatment. In 1980 and again in 1982 he
received the Mitchell Prize for essays dealing with the future of the
family in a changing economic and ecological context. In 1981 he
received a Silver Award from the International Film and Television Festival of New York for coauthoring the film "Don't Get
Stuck There; A Film on Adolescent Abuse." From 1975 to 1978 he
was a National Academy of Education Spencer Fellow, and from
1981 to 1984 he was a Kellogg Foundation National Fellow. His

1981 book *Successful Schools and Competent Students* received an Outstanding Book Award from the American Library Association.

Garbarino was director of the Maltreatment of Youth Project at the Boys Town Center for the Study of Youth Development from 1976 to 1979. As a member of the Board of Directors of the National Committee for Prevention of Child Abuse he chaired the Research and Program Evaluation Committee. From 1979 to 1985 he was a member of the faculty in the Department of Individual and Family Studies in the College of Human Development at Pennsylvania State University.

Edna Guttmann is a doctoral candidate in human development and family studies at Pennsylvania State University. She received her B.A. degree (1982) from the University of Haifa in Israel, in social work, and her M.A. degree (1985) from the University of Minnesota in family social science.

Guttmann's main professional activities have been in social work in general and in child and youth care work in particular, as they both relate to child and adolescent development and to the professional development of practitioners in this area. The research she has been and is involved with is ecological in nature and deals with the professional characteristics of social work practice and residential child and youth care, and with the development of children and youth as it differs across contexts of living. She has field experience in social work and residential youth work in Israel. Her publications, many coauthored with Zvi Eisikovits, from Haifa, Israel, include articles and chapters on the topics she is researching.

Janis Wilson Seeley is a doctoral candidate in human development and family studies at Pennsylvania State University. She received her B.A. degree (1978) from Kutztown State College in social sciences, with a concentration in social welfare, and her M.S. degree (1982) from the University of Maryland in family and community development.

Seeley's professional experience and research has focused on adolescent development and services to adolescents. She has worked as a counselor with runaway youth, educationally disadvantaged youth, and substance abusers. Seeley has also taught parenting skills and life skills to diverse populations including pregnant adolescents and teenage parents. Her research has focused on the issues of runaway youth and adolescent sexuality and pregnancy. She has written a chapter on runaways with James Garbarino and Anne Garbarino in the book *Troubled Youth, Troubled Families* (1986).

Advisory Panel

Richard Birkel
Pennsylvania State University
University Park, Pennsylvania

Marla Brassard
University of Georgia
Athens, Georgia

Dante Cicchetti
University of Rochester
Rochester, New York

Anne Cohn
National Committee for
    Prevention of Child Abuse
Chicago, Illinois

Bronwyn Della-Volpe-Robbins
Reading, Massachusetts

Paul DiLorenzo
Support Center for Child
    Advocates
Philadelphia, Pennsylvania

Byron Egeland
University of Minnesota
Minneapolis, Minnesota

M. Jerome Fialkov
Western Psychiatric Institute
Pittsburgh, Pennsylvania

Betty Friedlander
Tompkins County Court
Ithaca, New York

Robert Friedman
University of South Florida
Tampa, Florida

Ellen Gray
National Committee for
    Prevention of Child Abuse
Chicago, Illinois

Joann Grayson
James Madison University
Harrisonburg, Virginia

Tom Gregory
Boys Town, Nebraska

Bernard Guerney
Pennsylvania State University
University Park, Pennsylvania

Louise Guerney
Pennsylvania State University
University Park, Pennsylvania

Suzanne Hardin
Metro Council on Emotional
    Maltreatment
Kansas City, Missouri

Stuart Hart
Indiana University
Indianapolis, Indiana

Walter Jenewicz
Summit County Childrens
    Services Board
Akron, Ohio

Joanne Kassees
Parents Anonymous of
    Delaware
Wilmington, Delaware

Jill Korbin
Case Western Reserve
    University
Cleveland, Ohio

Ira Lourie
National Institute of Mental
    Health
Rockville, Maryland

W. Douglas McCoard
Huckleberry House
Columbus, Ohio

Susan McHale
Pennsylvania State University
University Park, Pennsylvania

Marie McManmon
Pasadena, California

Norman Polansky
University of Georgia
Athens, Georgia

Nolan Rindfleisch
Ohio State University
Columbus, Ohio

Ronald Rohner
University of Connecticut
Storrs, Connecticut

David Sandberg
Boston University
Boston, Massachusetts

William Tolan
The Meadows Clinic
Centre Hall, Pennsylvania

Alice Udall
Tucson, Arizona

Carolyn Van Buren
Barron County Special
    Education Center
Rice Lake, Wisconsin

Ralph Welsen
Bridgeport, Connecticut

Joan Vondra
University of Rochester
Rochester, New York

❈ ❈ ❈ ❈

The Psychologically Battered Child

*Strategies for Identification,
Assessment, and Intervention*

❃ 1 ❃

What Is Psychological Maltreatment?

- Each morning a mother threatens her four-year-old son with abandonment: "Maybe today is the day I go away and leave you alone. You'd better be good today, boy, or you'll never see me again."
- A father restricts his seven-year-old daughter to her room every day after school: "I don't want you getting involved with other kids; they're not good enough for you."
- Each time a ten-year-old brings home his report card from school, his parents look it over with expressions of disgust: "No son of ours could be such a dummy. We wish you weren't around all the time reminding us of the mistake we made."
- A three-year-old boy's father suspects that he is not the boy's father, that the boy's mother had an affair while he was away on business. Now he refuses to speak with the boy: "He's not mine; I don't want anything to do with him."
- A mother persuades her thirteen-year-old daughter to earn some money by having sex with the mother's "extra" boyfriends: "You're a little slut anyway, and I might as well get something out of being your mother."

All these parents are psychologically maltreating their children. What they are doing and saying jeopardizes the development of self-esteem, of social competence, of the capacity for intimacy, of positive and healthy interpersonal relationships. We know this in a general sense. We know that these five children are in danger. We know that they and their families need help. But what exactly is the problem? How do we relate these five cases of severe psychological maltreatment to the broader range of

1

behaviors that pose a threat to the emotional and intellectual development of the child?

It has been traditional in the field of protective services to differentiate between child "abuse" and child "neglect." The former term is usually defined to include direct actions by a parent or guardian that assault the child physically, sexually, or emotionally. The latter term typically is used to include failure to provide essential care. Abuse, neglect. Acts of commission, acts of omission. This conventional dichotomy is evident in previous efforts to define *psychological* maltreatment as well.

Researchers and theorists have offered several definitions of psychological maltreatment. Whiting (1976, p. 4), summarizing the results of community workshops that sought to define emotional neglect, reports these definitions: (1)"Emotional neglect is a result of subtle or blatant acts of omission or commission experienced by the child, which causes handicapping stress on the child and is manifested in patterns of inappropriate behavior. Court intervention may be applicable if a parent fails to recognize the need for or accept help or change." (2)"[Emotional neglect occurs when] meaningful adults [are unable] to provide necessary nurturance, stimulation, encouragement, and protection to the child at various stages of development, which inhibits his optimal functioning." Whiting concludes, however, that emotional neglect should be distinguished from emotional abuse. In her view, the term "emotional neglect" applies when parents resist or refuse cooperative intervention for a child diagnosed as emotionally disturbed. When deliberate parental action has caused emotional disturbance, the term "emotional abuse" is appropriate. More recently the Office for Study of the Psychological Rights of the Child (Hart, 1985) has taken this tack as well by formulating the concept of "mental health neglect" to apply to such situations.

Lourie and Stefano (1978), reporting on a workshop sponsored by the National Institute of Mental Health, also conclude that a two-level definition is necessary. In their view, mental health professionals need a broad definition, whereas those involved in legal action "against" perpetrators need a more explicit and limited definition to avoid having legal actions dismissed on grounds of vagueness. Their clinical definition focuses on "mental injury": "an injury to the intellectual or psychological capacity of a child, as evidenced by an observable and substantial impairment in his or her ability to function within his or her normal range of performance and behavior with due regard to his or her culture" (p. 203). Their legal definition, though vague, narrows the clinical definition to the most severe forms coupled with the absence of parental willingness or capacity to cooperate voluntarily in remediation.

In this book we have chosen to bypass the dichotomy between abuse and neglect. To be sure, some acts of psychological maltreatment are active in nature—verbal assaults, clearly intentional efforts to undermine the child's sense of self. Others seem more passive, reflecting a withdrawal from interaction. But the "active"/"passive" abuse/neglect distinction may obscure the multifaceted nature of much psychological maltreatment. For example, the actively abusive act of rejecting a child is linked to a withdrawal of attention in some cases but an increase in verbal assault in others. Though rooted in research, practice, and theory, the abuse/neglect distinction is, we believe, better replaced with the broader concept of child maltreatment. We adopt that stance with the recognition that in reviewing the work of other investigators and practitioners we may have to return to references to abuse and neglect separately to make sense of the findings. The first occasion for so doing comes when we turn to the definitions offered by state and federal government through laws and policies.

Some official definitions exist at both the federal and state levels in the various child abuse and neglect laws. For example, Pennsylvania's law (Act 124, 1975), often cited as exemplary, includes "serious mental injury" as part of the definition of an "abused child." Regulations to implement the Act define "serious mental injury" as

a psychological condition as determined by a psychiatrist, psychologist, or pediatrician apparently caused by acts or omissions of a parent or person responsible for a child (including the refusal of appropriate treatment) which: (1) renders the child chronically and severely anxious, agitated, depressed, socially withdrawn, psychotic, or in reasonable fear that his/her life and/

or safety is threatened; (2) makes it extremely likely that the child
will become chronically and severely anxious, agitated, depressed,
socially withdrawn, psychotic, or be in reasonable fear that his/her
life is threatened; or (3) seriously interferes with the child's ability
to accomplish age-appropriate developmental milestones, or
school, peer, and community tasks [Commonwealth of Pennsylvania, Department of Public Welfare, Child Protective Services,
Social Services Manual, section 2-23-41, 1976].

On the basis of her work with spousal abuse, which has
many similarities to child abuse, Walker (1984) offers a list based
on a model of "psychological torture" that includes "violence
correlates"—among them, physical attacks on the victim's
possessions, pets, plants, and loved ones—and "psychological
torture" in the form of isolation, induced debility (sleep and food
deprivation), monopolizing of perceptions, verbal degradation (for
instance, name calling or humiliation), hypnosis, drugs to alter
consciousness, threats to kill, and occasional indulgences.

Lest we appear to be reinventing the wheel as we struggle to
define psychological maltreatment, we should recall that most of
the major students of human development have dealt with it as an
issue in their work. Norman Polansky (personal communication,
1985) recalls Bowlby's description of its victims: "They come from
unsettled homes in which they have been (and perhaps still are)
subject to one or more of the following: irritable scoldings,
disparaging comparisons with others, quarreling parents, threats
of abandonment or loss of love, changes from one mother figure to
another, periods of separation with strange people in strange
places." What is more, child welfare professionals have been
wrestling with the concept of "emotional neglect" for decades (see
Mulford, 1958).

The *Interdisciplinary Glossary on Child Abuse and Neglect*
(National Center on Child Abuse and Neglect, 1978) offers several
definitions that have been incorporated into survey research on the
incidence of child maltreatment. The definitions of emotional
abuse include verbal or emotional assault, close confinement, and
threatened harm. The definitions of emotional neglect include
inadequate nurturance/affection, knowingly permitting maladaptive behavior (for example, delinquency), and other refusal to

provide essential care. The federally funded National Incidence Study (Burgdorff, 1980) employed these definitions in its efforts to discover the incidence and prevalence of all forms of maltreatment across the United States through an intensive search in twenty-six representative counties. It found that 2.2 per 1,000 children were subjected to emotional abuse and that 1.0 per 1,000 children were victims of emotional neglect.

Although the definitions employed by the National Incidence Study help quantify the problem of psychological maltreatment, there are objections. One objection is that the data bases underlying the assumption that psychological maltreatment exists are ambiguous. Although we all "know" that poor parental treatment produces developmental damage to children, research has been slow to document this cause-effect relationship. Emotionally disturbed children are not by definition psychologically maltreated. There are multiple possible origins for disturbed personality development.

As Lourie and Stefano (1978) have noted, children differ, often dramatically, in their responses to parental treatment; and the existence of "stress-resistant" children suggests that harsh and even hostile environments can produce pro-social, competent children (Garmezy, 1983). Indeed, some self-identified victims of psychological maltreatment testify to their apparent success in rising to the challenge and overcoming the threat that the maltreatment posed to their development (Osborne, 1985).

What is more, it is very difficult to separate out the distinctly "psychological" components of psychological abuse. How exactly do people commit psychological maltreatment? What are the behaviors, the "operational definitions," that researchers must have? What is verbal and emotional assault? How close is "close confinement"? What is inadequate nurturance and affection? What is included in "essential care"? These can be profoundly difficult questions to answer.

Any observation of psychological maltreatment depends heavily on social and cultural context. In general, it seems that behavior is considered psychologically abusive when it conveys a culture-specific message of rejection or impairs a socially relevant psychological process, such as the development of a coherent positive self-concept. Hart (personal communication, 1985) speaks of acts or omissions that "aim directly at the heart, at the self, that torpedo the ego." Erikson (1963) identifies as the principal challenge to culturally sanctioned child-rearing arrangements the task of creating a strong ego, "an individual core firm and flexible enough to reconcile the necessary contradictions in any human organization, to integrate individual differences, and above all to emerge from a long and unavoidably fearful infancy with a sense of identity and an idea of integrity" (p. 186). When families or societies sabotage this process, when they send destructive messages to children, we enter the realm of psychological maltreatment (Coopersmith, 1967). How can we understand these messages without the perceptual filter of culture? We cannot. How can we accommodate cultural and ethnic differences when defining such maltreatment (Garbarino and Ebata, 1983)? We must seek to define a set of categories general enough to reflect the universals of human nature.

Culture is not the only accommodation, however. If we are to move to an operational definition of psychological maltreatment, we must take into account a developmental perspective on the meaning and significance of behavior. Clearly, some forms of psychological maltreatment are more of an issue for young children than for adolescents, and vice versa. We may need age- or stage-specific definitions here to the same extent that we do in assessing social competence and other developmental phenomena. This issue blends with the issue of assessing severity. Is severity affected by developmental status? Are more developmentally advanced children more resistant to some forms of psychological maltreatment but more vulnerable to others? For example, are cognitively sophisticated children more vulnerable to subtle insult than unsophisticated children? Are infants more vulnerable to being ignored than adolescents?

The preceding catalogue of issues and questions demonstrates the formidable scientific, clinical, and policy challenges implicit in any effort to move psychological maltreatment to the forefront of mental health, child welfare, and protective service concerns. Yet, the advantages of psychological maltreatment as a central concept transcend the conceptual and technical challenges.

Interestingly, each advantage seems to convert a liability into a benefit.

First, the very "problem" that the socioemotional consequences of acts largely define the acts themselves turns psychological maltreatment into the central issue in most child welfare considerations. Preserving the physical organism is vital, of course. It is a necessary precondition for child welfare to exist. However, once physical survival is assured, the *subjective* reality of child development is the primary concern. How do children think and feel about themselves and their world? How do they define the treatment they receive at the hands of their parents and guardians? Bronfenbrenner (1979, p. 55) defines development in just such social psychological terms: "The developmental status of the individual is reflected in the substantive variety and structural complexity of the . . . activities which he imitates and maintains in the absence of instigation or direction by others." The core issue is self, in the sense of ego strength, self-concept, and social competence. ✳

Rather than casting psychological maltreatment as an ancillary issue, subordinate to other forms of abuse and neglect, we should place it as the centerpiece of efforts to understand family functioning and to protect children. In almost all cases, it is the psychological consequences of an act that define that act as abusive. This is true of physical abuse (consider, for example, the meaning to a child of an injury inflicted by a parent in rage compared with the same "injury" inflicted by accident in the course of an athletic event, recreation, or even medical attention); it is also true of sexual abuse (since sexual acts have little or no intrinsic meaning apart from their social psychological connotations—as the incredible variety of norms regarding sexual activity in childhood and adolescence across cultures suggests).

In our discussions we assume that the direct physical dangers involved in physical maltreatment and the moral dangers inherent in sexual exploitation are being dealt with by medical and protective services (including the criminal justice system). Our concern is with the specifically psychological dimensions of the problem, since they are the province of mental health, education, and social work professionals. To that extent our concern is limited in its social and cultural scope. However, as investigators who have carefully explored families involved in maltreatment report, rarely does one form of maltreatment occur alone (physical abuse without psychological abuse; sexual assault in the absence of emotional threat). When one form of maltreatment does exist in isolation from others, it is likely to be psychological in nature. Rarely if ever does a child experience physical abuse or neglect, or sexual assault or exploitation, in a relationship that is positive and nurturing. Indeed, even to pose the matter in such terms seems ridiculous.

In our definition, psychological maltreatment is a concerted attack by an adult on a child's development of self and social competence, a *pattern* of psychically destructive behavior, and it takes five forms:

> *Rejecting* (the adult refuses to acknowledge the child's worth and the legitimacy of the child's needs).
>
> *Isolating* (the adult cuts the child off from normal social experiences, prevents the child from forming friendships, and makes the child believe that he or she is alone in the world).
>
> *Terrorizing* (the adult verbally assaults the child, creates a climate of fear, bullies and frightens the child, and makes the child believe that the world is capricious and hostile).
>
> *Ignoring* (the adult deprives the child of essential stimulation and responsiveness, stifling emotional growth and intellectual development).
>
> *Corrupting* (the adult "mis-socializes" the child, stimulates the child to engage in destructive antisocial behavior, reinforces that deviance, and makes the child unfit for normal social experience).

These are basic threats to human development. Psychological maltreatment is the core issue in the broader picture of abuse and neglect. It provides the unifying theme and is the critical aspect in the overwhelming majority of what appear as physical and sexual maltreatment cases. The justification for this view is well established in the research on maltreatment of all forms. One source of support for this view derives from studies of what some have called "invulnerable" children or "superkids" or "stress-resistant children" (to use the preferred term; see Garmezy, 1983). The research documents that such children are *not* impervious to psychological maltreatment. Quite to the contrary, it suggests that such children are differentiated from other children exposed to stressful life events—such as sick parents and economically impoverished circumstances—precisely because the mistreatment or threat they experience at the hands of their environment is counterbalanced by compensatory doses of psychological nurturance and sustenance that enable them to develop social competence, that fortify their self-esteem, and that offer a positive social definition of self.

Where children are rejected, terrorized, ignored, corrupted, or isolated from sources of social support, they are vulnerable to negative influences in the broader social environment. Accordingly, we believe that the key to stress resistance is the absence of psychological maltreatment. This view is consistent with an "additive" model of socioemotional development (Gamble and Zigler, 1985; Rutter, 1971). In this view, threat, trauma, or deprivation in one domain of a child's life increases vulnerability to the effects of threat, trauma, or deprivation in another. For example, children who are subject to emotional deprivation at home are more vulnerable to negative experiences in day care than are children who benefit from enriched experience at home (Gamble and Zigler, 1985). Whereas children can absorb and overcome the experience of physical assault and sexual misuse if they are psychologically strengthened, they rarely can do so if they are psychologically mistreated as part of the experience. Mounting evidence on the beneficial impact of treatment for victims of sexual abuse seems to verify this proposition (Finkelhor, 1984). Similarly, emotional support in the process of disclosure and investigation can go far in reducing adverse consequences. We will return to these issues later in this volume, when we deal directly with issues of treatment.

Our definition of psychological maltreatment (as *patterns* of behavior involving rejecting, isolating, terrorizing, ignoring, and/or corrupting) places psychological abuse and neglect within a broader general definition of child maltreatment: "acts of omission or commission by a parent or guardian that are judged by a mixture of community values and professional expertise to be inappropriate and damaging," (Garbarino and Gilliam, 1980, p. 7). "Maltreatment" is thus intrinsically a *social* label. It is not enough that patterns of behavior are damaging; they must also violate some norm of appropriateness. In North America we damage children in many ways that do not constitute maltreatment. We circumcise baby boys, we pierce the ears of little girls, we expose young athletes to elevated risk of physical harm, we feed children high-cholesterol diets, we make children anxious and guilty about masturbation. These forms of damage are not yet defined as inappropriate, but definitions of the "appropriateness" of parental actions can change. For example, now that infant car seats are standard, whereas once they were optional and still earlier were unavailable, it is considered inappropriate for an adult to travel with an infant on his or her lap whereas once it was appropriate. Thus, an infant death in an automobile accident while riding on a parental lap rather than in a car seat is now "neglect related," where once it was a "preventable accident" and still earlier merely a "random accident." Similarly, paddling a child and shaking an infant were once considered "benign discipline" but now are defined as high-risk assaults. In both cases "perpetrators" are still generally absolved from "intent to damage" the child. Practitioners must make decisions about how far they *can* go and *should* go in labeling parental behavior as maltreatment. In doing so, *they* operationalize our definition. One could ask of our definition: Which is more important, community standards or professional expertise? To constitute psychological maltreatment, must behavior meet both criteria? To some extent, a complete answer can come only as we proceed with our analysis. But, as a start, we can say that we set the limits of definition so that behavior must *seriously* violate one and at least *moderately* violate the other criterion to constitute psychological maltreatment. In stating it this way, we are seeking to convey the notion that neither criterion is sufficient by itself. Both are necessary. But we do recognize that the more serious the violation of one criterion, the less serious the other violation need be.

In Chapter Two we explore our operational definition of psychological maltreatment through a series of case studies. Here, however, we will proceed to raise some further conceptual issues, through a series of eight questions.

Is rejection universally damaging and inappropriate? Researchers Rohner and Rohner (1980) have investigated the construct of rejection from an anthropological perspective by comparing parenting behaviors in several geographically and culturally disparate societies. From studies of the Colombian mestizo, the villagers of Tepoztlán, Mexico, and the Ik of Africa, among others, Rohner and Rohner conceptualized two distinct patterns of parental rejection. In the first, the mental attitude of hostility is converted into behavioral aggression toward one's offspring. In the second, the mental attitude of indifference is manifested behaviorally in neglect of children's physical and/or emotional needs. In each pattern the message conveyed to children is unambiguous: "You are neither valued nor loved." Mental cruelty is clearly implicated in such a scenario.

Despite the wide variability in society and culture, and despite individual differences among parents (in personality attributes, attitudes, and values), Rohner and Rohner were able to document a consistent set of factors that occurred with reports or observations of parental rejection. As in nearly every form of child abuse, rejecting parents appear generally overwhelmed by a convergence of social and economic hardships—too many children, inadequate material resources, too much stress, and too little emotional support. Specifically, these were the circumstances associated with increased risk for rejection: (1) restrictions against family-planning alternatives sanctioned by the society (implying a greater incidence of unwanted pregnancies), (2) an absence of adults in the home other than primary caregiver (so that caregivers had no opportunity for time alone or time away from home), (3) a lack of involvement by fathers as socializers of children, and (4) social and instrumental isolation of families in the community (families detached from friendship and assistance networks). These findings are hardly surprising and probably apply whether the topic under scrutiny is rejection, neglect, physical abuse, or some other manifestation of psychological abuse. Unless parents feel materially and psychologically secure enough to move beyond concern for themselves, they will not be able to function effectively as caregivers, as instructors, or as providers of emotional support for their children.

Given the defining characteristics of rejecting parents (hostile aggression, indifferent neglect) and given the environmental deficiencies that tend to accompany such behavior, it is only to be expected that Rohner and Rohner should document a host of adverse outcomes for the personality and behavior of rejected children. In general, youngsters who are rejected physically and/or psychologically by their parents are noticeably hostile and aggressive, have impaired self-esteem, and show either excessive dependency on parents and/or other adults or "defensive independence" (which appears to derive more from a negativistic reaction to their experiences than from a secure, constructive sense of autonomy). Furthermore, these children and teens appear emotionally unstable or unresponsive and come to perceive the world in negativistic terms. This last finding suggests that rejection wields a two-edged blade, eroding the confidence and self-esteem with which these children view themselves and distorting the lens through which they view their immediate and broader context.

Is the "double bind" a form of psychological maltreatment? Bateson (1972) has described a particular configuration of parental expectations and demands that places the child in a "double bind"; that is, a parent's behavior is so inconsistent as to be contradictory, creating for the child or teen what is truly a "no-win" situation. For instance, a mother walking with her son might move close to the boy, thus eliciting his gesture of putting his arm around her waist. She then subtly pulls away, so that he drops his arm—at which point she asks, "What's the matter, don't you love me any more?" A double bind may be as flagrant a contradiction as this one, or it may be as subtle as intimating that praiseworthy achievement in the school and larger community must be bought at the cost of compromising a strict code of loyalty to family.

This type of double jeopardy has clear parallels to the experimental phenomenon of "learned helplessness" in laboratory animals (Seligman, 1975; Seligman, Maier, and Solomon, 1971). Helplessness can be experimentally induced when animals are rendered unable to escape repeated presentation of a noxious stimulus (such as an electrical shock). No matter what the animal attempts, it can neither terminate nor control the occurrence of some distressing event. This is only half the story when children are caught in a double bind, however; for they are confronted with inescapable conflict or censure in *each* of the several alternatives they would seek to pursue.

Some children raised in such an environment—especially those whose mental health is already at risk because of biogenic factors—might become schizophrenic (Bateson, 1972). However, other children might respond to this form of psychological terrorism in ways that lead to enhanced psychological strength, particularly if these children have access to other sources of social support, to caring others, who can help them find a way out of the trap set for them by parents who create the double binds (Osborne, 1985).

Do children play a role in stimulating psychological maltreatment? Children, whether consciously or unconsciously, may trigger or even cause their own maltreatment. To a parent already overwhelmed by environmentally induced stress, attention-getting behavior and demands by the child may provide the impetus for violent parental reactions. Excessive activity, a naturally shy disposition, some mental or physical handicap—any of these might generate reactions that are easily translated into parental withdrawal, rejection, or neglect. Kadushin and Martin (1981) provide extensive testimony by abusive parents to illustrate the important (and often inadvertent) role that children can play in provoking maltreatment at the hands of their parents. One parent recalls: "My oldest child [Steve] is the extreme opposite of Carl [the abused child]—very timid and quiet and . . . I like his sensitivity. I liked him better from day one. . . . And Carl, I just don't understand him at all. It's like he's not like me at all. He rarely shows feelings, he is bullheaded, strong, real aggressive. And when I first came home from the hospital with Carl, all I could think of was protecting Steve from this intruder. I felt that the baby [Carl] was an intruder between him and me. So I guess I'm very partial to the older boy" (p. 241).

How do parents neglect the psychosocial needs of their children? How is lack of involvement or support made evident?

For some, emotional withdrawal accompanies more basic physical neglect. Indifference or hostility produces a total disregard for the physical and psychological needs of the child. In other cases the well-groomed, well-tended child is simply confronted with emotional coldness and distancing behavior by the parent: "Don't rumple your dress trying to climb into my lap." "Well-behaved children don't get angry; good children don't cry." "How many times have I told you not to touch *anything* in this house that isn't yours?"

Children learn by doing, by interacting with objects and with people. If parents or other adults severely restrict a child's opportunity to play, explore, make friends, visit neighbors, or participate in community organizations, they are thwarting the development of competence. If parents or other adults do not provide occasions for the child to exercise responsibility, to generate solutions to problems, to enjoy the pride of accomplishment, they are denying the experiences that promote a sense of personal efficacy. Evidence in support of these observations derives from studies of maternal restrictions during infancy and their presumed consequences for child development. Negative associations between the amount of floor freedom children are allowed (Ainsworth and Bell, 1974), the frequency of physical and verbal prohibitions (Tulkin and Covitz, 1975), maternal limitations on the child's freedom to explore the environment (Wachs, 1976), and various indexes of later cognitive development suggest that excessive parental regulation detrimentally affects the development of the child.

Can psychological deprivation produce physical consequences? Spitz's (1945, 1946) studies of children raised in orphanages and deprived of maternal involvement chronicle the deleterious consequences for children reared in socioemotional deprivation. Illustrating the extreme in potential outcomes, Spitz documented an infant mortality rate of over 33 percent in a sample of ninety-one orphans "in spite of good food and meticulous medical care" (1945, p. 59). In other studies both physical and psychological deficits have been found in children whose psychosocial needs are grossly ignored. In their long-term study of high-risk families, Egeland, Sroufe, and Erickson (1983) have identified a pattern that they term the "psychologically unavailable" parent. Children experiencing this emotional unresponsiveness fare poorly. In contrast to children whose parents provide predictable, responsive, and sensitive care, these children show problems in attachment and other forms of social and intellectual development. Many of the mothers termed psychologically unavailable evidence serious problems with depression. This finding is consistent with studies by Polansky, Chalmers, Buttenweiser, and Williams (1981), who found links between neglect and a pattern of depression and despair referred to as the apathy-futility syndrome.

Bullard, Glaser, Hagarty, and Pivchik (1967) have described in detail the medically recognized phenomenon of "nonorganic failure to thrive," which is particularly evident during late infancy and early childhood. Children suffering from this "malady" are typically undernourished physically, apathetic and lethargic, and developmentally delayed—often both physically and behaviorally. The diagnostic key is the child's responsiveness to treatment. Under watchful, therapeutic hospital care, the failure-to-thrive baby or child rapidly gains weight and animation. Withdrawn, uncomplaining, and unconcerned youngsters begin to participate in the activity surrounding them, even seeking out attention and favor. Nevertheless, lingering psychological symptoms—tantrums, secrecy, petty theft—belie hasty and overoptimistic pronouncements on the efficacy of compensatory experiences. Doubts remain about the degree of plasticity available and necessary to rechart the developmental course of a child exposed to early and pervasive socioemotional neglect.

Physical anomalies beyond simply low weight and developmental delays have been linked to severe neglect during childhood (Powell, Brasel, and Blizzard, 1967). One example is the phenomenon labeled "psychosocial dwarfism" or "deprivation dwarfism." Gardner (1972) elucidates some of the hypothesized precursors, possible biological processes, and physical and behavioral characteristics accompanying growth disorders of psychosocial origin. Abnormalities in sleeping, eating, and motor ability, as well as in physical growth and psychological functioning, were marked in his small sample of infants from "disordered" and neglectful family environments. Regarding the developmental outcome of the six "thin dwarfs" followed in this medical treatment study, Gardner notes: "In spite of . . . short-term gains [in weight, motor ability, and social responsiveness], few of the children recovered entirely from their experience of deprivation dwarfism. They tended to remain below average in height, weight, and skeletal maturation. Furthermore, the two we were able to follow until late childhood gave evidence of residual damage to personality structure and to intellect" (p. 78).

Can family disruption result in psychological maltreatment? In response to the surging statistics on divorce, researchers are increasingly devoting time and energy to understanding the effects of marital conflict on children. In studies of the precursors of delinquency (West, 1969, 1973), the situational determinants of competent parental functioning (Belsky, Gilstrap, and Rovine, 1984; Price, 1977), and the adjustment of children following a divorce (Hetherington, Cox, and Cox, 1977), similar findings appeared—namely, that a discordant and inharmonious marital relationship adversely affects child development (Bronson, 1966; see also Emery, 1982). Apparently, marital discord has a twofold pathway of influence on the children involved: direct effects of witnessing conflict between father and mother, and indirect effects of experiencing diminished parental efficacy in the caregiving role.

In psychological terms, a conflicted marital relationship, especially one severe enough to culminate in divorce, may imply self-guilt to the child (Hetherington, 1981; Wallerstein and Kelly, 1975), may furnish inappropriate models of interpersonal behavior, and may deprive the child of the nurturance and support that are contingent on the parents' own well-being (Belsky, 1984). Such a home environment, therefore, is psychologically injurious for children. Even though difficult children might contribute to such discord, they become the unwitting victims of the strained relations that ensue. Possible consequences include antisocial, aggressive, and other problematic behaviors in the children involved (for example, see Emery, 1982).

The developmental risks that a conflicted marriage presents for children are paralleled and magnified when the family structure is unstable—that is, when a child is removed from the family and placed in a series of foster homes. There is sufficient anecdotal evidence (for example, see Goldstein, Freud, and Solnit, 1973, 1979) concerning the "foster care shuttle" to suggest that instability and impermanence in family membership have potentially dire consequences. Parents who abuse their children, for example, frequently were themselves shunted from foster home to foster home. Psychological disturbance as well has been linked to a background of family instability, marital conflict, and separation from parental figures (Rutter, 1971).

The likely mechanisms connecting unstable family situations and poor developmental prognoses include disruption in relationships to primary attachment figures and inconsistency in experiences of child rearing. The literature on parent-child attachment (see Ainsworth, Blehar, Waters, and Wall, 1978) indicates that a secure relationship *maintained over time* with at least one adult is a fundamental precursor and correlate of later competence in psychosocial functioning. If a child is shuttled from one home to the next or, comparably, is exposed to a continual flux in institutional caregivers, such a relationship has little opportunity to develop and less so to persist for any appreciable amount of time. Hence, we find the deleterious outcomes for a subsample of repeatedly transplanted foster children and for the "maternally deprived" orphans studied by Spitz.

Does a sexually exploitative relationship between adult and child constitute psychological maltreatment? Sexual relations or sexually related activities between adults and children can be regarded as psychological victimization of the children involved when (1) the child is powerless and cannot give informed consent (Finkelhor, 1979, 1984) and (2) the child's emotional and social development is jeopardized. Children suffer an imbalance of social rank and power relative to adults and, at the same time, are handicapped by restricted information and experience as well as by cognitive limitations (depending on age and maturity). Because of the power that adults inherently possess, it is a facile and often subtle matter to tyrannize, cajole, or otherwise induce youngsters, who are both less influential and more ignorant, to conform to adult desires, even when these violate the strictest, most fundamental social and cultural standards. The issue of power is starkly apparent in the definition of sexual abuse adopted by the National

Center on Child Abuse and Neglect (1978, p. 42): "contacts or interactions between a child and an adult when the child is being used for the sexual stimulation of the perpetrator or another person *when the perpetrator is in a position of power or control over the victim*" (emphasis added).

In addition, sexual exploitation pits adults' self-interest against the developmental robustness of the children who become their victims. Densen-Gerber and Hutchinson (1979) eloquently attest to the emotional damage likely to ensue from what are clearly inappropriate sexual relations or activities. Victims of sexual abuse frequently experience emotional trauma resulting from shame, uncertainty, guilt, fear of breaking up the family (among victims of incest), and, for female teenagers, fear of pregnancy. The psychological risks are evident in reports that incest victims are more likely than the general population to engage in substance abuse; to exhibit depressive, anxious, and/or psychosomatic symptomology; and to commit suicide (see Garbarino and Gilliam, 1980). Social development, too, is imperiled by adult behavior of this sort (Kaus and Garbarino, 1985). In the case of incest, social roles within the family must become or already be strained when parent and child effect a travesty of the spousal relationship. Whether within or outside the home, sexually exploitative relations will tend to interfere with the development and maintenance of normal social relationships. This is particularly true for adolescents, as are the problems attendant on sexual abuse. Normal heterosexual experiences with peers (social interaction outside of school, dating, and the like) may be curtailed by an adult sexual partner who fears exposure or who experiences jealousy. Self-condemnation or denunciation by parents or friends often prompts the adolescent to leave home prematurely. Of the projected 800,000 teenagers who run away annually, the federal government estimates that one half to one third were victims of mistreatment (Garbarino, Schellenbach, Sebes, and Associates, 1986). Densen-Gerber and Hutchinson (1979) cite prostitution, pornography, and substance abuse as a subsample of the likely consequences for those who have fled their homes to escape sexually exploitative situations (thereby, ironically, putting themselves at risk of further exploitation).

Can and should we differentiate between psychological maltreatment and more general "negative influences," "risk factors," or "destructive social interaction"? This issue contains two additional questions. For purposes of intervention, should we have a narrow or a broad definition to sustain voluntary intervention? How does the definition differ for efforts associated with community mental health agencies versus legally mandated enforcement-oriented services? It is easy to be broad and all-encompassing with one's definitions when one's responsibilities are academic and intellectual. We feel more compelled to be specific and narrowly focused when we know that we must live with the bureaucratic, legal, and financial implications of those definitions. And yet we are convinced that the driving engine of progress in child welfare is provided by a conception of maltreatment in which "our reach exceeds our grasp." We deal with this conflict in Chapter Two. As a prologue, remember the importance of context in deciding what is and what is not psychological maltreatment. Most behavior can be understood only in the social, economic and political context in which it occurs. No simple answers suffice when we are confronted by the range of human experience documented in day-to-day lives of children.

For example:

A.S. Neill's (1960) Summerhill school (an aggressively permissive institution) proved to be successful with English children who had been reared in repressive Victorian-style families. But it appeared to be developmentally irresponsible when addressed to already "liberated" American children. Is it psychologically neglectful then, to provide a permissive school for contemporary American youth?

Recall Chaim Potok's (1967) novel *The Chosen*. In it a father embarks (out of love) on a campaign of silence with his genius son to teach the boy humility and to develop his *Menschlichkeit*—his sense of humanity. Was this pattern of more than a decade a case of chronic emotional abuse?

And what about parents who take a hard line with troublesome teenagers? For all that we have heard about runaways, a substantial number of youth on the streets are in fact throwaways, adolescents who have been expelled from their homes. Are such parents different from those in the "Toughlove" groups, collections of parents who band together to support each other in taking a tough stand toward their children's behavior—sometimes even throwing them out of the house but sending them into the care of another member's home? Is this a form of psychological maltreatment?

Is there a difference between psychological maltreatment and "growth-inducing challenge"? Psychological abuse attacks character and self; neglect fails to nourish character and self in important ways. Challenge, *when it occurs in the context of supportive relationships,* can induce the growth of character and an enhanced sense of self. Some years ago we observed the following homily posted in a cabin at a church camp. Despite its limitations as literature, it makes the point here.

Strong Words

Have you learned lessons only
from those who admired you
and were tender with you
and stood aside for you?

Have you not learned great lessons
from those who reject you and
brace themselves against you, or
who treat you with contempt, or
dispute the passage with you?

We should not protect children from growth-inducing challenges—things should not always be "nice." There is more to life than smiling faces with "Have a nice day" printed beneath them. That is not our goal here, of course. What we seek is a good society, one in which the institutional sources of psychological maltreatment are dismantled and replaced with justice and a humanly and environmentally sane and sustainable society.

The definition of maltreatment we presented earlier incorporates *both* community standards and scientific/professional expertise as criteria for judging the appropriateness and correctness of intervention on behalf of children (Garbarino and Gilliam, 1980). To fulfill the mission of pioneering advances in child welfare, we need to adopt broad definitions that we can justify on scientific grounds; we then need to use these definitions as a bargaining position in interactions with policy makers, with other practitioners, and with the general public. We view such a course as the engine of progress. Tentative, short-term compromises play a legitimate role when they move steadily in the direction of greater and greater protection based on increasingly high standards of care for *all* children in the family and in the institutional life of the community.

❧ 2 ❧

Developmental Stages and Psychological Maltreatment
Case Examples

In Chapter One we described five forms of psychological maltreatment and set these five categories in the context of an ecological model of child development, emphasizing the interplay of organism and social systems. From this perspective, development is intrinsically social (Bronfenbrenner, 1979; Garbarino and Associates, 1982). Development is emergent social competence, a growing sense of "self in the world" that is based in the day-to-day realities of ever wider spheres of social performance. Retaining this developmental focus, we now specify the behaviors that constitute rejecting, terrorizing, ignoring, corrupting, and isolating in each of the major stages in the first eighteen years of life: infancy (birth to age two), early childhood (ages two to five), school age (five to eleven), and adolescence (eleven to eighteen). Each of these periods has its own particular developmental issues and corresponding social correlates. Similarly, we recognize the need to deal with degrees of severity: mild, moderate, and severe. We describe as

The twenty case studies presented in this chapter are an amalgam based on cases identified by the authors, the project advisory council, and published sources. Cases 3, 6, 9, 11, and 13–17 are the result of the authors' own fieldwork. The other cases are based on material developed by others: Case 1, Maybanks and Bryce, 1979; Case 2, Bishop, 1983; Cases 4 and 12, DeCourey and DeCourey, 1973; Cases 5 and 7, M. J. Fialkov, personal communication, 1985; Cases 8 and 18, Marie Toby McManmon, personal communication, 1985; Cases 10 and 20, Dean, 1979.

"mild" those instances of psychological maltreatment that create the risk of limited psychic damage confined to one aspect of functioning (such as a lack of confidence in public settings); "moderate" refers to instances of maltreatment that may prevent a child from achieving minimal success in important settings (for instance, at school); the label "severe" refers to instances of maltreatment that will, in all likelihood, cause children to be crippled in one or more of life's primary settings—work, love, and play.

An Exercise in Developmental Specificity

What are the parental behaviors constituting psychological maltreatment across the period from infancy to adolescence? We know that we must look to the causes, context, and consequences of these behaviors in the family as a system, in the community, and in the child. But before we do that (in Chapters Three through Seven), we must ask about the operational definitions of psychological maltreatment in day-to-day parental behavior. Figure 1 provides a framework for exploring this question. What specific behaviors belong in each of the twenty boxes ("cells in the matrix," to use a more technically precise term)? How does "rejecting" translate into parental behaviors toward infants? How do these behaviors differ when they are directed toward adolescents? How, specifically, do parents go about "isolating" children at different developmental stages? These are the most obvious questions posed in and by Figure 1.

We have wrestled with these questions and now present our results. In each case we recognize that most forms of psychological maltreatment apply to some degree from infancy to adolescence. Many, if not most, behaviors are relevant to more than one life period, particularly for adjacent stages. Thus, although we may identify a parental behavior as especially important in the preschool period, we recognize that it also applies to the overlapping infancy and school-age periods. Our interest here is to highlight the differences, however; so we proceed with efforts to be developmentally specific.

Figure 1. Framework for Specific Behaviors Constituting Psychological Maltreatment by Age Group.

Developmental Period

Type of Psychological Maltreatment	Infancy	Early Childhood	School Age	Adolescence
Rejecting				
Terrorizing				
Ignoring				
Isolating				
Corrupting				

Rejecting

In general, rejecting involves behaviors that communicate or constitute abandonment. For example, the parent or caregiver may refuse to touch or show affection to the child or to acknowledge the child's accomplishments. Rejecting is considered "mild" when it is confined to isolated (though perhaps poignant) incidents. It becomes "moderate" when it is frequent and more generalized. When rejecting is categorical, absolute, and frequent, it becomes "severe."

Infancy. The parent refuses to accept the child's primary attachment. That is, the parent resists the infant's spontaneous overtures and natural responses to human contact so as to prevent the formation of a primary relationship. *Specific behaviors:* abandonment; refusal to return smiles and vocalizations.

Early childhood. The parent actively excludes the child from family activities. *Specific behaviors:* not taking the child on family outings; refusing the child's affiliative gestures (such as hugging); placing the child away from the family.

School Age. The parent consistently communicates a negative definition of self to the child. *Specific behaviors:* frequent use of labels such as "dummy" or "monster"; frequent belittling of the child's accomplishments; scapegoating the child as part of a family system.

Adolescence. The parent refuses to acknowledge the changing social roles expected of the child—that is, toward more autonomy and self-determination. *Specific behaviors:* treating the adolescent like a young child ("infantilizing"); subjecting the adolescent to verbal humiliation and excessive criticism; expelling the youth from the family.

Terrorizing

In general, terrorizing involves threatening the child with extreme or vague but sinister punishment, intentionally stimulating intense fear, creating a climate of unpredictable threat, or setting unmeetable expectations and punishing the child for not meeting them. In its "mild" form, it suggests arbitrariness and the use of scare tactics in discipline. When it involves direct threats to the child's everyday sense of security, it falls into the "moderate" category. To qualify as "severe," these tactics must involve dramatic, mysterious, or extraordinary threats or double binds.

Infancy. The parent consistently and deliberately violates the child's tolerance for change and intense stimuli. *Specific behaviors:* teasing; scaring; unpredictable and extreme response to the child's behavior.

Early Childhood. The parent uses extreme gestures and verbal statements to intimidate, threaten, or punish the child. *Specific behaviors:* verbal threats of extreme or "mysterious" harm (from ghosts, monsters, and the like); frequent raging at the child, alternating with periods of artificial warmth.

School Age. The parent places the child in intolerable "double binds" ("damned if you do, damned if you don't"). *Specific behaviors:* presenting extremely inconsistent demands or emotions; forcing the child to choose between competing parents; frequently changing "rules of the game" in parent-child relations; constantly criticizing, with no prospect of the child's successfully meeting expectations.

Adolescence. The parent threatens to expose the child to public humiliation. *Specific behaviors:* threatening to reveal intensely embarrassing characteristics or behaviors (for example, bed wetting or previous sexual experiences) to peers or other adults; ridiculing the child in public.

Ignoring

In general, ignoring refers to the parent's being psychologically unavailable to the child—that is, preoccupied with self and unable to respond to the child's behaviors. In its mild form, ignoring is evident in lack of sustained attention to the child during periods of contact (for instance, during meals or at times when parent and child are reunited after work or school). Moderate ignoring suggests prolonged periods of unavailability, with the implication that the parent erects a "barrier of silence." When children appear to have no real emotional or interactional access at all to parents, ignoring in its severe form is evident. In contrast to rejecting, which is active and abusive, ignoring is passive and neglectful in character.

Infancy. The parent fails to respond contingently to the infant's spontaneous social behaviors that form the foundation for attachment. *Specific behaviors:* not responding to the infant's spontaneous vocalizations; not noticing and responding to developing competence in the infant.

Early Childhood. There is a pattern of coolness and lack of affect in parental treatment of the child, a failure to engage the child in day-to-day activities, and distancing the child from social interactions. *Specific behaviors:* refusing to engage in conversation at mealtimes; leaving the child without emotionally engaged adult supervision for extended periods.

School Age. The parent fails to protect the child from threats or to intervene on the child's behalf when the parent is made aware of the need for help. *Specific behaviors:* not protecting the child from assault by siblings or other family members; showing no interest in evaluation of the child by teachers and other adults; failing to follow up on the child's requests for help in resolving problems with peers.

Adolescence. The parent abdicates the parental role and shows no interest in the child. *Specific behaviors:* refusing to discuss the adolescent's activities and interests; concentrating on other relationships that displace the adolescent as an object of affection.

Isolating

In general, isolating is evident in parental behaviors that prevent the child from taking advantage of normal opportunities for social relations. In its mild form, "isolating" suggests failure to provide normal occasions and opportunities for social interaction. It becomes "moderate" when it involves active efforts to avoid social interaction and "severe" when the parent thwarts all efforts by the child and others to make contact.

Infancy. The parent denies the child the experience of enduring patterns of active interaction with parents or parent substitutes. *Specific behaviors:* leaving the child in its room unattended for long periods; denying all access to the child by interested others—for example, close friends of the family or health care professionals.

Early Childhood. The parent teaches the child to avoid social contact beyond the parent-child relationship. *Specific behaviors:* punishing social overtures to children and to adults; rewarding the child for withdrawing from opportunities for social contact.

School Age. The parent attempts to remove the child from normal social relationships with peers. *Specific behaviors:* prohibiting the child from playing with other children; prohibiting the child from inviting other children into the home; withdrawing the child from school.

Adolescence. The parent tries to prevent the child from participating in organized and informal activities outside the home. *Specific behaviors:* prohibiting the child from joining clubs, after-school programs, and sports teams; withdrawing the child from school in order to perform household tasks (such as caring for siblings); punishing the child for engaging in normal social experiences (such as dating).

Corrupting

In general, corrupting refers to parental behaviors that "mis-socialize" children and reinforce them in antisocial or deviant patterns, particularly in the areas of aggression, sexuality, or substance abuse. Such behaviors tend to make the child unfit for normal social experience. In its mild form, the parents convey the impression that they encourage the child's unsuitable precocious behavior in the area of sexuality, aggression, or substance abuse. Reinforcing the child for behavior that is delinquent constitutes a moderate level of "corrupting." Creating and sustaining a pattern of behavior that risks permanent social dysfunction (for example, addiction, frigidity, compulsive sexual acting out, or repetitive acts of life-threatening violence) is evidence of severe corrupting.

Infancy. The parent places the infant at risk by reinforcing the development of bizarre habits and/or by creating addictions.

Specific behaviors: reinforcing the infant for oral sexual contact; creating drug dependence.

Early Childhood. The parent gives inappropriate reinforcement for aggression and precocious sexuality. *Specific behaviors:* rewarding the child for assaulting other children; involving the child sexually with adults or adolescents.

School Age. The parent rewards the child for stealing, substance abuse, assaulting other children, and sexual precocity. *Specific behaviors:* goading the child into attacking other children; exposing the child to pornography; encouraging drug use; reinforcing sexually aggressive behavior; involving the child sexually with adults.

Adolescence. The parent involves the child in more intense and socially unacceptable forms of sexual, aggressive, and drug/alcohol deviance. *Specific behaviors:* involving the adolescent in prostitution; rewarding aggressive, delinquent behavior directed at peers and adults or at "scapegoated" family members; encouraging trafficking in illicit drug use and alcohol abuse.

Case Studies

We now turn to a series of twenty case studies. Each illustrates one or more type of psychological maltreatment, and each focuses on a "target" child in one of the four developmental periods. The cases are ordered according to age of the target child, starting with infants and going on to adolescents. Table 1 classifies the cases by the type or types of psychological maltreatment they represent.

Case 1: Susan

Susan is a week-old infant born to Linda, who is seventeen years old. The mother was raped near the time of the baby's conception, and she feared that the girl might not belong to her boyfriend. She had doubts about going through with the pregnancy but delayed too long, so that an abortion was not possible. Around the time of the rape, her boyfriend left her because he did

Table 1. Twenty Cases Classified by Type of Psychological Maltreatment and Developmental Period.

	Rejecting	Terrorizing	Ignoring	Isolating	Corrupting
Infancy	Susan (Case 1) Frank (Case 3)	Betty (Case 2)	Susan (Case 1) Betty (Case 2) Frank (Case 3) David (Case 4)	Frank (Case 3) David (Case 4)	David (Case 4)
Early Childhood	Jane (Case 5) Patty (Case 7)	Jon (Case 6) Bobby (Case 8) Rhonda (Case 9)	Jon (Case 6)	Jane (Case 5) Patty (Case 7)	Rhonda (Case 9)
School Age	Cindy (Case 10) Ken (Case 12) Wanda (Case 13) Teddy (Case 15)	Ken (Case 12) Erin (Case 14) Teddy (Case 15)	Cindy (Case 10)	Cindy (Case 10) Mark and Bill (Case 11) Teddy (Case 15)	Mark and Bill (Case 11)
Adolescence	Shirley (Case 16) Ricky (Case 20)	Ann (Case 18) Johnny (Case 19) Ricky (Case 20)	Shirley (Case 16) Johnny (Case 19)	Johnny (Case 19)	Elsa (Case 17)

not want the responsibilities of being a father. At present Linda feels very weak after the delivery and rarely holds or touches the infant. She avoids eye contact with the child and will not feed her. She repeatedly says that she does not know what she is going to do with this "thing" and that there is no one to help her. Although the nurses have pointed out that she refuses to care for her child, the attending physician has given Linda a clean bill of health and wants to discharge her. After a conversation with one of the nurses about this case, the pediatric social worker has begun an investigation.

This case illustrates *rejecting* (the mother's refusal to care for the baby) and *ignoring* (the mother is psychologically unavailable to the child).

Case 2: Betty

Betty is the youngest of five children, aged eight months to nine years. She and her three-year-old sister seem the least well cared for of all the children. The mother, twenty-six years old, has been alone with them since their father, whom she had never married, left a year ago (four months before Betty was born). The mother rarely ventures out; and when she does, it is with all her children "in tow." The children are developmentally delayed and have difficulty relating to their peers.

The mother's memories from her own childhood are dominated by her fears of going outside the house. She recalls the dangerous streets and the unpleasant events that happened when she did dare to leave home. When she became pregnant at age sixteen, she and her boyfriend did not marry. When her oldest child was six, and after she and her boyfriend had had two other children, the boyfriend left. He said that he could no longer "live in a cage," referring to the mother's refusal to leave the house or to allow the children to leave it. The mother went on welfare and continued to live with her children, but the situation became worse. They began demanding to go out, making a mess in the house, and yelling at her. She felt that she wanted to get rid of them because they were making her life miserable; yet she knew that it was her duty to raise them and protect them. At about the age of eight and six, the two older children started running away to the street, and the mother felt she was going crazy. Each time they returned, she yelled at them, warned them, and sometimes even hit them to make them better understand the dangerousness of the streets. The more she screamed, the greater urge the children felt to run away from her. Now she is too preoccupied with the older children and herself to pay any attention to eight-month-old Betty. When the baby demands attention, the mother often yells at her and terrifies her to the extent that she becomes mute. When the mother expressed her fears to the public assistance worker, she was referred to the protective service agency.

Betty's case illustrates *ignoring* (the mother is psychologically unavailable to the infant) and *terrorizing* (yelling at the baby and terrifying her).

Case 3: Frank

Frank's mother was sixteen when he was born, and she did not want him. When he was two months old, she gave him to her parents and left town. After seven months Frank's grandparents decided that he was too much trouble for them to keep. They informed the local child welfare agency that they did not want him and placed him for adoption.

Frank is subject to persistent skin problems, and his dermatological problems (scaly, blotchy skin) have made it difficult to place him. The unwilling grandparents often left Frank alone, shut up in a room, for hours at a time. At eleven months of age, Frank is alternately listless and irritable. He sometimes cries when approached and sometimes seems oblivious to being left. The visiting nurse assigned to the case reports that Frank's intellectual and emotional development is delayed. Upon recommendation of the visiting nurse, the child welfare agency has now assumed custody of the boy.

Frank's case illustrates *ignoring* (the grandparents' long periods of inaccessibility to the child), *rejecting* (the mother's decision to abandon the child and the grandparents' decision to place him for adoption), and *isolating* (what appears to be a pattern of separating the child from social contact by leaving him shut up in a room alone for hours at a time).

Case 4: David

David's father worked long hours each day and was frequently out of town on business. His mother, a part-time secretary, had numerous affairs and often brought the men to her home. When David was eighteen months old, he called one of the visitors

"Dada." Terrified that David would expose her extramarital affairs to his father, she trained him to speak only when he was alone with her. She told her husband that David had a throat malformation and that she was seeking the best available˙treatment. To protect herself further, she would not permit David to play with other children in the neighborhood and rarely took him anywhere. Moreover, since her extramarital affairs did not satisfy her enough, she taught David ways in which he could gratify some of her sexual needs and made her attention to him contingent on it.

One day David's father came home unannounced and heard David talking to his mother. After being severely beaten, David's mother told her husband the truth and further revealed that she was uncertain whether he was David's father. David's father, who had previously been very attentive and caring toward David, reacted to his wife's declaration by withdrawing from interactions with David.

David is below developmental norms, is overdependent on his mother, and has become very destructive. A visiting aunt noticed these behaviors and encouraged David's parents to seek help for David. However, they refused to do so, and so the aunt notified the child welfare agency.

David's case illustrates *isolating* (the mother preventing David from speaking when his father was present), *ignoring* (David's father refusing to interact with him once he doubted paternity), and *corrupting* (the mother involving the infant in sexual activities).

Case 5: Jane

Jane was three years old when her parents divorced. After a year her mother married a man with three children of his own, and these children were added to the family. Jane, who was a very active and demanding child, became the focus of family conflicts. First her stepfather and his children, and then increasingly her own mother and brother, described her as aggressive, noncompliant, dishonest, and overall a disturbance to the family. Apart from Jane, the other children and the parents lived in harmony. When they went for vacations, they would leave her with her grandparents to avoid having the vacation "spoiled" by her behavior. When she escalated her overactive and acting-out behavior (now being unmanageable on a daily basis), the parents decided to place her in a residential institution.

Jane's case demonstrates *rejecting* and *isolating* (not allowing her to join in family activities).

Case 6: Jon

Jon's dad has very clear ideas about how children should behave: Jon, age four, should be kept on his toes. So his dad teases him a lot—in front of friends, guests, his mother, and his sister. When not teasing him, his father pays no attention to him at all, not wanting him to become spoiled. To keep Jon jumping, his dad also plays games with him. If Jon wins, his dad makes fun of him for being an egghead; if he loses, he makes fun of him for being a dummy. It is the same with affection. Jon's dad will call him over for a hug; when Jon responds, his dad pushes him away, telling him not to be a sissy. Jon is in a "double bind" and cannot win. At home he is tense, sucks his thumb, and is tongue-tied (which his dad teases him about). At nursery school he has begun to stutter and alternates between being whiny and acting aggressively toward other children.

Jon's case illustrates *terrorizing* (the father's teasing) and *ignoring* (the father's refusal to pay attention to the boy except to attack him).

Case 7: Patty

Four-year-old Patty was locked in her room as punishment for minor infractions of her strict parents' rules. When she was being punished, she was not permitted to eat her meals with the rest of the family. These punishments happened at least four times a week. When she "misbehaved" on a Saturday or Sunday, she had to stay in her room and eat separately from her family for the entire day. When she was not being punished, she was allowed to play in the living room but not outside or with other children. Patty often complained about headaches and dizziness to her nursery school teacher. When the teacher asked the parents about these symptoms, they explained their punishment techniques. The teacher then made a report to the local protective service agency.

Patty's case illustrates *rejecting* (not allowing Patty to interact with the rest of the family) and *isolating* (not allowing Patty to eat with the family or go outside).

Case 8: Bobby

Four-year-old Bobby is the only child of an unmarried twenty-one-year-old woman, Martha. Martha had been diagnosed by the local mental health center as paranoid schizophrenic and was under psychiatric care. However, treatment had not been successful, and Bobby was often the target of his mother's frequent episodes of rage and verbal attack. During these episodes Martha threatened Bobby with physical harm, death, and abandonment but never acted on her threats. Bobby, who was in day care, had fallen seriously below developmental norms; he did not initiate interactions with peers or teachers and refused their overtures toward him. He was extremely anxious and fearful, and his restricted play reflected feelings of fear, danger, and death. Concerned about his behavior, Bobby's day care provider contacted the day care council's social worker to investigate the home situation.

This case illustrates *terrorizing* (the mother terrorizes Bobby by threatening to harm him physically, kill him, or abandon him).

Case 9: Rhonda

Rhonda is the fifth of seven children. Her father recently lost his job and is home all day. Rhonda's parents do not believe in talking about feelings or saying things like "I love you" either to the children or to each other. They also believe that negative feelings should be ignored and suppressed. Four-year-old Rhonda has become the object of her father's attention during the hours when her mother is away at work and she (along with her two younger siblings) is home alone with her father. He began "cuddling" with her (which she enjoyed immensely because it was the first real warmth she experienced from her normally cool father) and has progressed to more and more intrusive sexual contact (including oral-genital sex). He has told her that a "bad man" will come at night and "cut her into little tiny pieces" if she tells anyone about what they do together. The girl has started sucking her thumb again, often has nightmares, and has begun "playing" with her baby brother's penis whenever she gets the chance. A visiting friend of the family expressed concern to the mother about her daughter's behavior, and a subsequent discussion with the family's doctor led to a protective service investigation.

Rhonda's case illustrates *terrorizing* (the threats of grotesque bodily harm) and *corrupting* (involving the child in oral-genital sex), as well as the obvious sexual abuse.

Case 10: Cindy

When Cindy was eight, her teachers became concerned about the treatment she was receiving at home. They believed that she might be a victim of "Cinderella syndrome," in which the parents and siblings scapegoated her. Cindy was the child in the family who always wore cast-off clothing, was required to do more household tasks than the other children, and was not given the same privileges and opportunities. The other children were allowed to join Brownie troops and Boy Scouts, but Cindy was not allowed to participate in any outside activities. The rest of the family ate in the dining room but Cindy ate in the kitchen standing at the drainboard. The mother has never visited Cindy's classroom or inquired about her progress.

The parents see Cindy as a difficult child who needs rigid discipline and control, and her brothers and sisters see her as "the problem of the family." Cindy herself, although she is depressed and unhappy about inability to participate with the family or other children, also feels that she is bad and does not deserve to be included.

The teacher's referral led to an investigation by the child protective service agency.

This case manifests *ignoring* (the parents' and siblings' unavailability to the girl), *rejecting* (the family's refusal to include her in the inner circle), and *isolating* (cutting her off from day-to-day family activities).

Case 11: Mark and Bill

Eight-year-old Mark and his ten-year-old brother, Bill, live with their mother and grandmother in a blue-collar neighborhood.

The father had a pattern of alcohol abuse and left shortly after Mark was born. The mother and grandmother rarely socialize and have centered their lives on the two boys. The boys are not allowed to play with the neighborhood children, and every day after school they go to a local park with their mother and grandmother. The women dress and bathe the boys, who have become very dependent on the two women, both physically and emotionally. Every night, Mark sleeps with his mother, and Bill sleeps with his grandmother. Bill has told Mark that he must never tell anyone else about this because people will think it is "weird and dirty." At school Mark is an aggressive child and often gets into playground fights with older, stronger boys. Bill is very passive and often lethargic and becomes sick to his stomach when any detail of the daily routine is changed. Eventually Mark's teacher asked the school social worker to make a home visit.

This case demonstrates *isolating* (keeping the two boys from normal social contacts) and *corrupting* (by "infantilizing" the boys to the point where they feel guilty about the sleeping arrangements).

Case 12: Ken

As a preschooler, Ken was greatly cherished by his parents. However, on entering school he lost his cherished position. Though apparently intelligent, Ken performed poorly in school. Teachers attributed his poor performance to his lack of effort (several years later he was diagnosed as dyslexic). Ken's father told him that he must get good report cards or he would be punished by having to eat a bar of soap for each bad grade he received. Consequently, Ken was sick six times a year, once each report card period. Ken's mother used a different approach. She continually derided him, compared him with other neighborhood children, scolded him, and admonished him. After the first two dismal years of school, the teachers abandoned their efforts to instruct Ken and ignored him in class. The other children in his class played tricks on him and called him "dummy." When he was nine, Ken began to develop an explosive temper. He got into many fights in school, swore at his teachers, and stabbed an aunt who was teasing him. During these episodes Ken was completely out of control. His guidance counselor finally contacted a family service agency for help.

This case reveals *rejecting* (his mother's verbal abuse) and *terrorizing* (the punishment of being forced to eat soap).

Case 13: Wanda

Wanda was an illegitimate child. Shortly after she was born, her mother left her with her grandmother and disappeared. Wanda grew up hoping that someday her mother would return with a husband, so that Wanda would have a family as other children did. One day Wanda's mother did return and wanted Wanda to live with her. Although Wanda was at first apprehensive about living with this strange woman, these feelings were overshadowed by her desire to be with her mother. This living arrangement did not last long. When Wanda could not meet her mother's expectations that she be mature and capable of providing companionship, she was returned to her grandmother's home. Throughout the following years, Wanda's mother would return, raising Wanda's hopes for a permanent reunion, and then abruptly leave again. Wanda felt bad about her mother but still held onto the hope that someday her mother would want her.

Around the age of ten, Wanda started stealing at school, lying, and hanging around with the neighborhood boys. School authorities were concerned about Wanda's behavior and referred her to the school psychologist.

This case reveals *rejecting* (Wanda's mother refuses to provide consistent care and maintain attachment).

Case 14: Erin

Erin has nightmares almost every night and is afraid to go outside her apartment. At age ten she has lived through a decade of life in a high-crime inner-city neighborhood. Last year her uncle, who lived next door, was killed by a mugger who robbed him on the stairs of the apartment building. Her best friend down the street was molested by a teenager, who threatened to kill the girl's cat if she told her parents. She told Erin about it after swearing her to secrecy, and now Erin is terrified that she will die if she goes outside. Every day on her way back from school, she sees the teenage neighbor on the street and he makes sexual gestures toward her and smiles. Her parents try to reassure her and to shield her from news of neighborhood violence, but to little avail. She often seems to daydream at school and at home. Pale and thin, Erin seems to be slipping away. At first her parents were solicitous, but now they alternate between being angry with her and depressed about her. The school guidance counselor has begun counseling sessions with Erin at school.

Erin's case illustrates *terrorizing* (the threatening environment personified in the sexually threatening teenage neighbor).

Case 15: Teddy

Teddy was separated from his mother at two and lived in a series of foster homes. When he was seven, his mother came to ask him whether he would like to live with her again. By this time he had a new half-brother and half-sister and a new stepfather (the boy's and girl's father). Teddy said that he did want to live with her. For a few months, everything was all right, but then the stepfather grew increasingly resentful of Teddy. He made Teddy ask for permission before doing anything—standing up, sitting down, or going to the bathroom. He refused to let Teddy join the Boy Scouts or go to his friends' houses to play. Teddy's mother (a problem drinker) did not want to take on any more trouble by opposing her husband. She had had a hard enough time getting him to agree to take Teddy in the first place. When the boy brought home things he had made in school or when he asked for help with his schoolwork, his stepfather made fun of his efforts or called him stupid. At age eleven, after four years of this treatment, Teddy was admitted to the emergency room of the local hospital because he had swallowed a can of turpentine. His parents described it as an accident, but the emergency room staff suspected that it had been a deliberate suicide attempt.

Teddy's case illustrates *rejecting* (the stepfather's refusal to accept the boy as part of the family), *terrorizing* (the constant belittling and torment), and *isolating* (refusing to permit the boy to have a normal social life).

Case 16: Shirley

Shirley was twelve years old when her parents divorced. She stayed with her father and younger brother, while her mother moved away with her boyfriend. For the first few months, things went fine in her father's house. Then he started spending more and more time with the women he was dating, and Shirley was left to care for her brother day and night. Finally, she decided to live with her mother, who had returned to town with a new husband. Four months later, Shirley discovered that her mother was pregnant and therefore went to live with her grandmother. After two months the grandmother complained that she could not handle Shirley and returned her to her father, who reluctantly took her back. He was preoccupied with the breaking up of his current affair and spent little time with Shirley. Shirley started shutting herself in her room and hanging around in the streets every night. She refused to care for her younger brother and skipped school frequently. Shirley came to the attention of the child welfare agency when she was picked up for truancy violations several times.

Shirley's case is an example of *ignoring* (father's remoteness) and *rejecting* (mother's abandonment).

Case 17: Elsa

Fourteen-year-old Elsa is the second of three children. Her mother is a heroin addict and her father is an alcoholic. Throughout her childhood Elsa was aware of her mother's drug use and her father's drinking. When Elsa's father is out on one of his binges, her mother often has men in the house overnight. Elsa has observed these men giving her mother money after she has had sex with them. Several times she has been awakened when these men entered her room and began touching her. On one such occasion, she called for her mother, who told her to shut up because the man had "paid good money for you." This man forced her to have sex and then gave her $10. After the third time this happened, Elsa decided to ask for $20. The man gave it to her, and Elsa's mother told her that from then on they would split the money she got. That night Elsa tried heroin for the first time.

Elsa's case illustrates *corrupting* (the mother introducing her to prostitution and drug abuse).

Case 18: Ann

Ann was adopted at age fourteen by her stepfather. Shortly thereafter, he assaulted Ann's mother and threatened Ann's older brother, who refused to be adopted, with a crowbar. For her own safety and that of her children, Ann's mother left her husband. However, since Ann had been adopted by her stepfather, he was entitled to visitation rights.

During visits he would tell Ann that her mother was mentally ill and needed to be hospitalized. He warned Ann to stay away from her mother or she too would become crazy. He also bought presents for Ann and wrote her romantic letters. After several such visits, Ann began talking in a strange voice, like a recorder, using her stepfather's exact words and language. Her posture became rigid and mechanical, and often she would sit for hours with a blank, fixed stare. Now Ann will not speak to her mother and has become plagued by suicidal thoughts. Unable to communicate with Ann, Ann's mother contacted a psychologist for help.

This case demonstrates that Ann's stepfather has *terrorized* her. He has brainwashed Ann into believing that her mother will harm her and has created a climate of fear for Ann.

Case 19: Johnny

Thirteen-year-old Johnny lives with his older sister, his mother, and an old-fashioned stepfather. The stepfather believes in setting strict limits for both of his children, but he is especially intent on disciplining Johnny. By threatening to hurt him, his father has made Johnny come home every day straight after school to chop wood for the house's wood-burning stove. The father watches Johnny from the house to ensure that the child is not being lazy or wasting time. When this job is done, Johnny has to clean the house and do other house-related chores. He is not allowed to see friends, since there is always some work to do, and after supper he must spend the rest of the evening in his bedroom.

On the rare occasions when the mother is home and the father is not, she allows Johnny to skip his chores. However, if the father finds out, Johnny will suffer "the consequences," and his mother will not intervene in his behalf. She feels that Johnny craves his father's attention but indicates that she will not discuss the matter with her husband because he might leave her. Their relationship, in general, seems conflicted; yet neither adult is willing to discuss the relationship. The case came to the attention of school authorities after Johnny had started a fire in the bathroom.

This case illustrates *terrorizing* (the stepfather's threats and constant supervision), *isolating* (the stepfather's refusal to allow Johnny to form friendships), and *ignoring* (the mother's unavailability and failure to provide support).

Case 20: Ricky

Ricky's hard-working, conscientious parents never showed affection toward their children, and they drove Ricky in the same way they drove themselves, requiring that he excel in everything and not involve himself in nonproductive activities. Ricky was the oldest and was therefore expected to perform at maximum capability at all times. The demands on the younger children were not so extreme, and their punishments for failure were less severe. Ricky was an honor student and an Eagle Scout. He had little interest in football but played because it was important to his father. Friendships were discouraged, and when Ricky was not at school, he was at home. He was also expected to participate in all the family activities.

At home Ricky was subjected to constant criticism because he never could meet his father's impossibly high standards. Although his friends, classmates, and teachers admired and approved of him, his parents considered him a failure and a disappointment. Moreover, he was never allowed to air his feelings at home. The father's control was total, and Ricky had been indoctrinated and conditioned to such an extent that he was unable to develop the normal escape mechanisms usually available to children in similar situations—running away, asserting himself, or rejecting his father's standards. Instead, after each complaint by his father, he tried harder and continued to experience the cycle of defeat, frustration, and rejection. The constant pressure began to be reflected in his performance. His grades slipped from A's to B's and C's, he began to lose weight, and his coach commented that he sometimes seemed disoriented and confused. Under increased pressures, he attempted suicide.

This case reveals *terrorizing* (the constant unrealistic and extreme demands to excel) and *rejecting* (defining him as a failure).

Conclusion

These twenty case studies and the matrix of behaviors presented in Figure 1 represent a first step toward operationalizing psychological maltreatment. Practitioners should determine how far their responsibility and competence extend. Which types of psychological maltreatment in what ages are within their jurisdiction and professional expertise? In order to identify cases of maltreatment, assess them, and intervene in them, we need to have a firm grasp on the issues of conceptual and operational definition (presented in Chapters One and Two), and we further need to know which types of maltreatment we can deal with.

One way to move forward to identification, assessment, and intervention is to go back to definition.

Think of a case or cases that you are familiar with, and fill in the corresponding cells in Figure 1. Then take a longitudinal perspective about this case (or cases), and think how each type of maltreatment would appear in the same child as he or she grows up. This exercise will lead to greater mastery of the definitions presented in Chapters One and Two.

❈ 3 ❈

Identifying Cases of Maltreatment

In Chapters One and Two we defined psychological maltreatment as rejecting, terrorizing, isolating, corrupting, and ignoring. Here our goal is to translate those definitions into practical strategies for identifying cases of psychological maltreatment in families and communities. By "community" we mean here, as well as in the next chapters, the geographical and social system within which the family lives—the system that is a combination of social units that are responsible for the main local functions. We use the broader terms "social environment," "social context," and "environmental context" interchangeably to denote the general environment of a family, to which "community" is subordinated.

Identifying cases of psychological maltreatment involves a consideration of "causes" and of "effects." By "causes" we mean the psychologically harmful actions directed toward the child by parents, siblings, and other family members. As described in Chapter Two, these harmful actions include behaviors that are developmentally dangerous, regardless of whether they have already produced visible and measurable harm to a child. By "effects" we mean the developmental consequences of maltreatment for the child, which are often manifested as disturbed patterns of behavior (withdrawal and apathy, aggression and hostility, or other maladaptive behaviors). Thus, identification involves the discovery of disturbed, delayed, or any other inappropriate behavioral patterns in children.

We begin by describing our ecological view of the family and, in so doing, provide a conceptual basis for the components and processes involved in identifying psychological maltreatment.

At the outset, however, we must differentiate psychological maltreatment from cases in which the child is emotionally or behaviorally disturbed and the parents do their best to help their child. We should also differentiate psychological maltreatment from occasional and situational mistreatment of the child. These are different, since part of the parent-child-environment picture has changed. When children are emotionally troubled, they may manifest the same characteristics as maltreated children; yet the parents will not be classified as ignoring, rejecting, or terrorizing. When the child is only occasionally mistreated, the consistency and severity of the maltreatment are reduced and so are the consequences.

Psychological maltreatment usually appears in the forms described in this chapter. On occasion, however, we find parents who maltreat the child, yet the child does not manifest any of the corresponding personal characteristics, perceptions, or behavior problems. Such a child appears to be "stress resistant" (Garmezy, 1983). In these cases we often can detect a supportive environment outside the family, which compensates for the maltreatment and sustains a semblance of normal development. The degree of family-level risk is crucial (Gray, Cutler, Dean, and Kempe, 1979; Nicholson and Schneider, 1978).

An Ecological View of the Family

When viewed from an ecological perspective, human functioning and development become inextricably social and interdependent. Environment shapes the self, and human functioning influences the social environment. Every person lives and develops within social systems that become increasingly broader in scope as development proceeds: starting from simple one-to-one attachments with caregivers and moving outward and onward to the community and the overarching culture (Garbarino and Associates, 1982). According to this framework, the family is a social system in its own right. It is embedded in the social environment of neighborhood and community. We see the family as a set of developing individuals who are constantly engaged in creating conceptions of who they are, as well as trying to comprehend the situations they encounter. When family members communicate with each other, their behavior communicates how they see themselves, but, more important, it communicates how they see the others. For example, if family members perceive another family member as an unworthy person, their behavior toward that family member may communicate rejection. Self-perception and the perception of others become central in understanding family communication in general, and communication in maltreating families in particular.

A person's behavior at any given moment is influenced by that person's current perceptions of self and other and by previously acquired and reinforced patterns of communication with the other person (see Blumer, 1969; Bronfenbrenner, 1979; Garbarino and Associates, 1982; Goffman, 1959; Manis and Meltzer, 1978; Turner, 1982). Thus, in order to understand a family's interaction patterns, we need to understand how the family members view themselves and each other; we also need to understand how the perception of self and others interacts with the previously developed patterns of communication and with general personal characteristics of the family members to create altogether unique patterns of interaction and mutual behaviors.

It becomes clear that, in order to identify psychological maltreatment and understand its dynamics, we need to understand each family member's perception of self and others and the interaction of these perceptions with personal characteristics. We also need to understand the overall communication patterns in the family, as manifested in the behavior of various family members. However, the understanding of psychological maltreatment goes beyond the interaction patterns within a family, since we view the whole family as a system related to its social environment. The relationship of the family system with its environment is mutual: environmental conditions influence family life, and changes that occur in the family facilitate environmental changes, as the environment tries to adjust itself to the new family patterns. Thus, the family and its environment mutually adapt in order to maintain the system-environment fit (see Bronfenbrenner, 1979; Garbarino and Associates, 1982). In psychologically maltreating families, this family-environment mutual fit acquires destructive characteristics or does not exist at all. Furthermore, the family system has a unique climate in it, derived both from its internal interaction patterns and from its modes of interaction with the environment. The case studies in Chapter Two give nice examples of the family characteristics and the relationship of the family with the environment when maltreatment has become a pattern.

The evolving picture of the ecological and interactional factors that play a role in psychological maltreatment is presented in Figure 2. This figure outlines our view of the relationships among the factors involved in psychological maltreatment in a parent-child relationship. The inner circle describes the processes that, in our view, characterize parent-child relationships in general and become dynamically evident in families where maltreatment occurs. Parental activities influence the child's perception of the parents as well as the child's personal characteristics. These, in turn, influence the child's behaviors, which, in turn, influence the parents' perceptions of their child and the parents' own personal characteristics. Parental perceptions and characteristics shape the parents' activities, which influence the child's perception of the parents—and so forth. This parent-child interaction circle is embedded in the family system with its unique climate, which is embedded in the larger environmental context. In each of these systems—the parent-child, the family, and the environment—both risk factors and preventive resource factors determine the likelihood, extent, and severity of maltreatment. Overall, certain characteristics of each of the factors in Figure 2 and their mutual interaction form the core of psychological maltreatment of children. Maltreatment of children is not limited to parent-child relationships. It may occur in other family relationships involving children, such as sibling relationships, and even in out-of-home settings (see Chapter Eight). However, this volume focuses primarily on identification of, assessment of, intervention with, and prevention of parental maltreatment.

As mentioned earlier, in order to identify psychological maltreatment, we must look at the specific characteristics of a family, its environment, and its individual members; we must understand the interrelatedness of these characteristics; and we

Figure 2. The Factors Involved in Psychological Maltreatment.

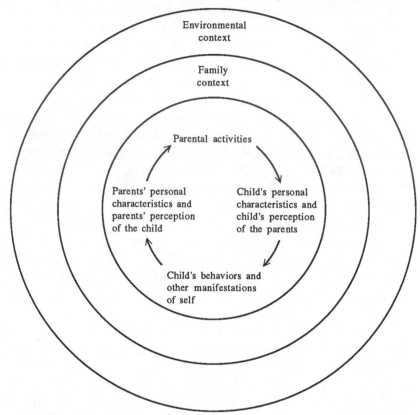

must collect more information about them. Let us now describe this identification process, moving from the broader contexts to the narrower ones—from the periphery of Figure 2 to its center.

Environmental Context for Psychological Maltreatment

Families in which psychological maltreatment occurs usually live apart from the "naturally corrective" and supportive influences of pro-social support systems (Elmer, 1967; Gil, 1970; Light, 1973; MacCarthy, 1979; Rohner and Rohner, 1980; Young, 1964). Often the family isolates itself from the community; but communities or neighbors also may reject and isolate the family (Polansky and Gaudin, 1983). In such communities there is no real sense of a collective responsibility and neighborhood identity; alienation and lack of belongingness prevail; and poverty, unemployment, crime, poor housing, and unavailability of services are dominant conditions of life (Brown, 1984; Brown, Whitehead, and Braswell, 1981). Psychological maltreatment is likely to be found more often in such distressed communities, where pervasive poverty and unemployment tend to create a sense of frustration and powerlessness among parents. Coupled with the prevalence of large families and heavy child care responsibilities and the absence of adequate health care, day care, and entertainment for children, this negative social climate establishes background for psychological maltreatment. It is a background of inadequate social resources (Belsky, 1980; Brown, 1984).

Stressed by their everyday living situation and overwhelmed by their child care responsibilities, these families tend to lose whatever positive constructive coping skills they may have possessed and slip into an escalating pattern of child maltreatment, involving rejecting, isolating, corrupting, ignoring, and terrorizing activities. They may have relationships with other families in the community. However, since all suffer from the same situation and none know how to get out of it, these networks do not function as positive social support. Rather, they serve as a mechanism for reinforcing the apathetic and futile world view that the world is unjust and that people like them will always suffer. These networks also reinforce the idea in the parents that child maltreatment is justified under such circumstances: for the sake of discipline or to prevent their children from adopting any form of social deviance, such as delinquency. These families are not socially isolated in a pure sense, but they are isolated from constructive pro-social support and from the world that is beyond their low-resource community. This negative social nexus is increasingly being referred to as "the underclass" in metropolitan centers.

Maltreatment, however, particularly psychological maltreatment, is not uniquely a phenomenon linked to low economic and social resources. Middle-class and upper-middle-class families who live in alienating neighborhoods or who adopt destructive lifestyles can be maltreating as well. In these neighborhoods, where there is a widespread belief in the value of privacy, families isolate themselves from one another, and each has to cope with the strains and stresses of life on its own. These families lack social support networks, and their isolation may give rise to maltreatment in times of crisis.

On the environmental level, then, two major contributing factors are evident. The first is the resourceless, impoverished family overwhelmed by the demands of life.

Betty's mother (Case 2) has been living on welfare and is overwhelmed by her responsibilities in taking care of five children. Further, she is the only adult to care for them, and there seem to be no resources in the community to assist her in her tasks. The family's isolation, coupled with the mother's reluctance to let her children go outside the house and their reaction to that restriction, has produced a dangerous situation. Since no support is available or accessible, the mother has lost her coping skills and has been terrorizing the older children and ignoring the infant.

The second type of maltreating family is the middle-class, alienated family that is engaged in a destructive lifestyle.

Ricky's parents (Case 20) have isolated themselves from the surrounding community by their work ethic and beliefs about family life. Family activities are intense and exclusive, and family members are discouraged from participating in other social groups. Similarly, outside friendships are viewed negatively and thus do not exist. The total control by the father, as well as the isolation of the family and Ricky from social situations, seems to have brought about the child's exhibition of disturbed symptoms.

Family Context for Psychological Maltreatment

As mentioned, families involved in psychological maltreatment are likely to operate in isolation from pro-social influences. They tend to lack an effective social support network and often resist such relationships (Fontana, 1973; MacCarthy, 1979; Rohner and Rohner, 1980). Isolated families also tend to distrust social services and sometimes even society in general. There is often a tense and aggressive climate in these families, and the whole home environment communicates psychic threat (Herrenkohl and Herrenkohl, 1981). The meaning of the family unit may be annihilated as a consequence of repeated reconstruction or breakdown of the family system, marital discord, mental and physical illness, or other problems. In such a family, members do not respect each other, find all contact aversive, and thus open the door for maltreatment (Bolton, Laner, and Gai, 1981; Gaines, Sandgrund, Green, and Power, 1978).

Even when the family continues to be meaningful to its members, maltreatment can occur as an expansion of marital conflict (Herrenkohl and Herrenkohl, 1981; Herrenkohl, Herrenkohl, and Egolf, 1983). In these cases the conflict enlarges to include the child or is attributed to the child's behaviors. Overall, the commonly identified family context of maltreating parents is one of stress characterized by distrustfulness and conflict.

The relationship between Johnny's parents (Case 19) has been identified as conflictual. The stepfather believes in setting strict limits for the children, and the mother lets Johnny skip his chores whenever the father is not around. The mother is afraid that her husband might leave her. They refuse to discuss their relationship, and in the meantime the father has been terrorizing and isolating Johnny, whereas the mother largely ignores him. The atmosphere in the family is one of threat, distrust (the father supervises Johnny while Johnny does his chores), passive conflict, and restricted freedom.

Another characteristic of maltreating families concerns their parenting skills and methods. Often the parents lack sufficient knowledge about child development to cope with the demands created by the child's needs and behaviors (Belsky, 1980; Herrenkohl and Herrenkohl, 1981). They may have irrational and exaggerated expectations of performance from their children and maltreat them when they fail to respond to these expectations (Gordon, 1979/80). Or the parents may not understand the importance of supervision for the child, the significance of regular eating and sleeping habits, or their role in stimulating and encouraging the child (Whiting, 1976). Further, the parents may hold one of two sets of attitudes toward their parenting skills: (1)

They may doubt the adequacy of their parenting skills and thus frequently and erratically vary the methods used to handle their children, thereby communicating an atmosphere of doubt for the children (MacCarthy, 1979). (2) Each parent may strongly believe in a different style of parenting, so that they have frequent disagreements or arguments about the correct parenting methods to use (Herrenkohl, Herrenkohl, and Egolf, 1983). Finally, the parents may lack knowledge of effective child management techniques. All such parents are vulnerable to becoming "entrapped" in a conflicted and unsatisfying parent-child pattern.

However, compensating factors tend to spare some of these families from frequent and severe episodes of maltreatment. We can identify four such compensating influences: (1) parents have the benefit of effective advice from their social network; (2) children engage in self-correcting development (linked to biological maturation or social influences) that alters behavior; (3) parents have sufficient competence and insight to proceed with self-analysis of emerging problems; and (4) parents are amenable to expert assistance. Families that slip into a pattern of psychological maltreatment tend to lack these compensatory influences. The following is an example of conflicted and unsatisfying parent-child patterns:

Ken's parents (Case 12) expect him to get good report cards every time and to be successful in everything he does. The boy, however, cannot meet their unrealistic expectations. Because they lack the parenting skills needed to cope with such a situation, they have rejected and terrorized him. Further, Ken has not had the compensatory influence of peers' or teachers' support and has developed an explosive temper. His parents do not know how to deal with his temper, and an enhanced pattern of maltreatment has been gradually created.

In short, a family atmosphere that is conducive to maltreatment tends to convey stress, tension, and aggression regardless of whether the family unit still has a meaning for its members. In identifying this atmosphere, one often finds inappropriate parenting skills as well. The overall picture is one of a tension-ridden family in which parent-child interaction has acquired chronic negative features that translate into maltreatment. Unless compensating factors can be found, parents tend to lack the coping skills needed to escape from the cycle of maltreatment. This pattern of family atmosphere reflects characteristics of the community context as well as the personal characteristics of the parents in interaction with their specific child.

Parental Factors Related to Maltreatment

Parental Behavior. Several classifications of the behaviors of psychologically maltreating parents have been suggested (see, for example, Garbarino and Vondra, 1986; Jacoby, 1985; Rohner and Rohner, 1980). In summarizing them, one finds a continuum of parental attitudes and behaviors, ranging from the parents' "being unavailable to meet the child's needs" to "making partial and inappropriate responses to the child" and extending to "responding harshly and destructively to the child's needs."

1. Parents are unavailable to respond to the child's needs. Such parents mainly ignore and reject their children. When they are unavailable to meet their children's physical needs, they fail to feed the children appropriately, to dress them as needed, or to enable them to get enough sleep or health care (Fontana, 1973; Herrenkohl and Herrenkohl, 1981; Jenewicz, 1983). They may couple these ignoring and rejecting behaviors with inadequate supervision of the child. Ultimately, they leave the child's needs uncared for.

The parents may also be unavailable to meet their children's psychological needs (Egeland, Sroufe, and Erickson, 1983)— rejecting (Rohner and Rohner, 1980), depriving and distancing (Jacoby, 1985), and neglecting (see Egeland, Sroufe, and Erickson, 1983; Watkins and Bradbard, 1982) their children. In our terms, parents who are psychologically unavailable tend to ignore, isolate, and reject their child. When trying to identify these families, we often find a lack of physical and verbal closeness to the child, as well as an unawareness of the child's need for warmth, support, and love.

Shirley's parents (Case 16) were unavailable to respond to her physical, psychological, and developmental needs (ignoring and rejecting). Her father was too preoccupied with his affairs and her mother with a new husband. They both have failed to pay the needed attention to their child. Because the grandmother could not handle Shirley's adolescent behaviors, the girl returned to her father but was actually left on her own. Being uncared for, she started hanging around in the streets and skipping school.

2. Parents give partial and inappropriate responses to the child's needs, mainly rejecting and corrupting the child. The parents try to meet the child's physical and psychological needs; yet they lack sufficient resources, knowledge, and skills for doing so effectively. More specifically, they may impose too many responsibilities on the child and become angry whenever the child fails to perform. At the same time, they may set too many rules and limits for the child, and thereby leave no option in the child's hands but to break the rules and fail to perform (Herrenkohl, Herrenkohl, and Egolf, 1983). Similarly, the parents may set excessively high demands for performance by the child that make it impossible for the child to meet the parents' levels of expectations (Gordon, 1979/80; Jenewicz, 1983).

Another inappropriate response is infantilization. Instead of placing excessively high demands on the child, the parents underestimate the child's physical abilities and mental capacities and consistently prevent the child from actualizing his or her potentials. Sometimes the reason for infantilization is the parents' wish to maintain their control over the child or their fear of becoming old by seeing the child growing up. Parents who are emotionally needy and who become overdependent on their children may be at special risk here (for example, parents who never resolved separation from their own parents or whose parents died early in life). Lack of knowledge about children and how to raise them may contribute. Regardless of the reasons for parental infantilization, however, this behavior places constraints on normal child development.

A third type of inappropriate response, corrupting or mis-socializing, occurs when parents teach the child values that deviate from normative community values. In some instances the child is

raised on values that differ markedly from those of the community—for example, values favoring drug abuse, sexual misconduct,
or delinquent activity (Garbarino and Vondra, 1986)—and
therefore place the child in jeopardy. Children who are corrupted
or mis-socialized tend to become maladjusted and, to some extent,
may even be a threat to themselves.

Parents who give inappropriate responses often do so
because they lack respect for the child's personality, thoughts,
feelings, and behaviors. Such parents often undervalue the child's
accomplishments; dismiss the child's feelings as "childish,"
unimportant, or even bothersome; and fail to consider the child's
limitations and weaknesses (Patterson and Thompson, 1980). They
may become sarcastic toward the child and convey an overall
message of personal insignificance and worthlessness. They teach
children that they are not to be respected and valued.

Finally, parents may be inconsistent in their parenting style,
thereby giving the child conflicting and contradicting messages. As
a result, they tend to prevent the child from fulfilling his or her
needs for exploration, safety, and certainty (Fontana, 1973). The
parents' responses become unpredictable to the child, something
that should not be trusted. The parental figure becomes a symbol
of unreliability. These parents often give contradictory responses
to the child. They may mix periods of hugging and rewarding
with periods of screaming; or they may scream at the child for
doing something, whereas on a different occasion they hugged the
child for doing the same thing. The gap between the child's
expectation for a certain response and the actual response that he
or she gets might be considered one of the sources of later
maladjustment.

Frequently parents who give partial and inappropriate
responses to the needs of their child display not one but several of
the previously mentioned behaviors. They tend to impose too
many responsibilities, set excessively high demands for performance, be inconsistent, and lack respect for the child. They may
also mis-socialize the child and infantilize him or her at the same
time. The following is an example of inappropriate parental
responses:

Mark (Case 11) and his brother, Bill, have been infantilized by their mother and grandmother. By treating the two boys as if they were toddlers, when they are actually eight and ten years old, the women also demonstrate a lack of respect for these children's developmental needs. To some extent, the two women also have mis-socialized the boys, keeping them away from social contacts and conveying to them the message that the outside world is dangerous.

3. Parents make harsh and destructive responses to the needs of their child, mainly terrorizing but also degrading, threatening, and exploiting their children (Garbarino and Vondra, 1986), as well as depreciating and dominating them (Jacoby, 1985). Overall, these parents verbally abuse their child, using words such as "never" and "always" to strengthen their verbal abuse; or they may threaten and terrify the child (Krugman and Krugman, 1984; Whiting, 1976) or confine the child and forbid any social contact (Fontana, 1973). As a result, the child learns that the world and they, as parents, are entities to be feared. These parents demand total compliance and cannot tolerate any behavior that deviates from their expectations. Even when the child reaches their expectations, they are likely to find some other reason that would justify maltreatment.

Teddy's stepfather (Case 15) terrorized the child until Teddy made a suicide attempt, which led to the identification of the case. Restrictive and hostile to the child, the father terrified and humiliated Teddy by forcing him to ask permission before doing anything. He also forbade social contact and consequently isolated Teddy from compensating influences. Simultaneously, the father made fun of Teddy and called him stupid, thereby strengthening the verbal abuse and furthering the maltreatment.

Parental Perceptions of the Child. Each of the three categories of parental behavior has a corresponding parental perception of the child. At one end of the perception continuum (corresponding to physical and psychological unavailability), parents view children as being able to get along on their own. They tend to be unaware of the child's needs and often feel that no problems exist in the family in general and with the child in particular (Fontana,

1973; Patterson and Thompson, 1980; Whiting, 1976). At the other end of the continuum (corresponding to giving harsh and destructive responses to the child's needs), parents perceive the child as being "very bad," "much too demanding," "provocative," and "a big problem" (Herrenkohl, Herrenkohl, and Egolf, 1983). He or she is just a burden. Along this continuum, varying degrees of perceived child-related problems can be found (corresponding to giving partial and inappropriate responses to the child's needs). All these perceptions convey one central idea—that the unliked child is different from the rest of the family in negative and troublesome ways.

Cindy (Case 10) was perceived by her parents and siblings as a difficult and troublesome child. They all thought they had to exert rigid discipline and control over her in order to keep her out of trouble. As a result, they isolated her from external social contacts and scapegoated her at home. When asked about her behavior, upon identification of the scapegoating, they said that she had always been such a problem that the only possible way to handle her was to cut her off from everyday family activities.

The child who is perceived as unusual (as Cindy was) is typically also perceived as eliciting and enhancing the maltreatment by his or her own behaviors and personality. The perceived unusualness of the child tends to become the parents' justification for maltreatment. This perception is one of the identified characteristics of psychologically maltreating parents.

Parents' Personal Characteristics. When we identify parents who maltreat their child, we are likely to find not only specific behaviors and characteristic perceptions of the child but also a number of related parental personal characteristics. These personal characteristics can be summarized as follows:

1. The parents themselves have been psychologically maltreated as children. Often they have received inadequate nurturance, support, and encouragement from their parents and have become emotionally needy, disturbed, and unstable adults (Belsky, 1980; Fontana, 1973; Gordon, 1979/80; Jacoby, 1985; MacCarthy, 1979; Sweet and Resick, 1979). These parents often rely on their children to satisfy their own dependency needs, needs left

unsatisfied during their childhood. They tend to "parentify" children and frequently ask for comfort and support from them. When the child, naturally, fails to meet the parents' needs, they feel insecure and betrayed by their own child. The feelings of betrayal and insecurity on the parents' part form the ground for maltreatment.

These parents are often characterized also as impulsive, low in self-esteem, and uncertain about their own identity. They may use projection and externalization with regard to the child. In other words, they tend to be unsure of themselves and to blame the child and the environment for their own failures.

Wanda's mother (Case 13) is an unstable, impulsive individual who has left her child and then returned and then, unexpectedly, left again. She expected Wanda to meet her companionship needs; when the child failed to do so, the mother simply left her. Having grown up in an impoverished environment herself, the mother had experienced psychological maltreatment as a child. The first boy she met became Wanda's father. At present, in part because of her "undeveloped" personality, she tends to reject her daughter.

Interestingly, early inquiries into the "battered child syndrome" reported a similar sort of psychological maltreatment in the background of parents (not, as is commonly believed, a pattern of physical brutalization). Steele and Pollack's (1968) classic study is clear on this point.

This "personality type" can also be understood from a social learning perspective. Parents have likely learned these behaviors, at least in part, through observing the model of their own parents. Furthermore, their current style of behavior might be positively reinforced within the family system (Sweet and Resick, 1979). Yet, regardless of the explanatory scheme that we choose, these parents are usually identified as having emotional problems and being unstable and unreliable.

2. The parent is addicted to drugs or alcohol. Drug- or alcohol-addicted parents are often out of control when responding to the child's activities, have marital conflicts, or are unable to care for themselves and the child. Moreover, they tend to ignore and

neglect the child and to disregard their parenting responsibilities (Jenewicz, 1983).

3. The parent creates an "interactional stress environment" (Jenewicz, 1983), where the parent-child relationship is constantly tense and both feel that the relationship might explode at any moment. The parents maintain disorganized lives, as well as large and chaotic families, and are usually also involved in parent-child power struggles. They create and sustain a social climate of instability and "messiness." Often both the drug abuser and the parent who creates an "interactional stress environment" are members of impoverished families.

Elsa's parents (Case 17) both suffer from drug and alcohol problems. As a consequence, they have neglected Elsa's developmental and psychological needs. Moreover, the parents lead two separate lives, thus creating a stressed family environment; and the mother's involvement with prostitution has decreased her care for her daughter and has led the girl herself to prostitution and drug abuse.

4. The parent is mentally ill or mentally retarded. Such parents are often identified by the lack of sufficient psychological and social resources to meet the child's needs adequately.

Bobby's mother (Case 8) had mental health problems and was under treatment. Because of her own difficulties, she lacked the resources to handle her child and often terrorized him by her verbal abuse. She would threaten him whenever she was in an episode of rage related to her paranoid schizophrenic characteristics. The child's needs were unmet to such an extent that he fell below developmental norms and was extremely fearful and anxious. The mother's treatment of Bobby was identified after his behavior became dysfunctional and bizarre.

Children's Behavior, Perceptions, and Characteristics Related to Maltreatment

Infants, young children, and adolescents respond differently to psychological maltreatment, as individuals and as representatives of developmental categories. Their responses vary along developmental stages and across contexts: an infant will respond differently from an older child, and a child in one family or community context will respond differently from a child in another context. Because their developmental levels and contexts differ, they perceive the parents accordingly and manifest developmentally and contextually specific behaviors.

Infants. Psychological maltreatment of infants usually occurs in the form of rejection, unavailability (ignoring), malnourishment, and inconsistency (Fontana, 1973; Rohner and Rohner, 1980). The parents may disregard the infant's basic physical needs, hold back love and warmth, or be inconsistent about meeting the infant's needs. They may shut off the infant's needs for exploration and manipulation of the environment by forbidding movement and access to objects, and they may avoid physical contact with the baby. The infant's perception of such parents is manifested through apathy, crying and irritability, refusal to calm down, and avoidance of the parents. In addition, "turntaking" (Brazelton, 1982; Kaye, 1982)—in which the parents' words and movements are tied to and harmonious with the infant's—is erratic, off-timed, or missing. The infant may even undergo the process of "nonorganic failure to thrive" (Gordon, 1979/80; MacCarthy, 1979), characterized by insufficient weight gain and impaired health, slow physical growth, retarded language development, distorted social responses, and apathetic solitariness. Physical and psychological nurturance are linked during infancy.

Overall, these infants, even when they are physically cared for and only psychologically maltreated, are likely to be anxiously attached to their parents, irritable, and inadequate in their social responses. In other words, they may make an attempt to be near the parent but move away when the parent tries to get closer. They may stay near the parent but avoid eye contact, or they may ask to be picked up but then may kick the parent, or they may try to avoid any kind of contact with the parents. They may be more responsive to other adults than to their parents; or they may show negative affect to all the people surrounding them (Ainsworth, Blehar, Waters, and Wall, 1978; Egeland, Sroufe, and Erickson, 1983).

In short, psychologically maltreated infants can be indentified by the lack of harmony in their relationships with their parents and by their socially inappropriate and irregular responses.

David (Case 4) was forbidden by his mother to talk with strangers and with his own father. He was also not allowed to play with other infants and was usually kept at home. His father, in turn, withdrew from interactions with the infant. Being isolated by the mother and ignored by the father, David began to manifest disturbed patterns. He has been diagnosed as developmentally delayed, destructive, and overdependent on his mother.

Children. Children who are psychologically maltreated by their parents, or even by an older brother or sister, tend to feel unloved, unwanted, inferior, inadequate, and unrelated to any social system (Rohner and Rohner, 1980; Whiting, 1976). They are likely to develop low self-esteem (Egeland, Sroufe, and Erickson, 1983; Jacoby, 1985; Watkins and Bradbard, 1982) and a negative view of the world (Jenewicz, 1983). In other words, they perceive themselves as unworthy individuals and the world as a place that is hostile to them and causes them to be failures.

These children frequently become anxious, aggressive, and hostile. They suffer from constant fear and feel ready to "hit back." Some children internalize their anxieties and aggressions and are ready to "hit themselves back." Other children externalize those anxieties and aggressions and thus become ready to "hit back" the people in their environment. Those who internalize manifest self-destructiveness (causing self-pain), depression, suicidal thoughts, passivity, withdrawal (avoidance of socializing with people), shyness, and a low degree of communication with others. They may also have nervous habits, nightmares, and somatic complaints, such as headaches (Aber and Zigler, 1981; Fontana, 1973; Krugman and Krugman, 1984). Children who externalize tend to be impulsive and overactive, lacking in self-control and often violent toward other people and their environment; in other words, they behave only according to impulses and not according to social norms (Fontana, 1973; Rohner and Rohner, 1980).

Psychologically maltreated children, because they perceive the world as hostile to them, tend to lose their belief in people and become distrustful of them. Further, they may perceive their parents as cruel, unpredictable, and untrustworthy individuals (Fontana, 1973). Simultaneously, the children perceive themselves as inferior and different from other family members and children. Having incorporated a negative self-image, they tend to feel that they deserve the maltreatment, although not all of them and not always (Jacoby, 1985).

Jane (Case 5) was the focus of family conflicts and was rejected by her family and isolated from them. She felt unwanted and inferior. Sometimes she believed that she deserved this treatment; at other times she bitterly resented it. Jane externalizes her feelings and, consequently, has been identified as aggressive, noncompliant, dishonest, and overactive.

The child's personal characteristics and perceptions help us to understand his or her behavior. The behavior of the psychologically maltreated child is often identified as dependent, on the one hand, and angry and aggressive, on the other (Egeland, Sroufe, and Erickson, 1983). If externalization is the method used, the child may behave in a noncompliant, overactive, and destructive manner; if internalization is used, the child may manifest indifference, submissiveness, and hostile withdrawal. The child who externalizes will usually be disobedient and loud, will try to do many things all at once and jump from one to the other, and will attempt to destroy objects and interrupt social interaction. The child who internalizes will be apathetic, will behave according to group decisions rather than self-thought, and will angrily avoid social contacts. Among normal children aggression, whether manifested as violence or as withdrawal, is directed toward the specific frustrating person, and it ends when the child gets what he or she wants or when a specific need has been met (Santostefano, 1978). In contrast, among psychologically maltreated children, aggression is usually not specifically directed but rather widely spread, and it is continuous; it is a state of living rather than a response to a particular situation.

Some children have low levels of social responsiveness or hesitant response patterns. They tend to approach unfamiliar adults, seek their attention, yet avoid physical contact with them (Balla and Zigler, 1975; Harter and Zigler, 1974). Other children may cling to adults other than their parents but nevertheless remain aloof with peers (MacCarthy, 1979). In each instance their social behavior can be identified as situationally inadequate. Often the child fails to respond to environmental rewards (Watkins and Bradbard, 1982) and lacks the skills needed to cope with the social context (Egeland, Sroufe, and Erickson, 1983). In other words, the child will often be indifferent to positive feedback or to his or her own success and will not know how to respond to social challenges or peer rejection.

In the child's behavior toward the parents, similar characteristics are usually identified. Frequently afraid of the parents, the child may try to avoid them as much as possible, so as to avoid the rejection and harm (Egeland, Sroufe, and Erickson, 1983; Fontana, 1973). The child may also try to take care of the parents' needs, hoping that this behavior will reduce future maltreatment. Yet we can identify children who are aggressive or withdrawn with the parents, as they are with other adults. They may rebel completely against parental authority or consistently be provocative toward the parents. These tactics, in turn, enhance the parents' negative perceptions of their child, which, consequently, strengthen child maltreatment, as shown in Figure 2.

In sum, the psychologically maltreated child is often identified by personal characteristics, perceptions, and behaviors that convey low self-esteem, a negative view of the world, and internalized or externalized anxieties and aggressions. Whether the child clings to adults or avoids them, his or her social behavior and responses are inappropriate and exceptional.

Patty (Case 7) was consistently rejected and isolated by her family. She was often locked in her room and punished for what her parents regarded as "misbehaving." Patty felt that she was unloved by her family and that she did not belong in the family. Her anxiety, which resulted from her low status in the family, was internalized and manifested in headaches and dizziness. Patty has been diagnosed as suffering from psychosomatic problems.

Adolescents. Adolescents who are psychologically maltreated tend to exhibit patterns similar to those exhibited by children, except that these patterns are often stronger and more elaborated and perhaps less linked to the parents. Like children, psychologically maltreated adolescents often feel worthless, unloved, and not belonging. Sometimes they perceive the maltreatment as unjust rather than as something they deserve (Brown, Whitehead, and Braswell, 1981). We can hypothesize that adolescents who have been maltreated since they were children might maintain the perception that they deserve it, whereas adolescents who have only recently been subjected to maltreatment might perceive it as evil. However, no data exist to support this plausible hypothesis.

Adolescents may become truant or runaways, get involved with delinquency or substance abuse, rebel against authority, or even become purposefully destructive. Alternatively, they may become depressed, attempt suicide, develop eating or other somatic disturbances, and become emotionally troubled and unstable.

Believing the world to be hostile and their parents untrustworthy, these adolescents are likely either to isolate themselves from the world, family, and peers or to become part of an antisocial group of teenagers. These actions represent the adolescent's way of protesting against parental injustices or achieving some revenge. Adolescents, unlike younger children, may also understand that their parents have problems that help "explain" maltreatment; yet youth are often puzzled and perplexed by the whole situation and do not know how to change it or feel inadequate to do so.

The adolescent's behavior toward the maltreating parents is usually at one extreme or the other, avoidance or aggressiveness. Less effort than in the childhood stage tends to be put into taking care of the parents' needs. On the contrary, some attempts may be made to confront the parents. The following is an example of a terrorized adolescent, who, consequently, became socially withdrawn:

Ann's stepfather (Case 18) tried to distance Ann from her mother by telling her that terrible things would happen to her if she maintained her relationship with her mother. At the same time, he tried to buy her loyalty with presents. Ann's reaction to the psychological maltreatment was manifested in withdrawal, a rigid posture, and a change of voice. She has undergone a complete withdrawal from contact with her mother.

Overall, the maltreated adolescent is similar to the child, with probably two major exceptions: the consequences of the maltreatment may have become more of an integral part of the adolescent's personality, especially if the maltreatment started in childhood, and responses to the maltreatment tend to be more severe and disturbed than the child's responses.

Methods of Information Gathering

Once a family has been suspected of maltreatment, we need to collect more information in order to confirm the suspicion, assess the problem, and prepare for effective intervention. In Chapter Four, we discuss specific instruments and assessment techniques. Here we examine the initial way of assessing the problem.

Information should be collected to shed light on the factors described in this chapter. Information is needed from all the people and contexts that might be directly and indirectly involved in the maltreatment: the child, the parents, other family members, the school or day care center, and any relevant community or social services. Similarly, the responsible practitioner should have or create an opportunity to observe the family and the child's interaction with peers.

Gathering Information from the Child. In correspondence with the theoretical model underlying this chapter (see Figure 2), we want to gather information from children about their perceptions of self and others, their behaviors, parental activities as understood, and relevant environmental aspects. We will use this information to look for compensating and potentiating factors with regard to the suspected maltreatment and to try to determine who the maltreating person is and which types of maltreatment exist: rejecting, terrorizing, ignoring, isolating, and/or corrupting.

With older children and adolescents, interview methods might be used. Children can be asked to describe their parents and portray their ideal parents. They can also describe specific events from their everyday life, focusing on themselves, other family members, misbehaving episodes, methods of punishment used, or patterns of family communication. Children usually like to tell stories about their family and can be asked to do so. They can further describe specific times during the day, such as mornings or bedtimes, when problems are likely to emerge. Once the worker has a general picture of the child and the family and of the circumstances surrounding the maltreatment, the interview can become more specific and focused more on the maltreatment. The child and the worker can role-play a typical incident involving maltreatment, alternating the roles of the parent and the child. They can also use some of the projective methods described in the next paragraph, as well as in Chapter Four, depending on the child's developmental level and preference.

When information must be obtained from younger children, interview methods may be less helpful, although they can certainly reveal some of the needed information. In those cases nonverbal and projective methods should be used. The worker can play with the child, using "pretend play," "family dolls," or doll-house or puppet play. The child can be further asked to make a picture of the family or to draw the family doing something (Kinetic Family Drawing). Projective storytelling and sentence completion can be used as well. In general, these methods are useful for gathering information from children who find it hard to talk about themselves and their families. The themes to be included in the nonverbal and projective methods are the same as in the interview: children's perceptions of self and parents, children's and parents' behaviors, and everyday occurrences and patterns. Using these and similar methods of gathering information from the child, the worker should be able to gain some understanding of the family's interaction patterns and the child's role in that family.

Gathering Information from Parents and Other Family Members. Parents who are suspected of psychological maltreatment or who are likely to know about the maltreatment of their child by another family member should be part of the process of information gathering. In general, the most useful method for getting information from the parents is to interview them about themselves, the family, the environment, and the child. Because of the sensitivity of the issue, indirect and open questions usually are preferable to direct questions.

The parents, interviewed together or separately, can be asked about the current familial and child-related situation, as well as about the emergence of that situation. More specifically, the worker can ask them about everyday patterns, their satisfaction with their family life, their understanding of their behavior, the social networks of the child, and their own networks. Other questions can focus on the parents' perception of their child, his or her behavior and problems, their communication with the child, discipline methods used with the child, and patterns they want to see changed. Again, questions about specific events and times of the day may clarify the picture.

Another part of information gathering from the parents has to do with family history: whether the child was planned and wanted, the circumstances surrounding the birth, typical behaviors of the infant and the parents' responses to them, parenting ideologies and commonly used methods, developmental milestones of the child, and any other major occurrences they remember. Parents also should be carefully asked whether family members have had physical or psychiatric problems or have ever engaged in criminal activities.

Some parents may find it embarrassing or threatening to talk about their family and child or may become confused and incoherent in their descriptions. This in itself is an indicator of problems. In order to clarify the patterns of this family, nonverbal and projective methods, as described previously, might be helpful. In addition, the worker can observe the child and a parent-child or family interaction, noting communication and relationship patterns. Once the worker has developed some specific ideas about the dynamics and patterns of a family, more focused questions about the types of maltreatment can be asked. However, one should be very careful in asking those questions because the issue is extremely sensitive.

Gathering Information from the School and Other Community Services. From the family doctor, the pediatrician, school or day care personnel, or other professionals, we can obtain further information about the child's life, family habits, strange occurrences or behaviors, and social networks. More specifically, we can learn whether the child had or has serious injuries and illnesses and how the family reacted to them; whether the child and family are distanced from the other children and families in the neighborhood; whether the family utilizes any community resources; and whether the family is known at the day care center or school and to the other neighborhood families. From the school we can learn the extent to which a child misbehaves, is late or absent, arrives early and hangs around late, or is inadequately fed and dressed. We can also learn about the child's relationship with other children and the family's attitude toward school. It might be helpful to observe the child at school and consult with the school counselor for further information. Overall, the information we gain from community professionals may verify the existence of psychological maltreatment and is likely to clarify the social context of a family, the parents' methods of parenting, and the child's corresponding responses.

Conclusion

By the end of the identification process, we should have developed sound hunches about the form and type of the existing psychological maltreatment. We also should have some understanding of the family's environmental context (whether it potentiates or compensates for maltreatment); the family context (climate and interaction patterns); the child's behavior, personal characteristics, and perceptions; and parental activities, personal characteristics, and perceptions.

In order to apply the themes of this chapter to your work, consider the following questions: How did you identify some of your own cases of psychological maltreatment? Start by examining

Table 2. Components Involved in Identification of Psychological Maltreatment.

Environmental Context	Family Context	Parents	Child
1. Community isolates family: poor, alienated community; large families; no social resources 2. Family isolates itself: middle class, values privacy, has destructive lifestyle	1. Annihilation of meaning of family unit 2. Expansion of marital conflict, stress 3. Parents lack understanding of child development, exaggerated expectations 4. Parents lack adequate parenting skills	*Behaviors* 1. Unavailable to respond to child's physical and psychological needs 2. Give partial and inappropriate responses to the child's needs: make too many demands infantilize corrupt, mis-socialize lack respect are inconsistent 3. Give destructive responses to child's needs *Personality* 1. Maltreated as children 2. Addicted to drugs or alcohol 3. Create interactional stress environment 4. Mentally ill, mentally retarded	1. Infants: show nonorganic failure to thrive, irritability, inadequate social responses, lack of harmony in relationship with parents 2. Children: feel unloved, inferior, low self-esteem, negative view of the world; anxiety and aggressiveness turned inward or outward; inadequate social behavior 3. Adolescents: feelings similar to children's, but response may be more severe; may become truants, runaways, destructive, depressed, suicidal

the presenting problem and follow this line of diagnostic development to the characteristics of the community, family, parents, and child. Which characteristics of what systems/persons have led you to decide that this is a case of psychological maltreatment? Once you have identified a case of maltreatment, what further information do you need the most? Why? How did you go about getting it? How could you go differently about getting it? What further information do you need the least? Why? From which systems did you receive all your further information? In your experience, what are the best ways to collect information efficiently and to ensure that that information will be accurate? What should one avoid when collecting information? We have identified certain characteristics of maltreating communities, families, and parents and of maltreated infants, children, and youth. (All these characteristics are summarized in Table 2.) Can you identify other characteristics that we have not discussed in this chapter? What additional systems of information collection do you usually use?

At this point, after considering the factors involved in identifying maltreatment, as well as the process of doing so, we have developed some understanding of a family and its child. Yet, before intervening with the case, we will need to carry out a more formal assessment of it—an assessment that will enable us to understand a family more fully and in a way that is conducive to intervention.

❀ 4 ❀

Assessing the Causes and Effects of Maltreatment

Once we have identified a case of psychological maltreatment and gathered basic descriptive information, a more formal assessment of the factors discussed in Chapter Three is in order. This assessment will consider the characteristics of the community and family in which maltreatment has occurred, as well as the immediate and future consequences of the maltreatment for the child. More specifically, the assessment is an attempt to do two things: (1) to clarify, explain, and evaluate the relationships among the processes that characterize the child, the family, and their social environment; (2) to discover how these processes can be used in intervention aimed at replacing maltreating patterns with healthier ones. Assessment, then, becomes the bridge between defining, identifying, and collecting information about psychological maltreatment of children, on the one hand, and intervening with the community, family, and child, on the other. It casts the practitioner in the role of "applied researcher."

In order for the assessment to achieve its goals of explaining processes and orienting intervention, we need to consider several issues before discussing practical assessment instruments and methods: the potentials and limits of information; the role of practitioners in ensuring comprehensive assessment; the relationship between the identified characteristics of a case and its assessment; and "borderline cases," where no clear evidence of psychological maltreatment exists.

71

Issues in Assessment of Psychological Maltreatment

Potentials and Limits of Information. Information serves as the foundation for intervention by human service delivery systems. As we think about information as a resource in intervention, we must recognize three themes.

1. Lay and professional expertise are complementary. Professional knowledge and expertise are limited and vary across and within practitioner groups. Therefore, we need a variety of assessment approaches, ranging from techniques that require a high level of training and expertise to approaches suitable for use by paraprofessionals and nonprofessionals. In some cases even the most simple assessments, assessments with "face value," will do the job. A classic illustration came out of World War II "personnel" screening. In developing an instrument for use in assigning military personnel to Arctic bases, complex procedure proved to be necessary. A one-item questionnaire did the job: "Do you enjoy working outside in cold weather?" We have analogous findings from the field of child maltreatment.

Henry Kempe (personal communication, 1985) reports that nurses on maternity wards and in delivery rooms can make excellent assessments of the prognosis for maternal functioning. Byron Egeland (personal communication, 1985) found that the best predictor of subsequent maternal functioning was a three-point scale rated by hospital nurses: "How interested in her baby does this mother seem?" 0 = not interested; 1 = somewhat interested; 2 = very interested. The point here is not that sophisticated assessment instruments are irrelevant but that we can sometimes make good assessments just by asking simple questions and searching, perceptively, for the answers. "Simple" clinical insight (such as is commonly found among nurses in direct contact with families) may well do the job, particularly when the larger picture includes "objective testing." Thus, it is important to include assessment instruments that vary in degree of sophistication. A comprehensive evaluation of each case requires that we be open to all sources of information.

2. Psychological maltreatment is often difficult to predict. Pencil-and-paper questionnaires designed to identify parents who

will eventually maltreat their children have proved ineffective. Such instruments can identify most of the pool of families from which actual maltreatment cases will eventually come. But there are many mistakes: some parents who are maltreaters slip through ("false negatives"), and many parents who are not maltreaters are identified as such ("false positives").

No one source of information gathered "objectively" is likely to succeed in screening. Rarely, even, can such pencil-and-paper questionnaires predict which individuals among a high-risk group will actually maltreat their children. Similarly, it is difficult to determine whether or not a parent will continue to maltreat a child (Starr, 1982).

To deal with the challenge of prediction, we must have as much information as possible, and over as long a time span as possible—information about the enduring patterns of parental and child behavior, about the ways the parent responds to key situations, about the forces in the parent's enduring environment that reinforce and sustain both the patterns of behavior and the facing of key parenting situations. Even with such comprehensive information, we can make only probabilistic statements rather than definite predictions. The closer the sources of information to the actual conditions of family life, the better the predictive power.

3. Information about child maltreatment is extremely complex. It consists of both regular feedback on parent-child relations and general knowledge of appropriate norms, expectations, and techniques concerning child rearing. Adequate information depends on three factors: regular observation and discussion of parent-child relations; informal folk wisdom based on extensive, historically validated firsthand experience; and formal, professional expertise, particularly in the area of solving behavior problems. The need for information is related directly to the situational demands of the parent-child relationship. As these demands increase, so does the need for information. Formal institutions can also become effective sources of information if they are linked to the family's social network, either directly through the parent or indirectly through the parent's relationship with some other person. Information is a social phenomenon, and

its quality increases when it comes out of real insight into the events and meaning of day-to-day experience.

Role of Practitioners in Ensuring Comprehensive Assessment. Ideally, psychological maltreatment is assessed by interdisciplinary or multiprofessional teams. These teams might include child welfare workers, social workers, teachers, psychologists, psychiatrists, attorneys, pediatricians, nurses, and paraprofessional staff, depending on the type of agency with which they are affiliated. The major advantage of conducting an assessment in teams is the potential for variety and comprehensiveness: practitioners can evaluate a case in the light of their own expertise, and ultimately an integrated assessment can emerge from the dynamic of all the individual, professionally unique evaluations.

More specifically, every practitioner administers the instruments that deal with topics in his or her area of expertise, interprets them, and then integrates the conclusions with the conclusions derived from other instruments, administered by other professionals. On the basis of these integrated evaluative conclusions, the team determines the direction of intervention and proceeds to plan for it. In agencies where interdisciplinary teams work with cases of psychological maltreatment, each practitioner's role is professionally unique, and the limits of any one approach are balanced by the strengths of others.

If one message has emerged from the past two decades of clinical work with child maltreatment cases, it is to avoid professional isolation. If a formal interdisciplinary team is not in the institutional cards, professionals should seek informal collaboration. The wisdom of this statement is borne out ever more strongly as child abuse and neglect matures as a field for professional activity. In isolation the problem of "burnout" intensifies. (For a more complete discussion of this point, see Helfer and Kempe, 1980, and Copans, Krell, Grundy, Rogen, and Field, 1979.)

The role of the practitioner, then, depends on the situation in which assessment occurs. The goal, however, is always to achieve as much comprehensiveness as possible—whether by using a variety of instruments, administering the same instruments to various family and community members, or combining informal family interview and observation with the formal assessment. In this chapter we make an effort to be comprehensive in the topics we cover—namely, each of the factors contributing to psychological maltreatment (factors discussed in Chapter Three). However, so many assessment instruments are available for the purpose of evaluating each factor that we find it impossible to be comprehensive in that sense. For this sort of comprehensiveness, consult a handbook on assessment (for example, Knoff, 1986).

For each factor we describe one or more assessment instruments with generally recognized validity and wide use. (For information on sources where these instruments can be obtained, see Resource A, Part 2.) Some of the instruments we discuss have been used to differentiate abusive from nonabusive families. Others have not; but, on the basis of their regular use with clinical and nonclinical populations, we believe that they may be useful in understanding maltreating families.

Relationship Between Identified Characteristics of a Case and Its Assessment. Identification is a conclusion about whether the family meets our definition of psychological maltreatment; assessment is an exploration of the dynamics of family life as it exists in a community context. For example, the description of Johnny's family (Case 19) indicates that the family is isolated in the community. Accordingly, we would first want to evaluate the extent and nature of this isolation and find the possible intervention points. Second, we would want to evaluate the overall family climate and structure, because it seems that some of the mechanisms facilitating the maltreatment exist on this level. Third, we would want to assess the character of each parent-child relationship, as it arises from values, perceptions, and parenting skills. On this level we are interested in the differences between the parents' treatment of Johnny and their treatment of his sister, and particularly in the father's parenting attitudes and practices. Again, we would be interested in discovering points of potential change. Finally, we would try to evaluate the consequences of the maltreatment for Johnny's character and development. We *must* have this "child's-eye level" assessment if we are to fulfill our mandate to be child oriented in our decision making when it comes to intervention.

The preferred route of assessment arises from the process of identification. It reflects realistic decisions about the availability of professional resources and expertise. Because assessment is an exploration, the route chosen is always open to modification as preliminary efforts yield new insights about family dynamics or community context.

Borderline or Ambiguous Cases. Often a troubled family is identified, but we do not have clear evidence of psychological maltreatment. In other words, we have not clearly found the parents or the whole family to be rejecting, terrorizing, ignoring, isolating, or corrupting their child(ren); yet the family and the child(ren) seem troubled, and we somehow sense that psychological maltreatment is occurring or is likely to emerge. In such cases we suggest proceeding with an asessment of the family, the parents, and the child(ren), according to their identified characteristics, as the basis for intervention. Such an intervention will serve as prevention or will work against the maltreatment too subtle or ambiguous to pinpoint in the initial process of identification. This approach gives credence to the reality of practitioner insight. It also recognizes that "unsubstantiated" cases are often "in need of services" and that an exploratory assessment may proceed on a "hunch," a "hypothesis," or a "feeling." As long as this exploratory assessment guides intervention, it can proceed. Only where there is a blind mechanistic link between identification and intervention (particularly coercive intervention) is action in borderline or ambiguous cases subject to being ethically compromised. But here as elsewhere the operative criterion is the well-being of the child rather than a legalistic commitment for formal process.

Assessing Environmental Context

When we assess the family's social environment, we seek to analyze the degree of isolation and resourcelessness, in contrast to social connectedness and access to social support. As we do so, we seek to answer the following questions:

What are the community's beliefs about the care of children (recognizing the power of values and norms in turning otherwise deviant experience into an event that is "normal")?

To what extent and how is the family isolated and lacking social resources? What are the environmental factors that tend to increase the family's isolation, poverty, and resourcelessness (remembering that social impoverishment is both a cause of and a constraint on intervention)?

What are the environmental factors that increase the extent and severity of the maltreatment (remembering that the "stress resistance" of children is very much a social phenomenon)?

What is the community's contribution to the family's environmental situation, as compared with the family's own contribution to it (recognizing that both "directions of effect" exist and have ramifications for intervention)?

What pathways can be found, in the community and in the family, that will help in changing their mutual relationships (remembering that social resources are essential to provide the ongoing structural support necessary to sustain changes in family functioning)?

Such an assessment of the family's environmental context is likely to result in an understanding of environmental processes that maintain and facilitate the psychological maltreatment, processes that have the potential to reduce maltreatment and promote healthy growth patterns, and processes (for example, key persons who can serve as "natural neighbors" and members of a supportive social network) that can be utilized for intervention.

The five children in Case 2 live in a poor community with very few resources. There is one private day care center and no preschool. The children and the mother have to travel by public transportation to another community for health care and consequently go very seldom. The family is isolated from the social environment, and the only social support is the grandmother, who often becomes a burden. They do not belong to a church. The material and social resourcelessness of the environment exacerbates occurrences of maltreatment. However, a community center will soon open nearby. Persuading the mother to participate in its activities might be a step toward social integration.

Assessing Family Context

In a psychologically maltreating family, the family climate is often characterized by tension, conflict, aggressiveness and mistrust, broken communication, chaos or extreme rigidity, separatedness or extreme cohesion. Three existing instruments may be useful in evaluating family climate: the Family Environment Scale: (Moos, 1975; Moos and Moos, 1976), Family Adaptability and Cohesion Evaluation (Olson, Russell, and Sprenkle, 1979, 1983), and the Interparental Conflict and Influence Scales (Schwartz and Zuroff, 1979).

Family Environment Scale. The Moos scale assesses the social environment of a family in three dimensions: interpersonal relationships among family members, directions of personal growth emphasized in the family, and the family's organizational structure. The scale is capable of differentiating among expression-oriented, structure-oriented, independence-oriented, achievement-oriented, conflict-oriented, and moral-religious–oriented families; and, when administered to both children and parents, it is sensitive to parent-child differences in family perception. It also differentiates disturbed family environments from normative ones; and, when available to a caseworker, it can help in exploring the family as a social system.

The Moos scale is based on an "ecological" approach to human systems and environments and to the helping professions (for example, see Germain, 1979; Moos, 1975). This approach focuses on the processes through which people seek to achieve "goodness of fit" between themselves and the physical and social environment. They actively try to adapt to the environment, as well as to adjust it to their needs. The environment, in turn, supports or fails to support human growth, autonomy, competence, and needs and thus enhances or impedes people's adaptation and development. Once the person-environment fit breaks down, helping professionals can use the FES as a diagnostic tool to explore the dimensions of breakdown as a basis for intervening to regain this fit, to help the person and family readapt, and to restart the processes of growth.

Moos (1975) developed the FES by analyzing patterns in the statements of about 285 families representing a wide range of socioeconomic and ethnic groups and sampled from both normative and clinic populations. The families evaluated themselves by means of ninety true-false statements; observers rated the families as well to provide an independent reality check. The FES includes ten subscales within the three categories of family: Relationships, Growth, and Structure. Subscales 1-3 constitute the "Relationship" category—the extent to which family members feel that they belong to and are proud of their family, the openness for expression in the family, and the nature of conflictual interactions in it:

1. *Cohesion:* the degree to which family members are committed to the family, are helpful and supportive to one another.
2. *Expressiveness:* the degree to which family members are allowed and encouraged to act openly and express their feelings directly.
3. *Conflict:* the extent to which anger and aggression are openly expressed in the family and the degree to which conflictual interactions characterize the family.

Subscales 4-8 constitute the "Personal Growth" category— the developmental processes fostered by the family:

4. *Independence:* the extent to which family members are encouraged to be self-sufficient, make their own decisions, think independently, and be assertive.
5. *Achievement Orientation:* the extent to which the family emphasizes achievement and competitiveness.
6. *Intellectual-Cultural Orientation:* the degree of family involvement with social, political, intellectual, and cultural activities.
7. *Active-Recreational:* the extent to which the family is involved with sporting and recreational activities.

8. *Moral-Religious Emphasis:* the extent to which the family discusses and emphasizes ethical and religious issues and the family values.

    The last two subscales constitute the "System Maintenance" category:

9. *Organization:* the extent to which order and organization are important in the family; the structuring of activities, financial planning, and the explicitness and clarity of rules and responsibilities.
10. *Control:* the extent to which the family is organized hierarchically by rigidity of rules and procedures, and the degree to which family members order one another around.

In sum, the FES is capable of assessing a family's environment in terms of interpersonal relationships, personal growth, and system maintenance. The scale is reliable, and each subscale tends to measure a distinct aspect of the family's environment. In the technical language of test construction, the internal consistency of the ten subscales is .64 to .79, test-retest reliability is .68 to .86, and the subscales correlate with one another with an average correlation of $r = .20$. Some researchers and clinicians have raised questions about the validity of the FES; nevertheless, it has been widely and successfully used to evaluate the environmental climate of families. The scale can be used to compare the perceptions of family members, or a total score can be averaged for a certain family, for the purpose of comparing it with existing normative data. By assessing the family environment, the FES has the potential to guide intervention aimed at the whole family as a system.

The environmental climate of Johnny's family (Case 19) seems to be characterized by relationships of threat, conflict, and distrust; by a low personal-growth orientation; and by a fixed structure, which maintains the current situation. Family relationships seem to be low in cohesion and expressiveness and high in conflict, which is expressed passively. In order to assess personal-growth orientation, more information is needed about the family's emphasis on independence and achievement; however, objective assessment is likely to find that personal development is not a major factor in this family. Organization and control (the system maintenance factors) are highly stressed in the family and thus increase the difficulty of intervention.

Family Adaptability and Cohesion Evaluation Scale. FACES measures family members' perception of their family as a social system. It focuses on their evaluation of the family's cohesion (external and internal boundaries, coalitions, shared activities, independence, decision making) and the family's adaptability (power structure, negotiation styles, role relationships, relationship rules, feedback). Extremes of cohesion and adaptability are regarded as dysfunctional. The scale is capable of identifying parent-child differences in perceiving the family system.

The scale is based on the application of a systems framework to the understanding of family relationships (see, for example, Broderick and Smith, 1979; Kantor and Lehr, 1975). This framework views the family as a system composed of interacting individuals. The system has internal boundaries (differentiating among its subsystems), as well as external boundaries (separating it from other systems). Positive or negative feedback loops in communication help the family to process environmental input. The family's major goal is to maintain itself in a state of relative stability.

From this framework the major dimensions that emerge concerning family functioning and behavior are Cohesion; Adaptability; and Communication, the mechanism by which the cohesion and adaptability levels change (Olson, Russell, and Sprenkle, 1983). Cohesion is defined as the "emotional bonding members have with one another, and the degree of individual autonomy a person experiences in the family system" (Olson, Sprenkle, and Russell, 1979, p. 5). Adaptability is defined as the "ability of a marital/family system to change its power structure, role relationships, and relationship rules in response to situational and developmental stress" (p. 12). The four levels of family

Cohesion are, from the lower to the higher end of the scale, "disengaged," "separated," "connected," and "enmeshed"; the Adaptability levels range from "rigid" to "structured," to "flexible," to "chaotic." These levels result in sixteen categories of family functioning (see Table 3). FACES thus identifies four types of extremely dysfunctional families with very high or very low levels of cohesion and adaptability, four types of balanced families, and eight in the middle range.

Table 3. A Model of Family Relationships.

| | | low ← *Cohesion* → high | | |
	Disengaged	Separated	Connected	Enmeshed
Chaotic	extreme	midrange	midrange	extreme
Flexible	midrange	balanced	balanced	midrange
Structured	midrange	balanced	balanced	midrange
Rigid	extreme	midrange	midrange	extreme

(left axis, bottom-to-top: low → high, Adaptability)

Source: Adapted from Olson, Russell, and Sprenkle, 1983, p. 71.

The initial version of the FACES had 111 statements, which the family members rated according to the degree that they were applicable to their family. These items constituted nine subscales of Cohesion (emotional bonding, independence, boundaries, coalitions, shared time and shared space, friends, decision making, interests, recreation) and seven subscales of Adaptability (assertiveness and aggressiveness, control, negotiation styles, role relationships, relationship rules, positive and negative feedback). On the basis of ratings by family members, the family was defined as balanced, midrange, or extreme; or as "chaotically enmeshed," "flexibly connected," "rigidly disengaged," or "structured-separated," for example.

A new version of the initial FACES, called FACES II, has been developed (Olson, Portner, and Bell, 1982). The revised scale measures the same Cohesion and Adaptability domains of family systems; its major advantage is that it contains only 30 items (rather than 111), which makes it more economical and easy to administer and score. Evaluation of the 111-item instrument revealed that many items were sufficiently overlapping to permit deletion in the interest of efficiency.

In sum, FACES or FACES II is capable of assessing a family's degree of cohesion and adaptability, as well as determining the extent to which it is dysfunctional. (In technical terms, the internal consistency of the scale is .75 for Adaptability and .83 for Cohesion.) It can be used to compare family members' perceptions or to determine the family's overall level of functioning by its total score as averaged on its members. Thus, using the scale can help a practitioner decide in which direction the family's communication should be channeled so that it will return to normative functioning.

Ricky's family (Case 20) seems to be closed within itself (enmeshed) and strict on rules and responsibilities (rigid). If one rates the family on the Cohesion subscales, it emerges as low in emotional bonding, high in dependence, low in internal boundaries, and low in shared time and space. On the Adaptability subscales the family emerges as high in control, aggressiveness, and role relationships. Thus, it tends to be a "rigidly enmeshed" family, one that is extreme in its dysfunctionality. Intervention might therefore seek to decrease cohesion and increase adaptability.

Interparental Conflict and Influence Scales. The IPC measures conflict between the parents and the degree of influence that each parent has in family decision making. More specifically, the Conflict Scale measures the content and frequency of overt conflict and arguments between the parents in the last five years. The Influence Scale deals with each parent's perceived influence in family decision making. Schwartz and Zuroff (1979) developed the scales on the basis of theoretical considerations concerning parental conflict and decision-making power. The selected items were validated against an external criterion (another measure of conflict, which has already proved valid) and then cross-validated on a new sample.

The Conflict Scale includes thirty-seven items dealing with four main areas of interparental conflict: (1) finance and spouse responsibilities—budgeting, luxury spending, satisfaction with family income; (2) spouse's personal characteristics—ignoring spouse's needs, personal crudeness, acceptability of specific friends; (3) child-rearing practices—children's household duties and responsibilities, methods of discipline, homework requirements; and (4) joint family activities—vacation plans, frequency of visiting with relatives, family versus individual recreation. Each family member or a practitioner who is familiar with the family rates the degree of existing conflict with regard to each item. Research has shown the scale to be stable in identifying the areas of conflict and assessing its degree (test reliability over one week— the extent to which the same results were yielded after a week—was found to be .86).

The Influence Scale contains thirteen items dealing with the relative power of the mother and the father in decision making about finance (for example, how much life insurance to buy), spouses' personal characteristics (for example, choice of parents' friends), child-rearing practices (for example, children's duties and household responsibilities, children's bedtimes), and joint family activities (for example, where to live, vacation and leisure-time activity). Each family member or a practitioner who is familiar with the family rates each item from "father makes most of the decisions" to "equal and shared decision making" to "mother makes most decisions." (Test-retest reliability over one week was found to be .91, showing that the scale is rather consistent in identifying and assessing the power structure in decision making between the parents.)

Both the Conflict Scale and the Influence Scale are useful in understanding the parents' as well as the child's perceptions of the ongoing conflicts between the parents and the overall family power structure. The following is an example of some evaluative statements regarding parents' relationships:

The relationship between David's parents (Case 4) seems to be conflictual especially in the area of "spouse's personal characteristics." The father has even expressed his dissatisfaction with his wife's behavior by physically abusing her. In the area of decision making, it seems that the wife has more power, although more information needs to be collected. The mother does seem to be the final authority in rearing David, a characteristic that has initiated and still maintains the conflicts.

Assessing Parental Factors and Parent-Child Interactions

Parent-child interaction in psychologically maltreating families usually involves patterns of broken communication, negative attitudes toward each other, and little respect for each other's uniqueness. As we saw in Chapter Three, the parents may be physically and/or psychologically unavailable to the child, may respond partially or inappropriately to the child's needs by infantilizing or mis-socializing, or may provide harsh and destructive responses to the child's needs by degrading, threatening, or exploiting. In other words, the parents ignore, isolate, reject, corrupt, or terrorize the child. They perceive the child as different and exceptional, even as the one who elicits the maltreatment. Children, in turn, view their parents as authoritarian and unjust, although some maltreated children believe that they deserve such treatment.

The parents' lack of knowledge and skills, together with their feelings of inadequacy (and, in most cases, their marital conflicts), contributes to their extreme perception of the child and their behaviors toward the child. Thus, the second set of instruments deals with the assessment of these parental factors and their interrelatedness. The instruments we will look at are these: Parental Acceptance-Rejection Questionnaire (Rohner, 1980; Rohner and Rohner, 1980), Children's Reports of Parental Behavior Inventory (Schaefer, 1965a, 1965b), Bronfenbrenner's Parental Behavior Questionnaire (Devereux, Bronfenbrenner, and Suci, 1962; Siegelman, 1965), Michigan Screening Profile of Parenting (Helfer, Schneider, and Hoffmeister, 1978), Maternal Characteristics Scale (Polansky, Borgman, and De Saix, 1972; Polansky, De Saix, and Sharlin, 1972), Childhood Level of Living Scale (Polansky, Borgman, and De Saix, 1972; Polansky and Pollane, 1975).

Parental Acceptance-Rejection Questionnaire. This questionnaire looks at perceptions of parental treatment of the child in
terms of warmth/affection, hostility/aggression, indifference/
neglect, and undifferentiated rejection. It is a self-report instrument for parents to use in evaluating their treatment of their
children or their own parents' treatment of them as children, or for
children to use in reporting their perceptions of their parents' way
of handling them.

The questionnaire is based on Rohner's (1980) parental
acceptance-rejection theory, a theory of socialization that seeks to
explain both the antecedents of parental acceptance-rejection and
its consequences for the child's emotional, cognitive, social, and
behavioral development. Acceptance-rejection is conceived as a
continuum of parental behaviors. On one extreme stand parents
who show their love and affection toward the child verbally or
physically. On the other are parents who dislike, disapprove of, or
resent their children. Parental rejection may take the form of
physical or verbal hostility and aggression or of indifference and
neglect. Paralleling this continuum of parental behaviors, children
tend to feel loved and accepted in decreasing degrees until they feel
unloved and rejected. According to this theory, rejected children
are likely to manifest hostility, dependency, neuroses, delinquency
and conduct problems, psychosomatic reactions, emotional
problems, poor self-concept formation, academic problems, or
disturbed body image.

The three forms of the Acceptance-Rejection Questionnaire
attempt to assess the degree to which the parents perceive
themselves as warm, hostile, neglectful, or rejecting; the degree to
which they perceive their own parents in these terms; and the
children's perception of the parents as warm/affectionate (for
example, "My mother makes me feel wanted and needed"),
hostile/aggressive ("My mother goes out of her way to hurt my
feelings"), indifferent/neglectful ("My mother ignores me as long
as I do not do anything to bother her"), or rejecting ("My mother
doesn't really love me").

Thus, the Parental Acceptance-Rejection Questionnaire is
capable of identifying hostile, neglectful, and rejecting parents,
both from a parent's and from a child's viewpoint. (In technical

terms, the internal consistency of the scales is good. For the child's version, it ranges from .72 to .90; for the parental version, it is .86 to .95.) The scales can provide a direction for intervention with the parents, designed to increase accepting behaviors and decrease rejecting and neglectful behaviors.

Ken's parents (Case 12) manifest stylistic differences in their expression of rejection. The mother's self-report shows high rejection, perhaps even indifference, but relatively low aggression. The father's self-report reveals high hostility and aggression, coupled with low warmth. He would be classified as hostile-aggressive and the mother as rejecting. The child's self-report portrays the parents as low in affection and high in hostility, indifference, and rejection. These findings initiate the exploration that leads to a plan for intervention with the parents.

Children's Reports of Parental Behavior Inventory. This inventory taps children's perceptions of their parents' behavior in terms of love versus hostility and autonomy versus control. Similarly, it can measure the parents' perception of their behavior with the children on these dimensions.

The inventory is based on the idea that a child's adjustment level and behaviors are related more to his or her *perception* of the parents than to the parents' *actual* behavior. The scales of the inventory were derived from a study of psychologist ratings of parental behavior (the statistical model used was a factor analysis). Three major factors have emerged in this process: (1) *acceptance versus rejection:* positive evaluation of and emotional support to the child, versus ignoring, neglecting, and rejecting him or her; (2) *psychological autonomy versus psychological control*: offering the child the psychological autonomy needed to develop as an individual apart from the parent, versus controlling the child through protectiveness, intrusiveness, and possessiveness; (3) *firm control versus lax control*: punishment and strictness versus autonomy and lax discipline. Some of the scales based on the three factors are (1) positive evaluation ("often praises me"), sharing ("enjoys talking with me"), expression of affection ("speaks with a warm and friendly voice to me"), rejection ("acts as though I am in the way"), neglect ("forgets to get me things I need"), ignoring ("doesn't talk with me very much"), (2) extreme autonomy ("allows me to go out as often as I please"), encouraging sociability ("enjoys it when I bring friends home"), encouraging independent thinking ("asks me what I think"), possessiveness ("would like me to spend most of my free time with him or her"), intrusiveness ("asks other people what I do away from home"), protectiveness ("worries about me when I'm away"); (3) lax discipline ("excuses my bad conduct"), strictness ("has lots of rules and regulations for me"), control through guilt ("thinks I am not grateful when I don't obey"), irritability ("loses his or her temper when I don't help around the house"). Each scale contains ten items. (The average internal consistency of these scales is .76, ranging from .38 to .93.)

In short, the Parental Behavior Inventory, whether filled out by parents or by their children, assesses the major characteristics of the acceptance-rejection and autonomy-control continuum of parental behavior. It can evaluate the degree of parent-child differences in perception as well as guide the intervention with both sides.

Patty's parents (Case 7) exercised firm control over her. They locked her in her room as punishment and were strict in setting rules she had to obey. They were also psychologically controlling in their child-rearing practices and opposed her growth needs. Finally, they rejected her by not allowing her to interact with the rest of the family. Overall, then, the parents can be placed on the negative side of parental behaviors, and all three dimensions (rejection, psychological control, and firm control) need to be addressed in intervention.

Bronfenbrenner's Parental Behavior Questionnaire. This questionnaire explores children's perceptions of parental practices. Like the Parental Behavior Inventory, it is based on the phenomenological idea that the child's *perception* of how the parents act is crucial for understanding child development. The questionnaire can also be filled out by parents, who are asked to rate their own behavior toward the child.

The forty-five-item Parental Behavior Questionnaire consists of three parental behavior dimensions: loving, punishing, and demanding. The *loving* dimension measures the degree to which the parent is available to counsel, support, and assist the child; the degree to which the parent enjoys being with the child and is affectionate toward and concerned with the child. The *punishing* dimension looks at the extent to which the parent uses physical and nonphysical punishment without concern for the child's needs and feelings and without any apparent reason. It also measures the degree of parental rejection and hostility. The *demanding* dimension deals with the extent to which the parent is controlling, demanding, protecting, and intrusive. It also includes the degree to which the parent is achievement oriented, explains the reason for punishment to the child, and becomes distant and upset when the child misbehaves.

These dimensions are composed of fifteen variables: nurturance ("comforts me"), affective reward ("praises me"), instrumental companionship ("helps me"), affiliative companionship ("enjoys talking with me"), prescriptiveness ("expects me to help"), social isolation ("punishment is not being allowed to play with friends"), expressive rejection ("nags at me"), physical punishment ("spanks me"), deprivation of privileges ("punishing by taking my favorite things away"), protectiveness ("worries that I can't take care of myself"), power ("insists that I get permission before doing things"), achievement demands ("insists that I do better than other children"), affective punishment ("makes me feel ashamed when I misbehave"), principled discipline ("is just when punishing me"), indulgence ("lets me off easy when I misbehave"). On each item the child or the parent chooses one answer out of four options, ranging from "never" to "always."

Research on this instrument has demonstrated the reliability of this measure (Siegelman, 1965). (Factor-score reliabilities range from .70 to .91, and these internal-consistency coefficients were in general found higher than the reliabilities of the individual scales.)

On the whole, the Parental Behavior Questionnaire is useful in assessing components of psychological maltreatment, both from a parent's and from a child's viewpoint.

Mark's and Bill's mother and grandmother (Case 11) are loving but, at the same time, overprotective and possessive.

Although they do not punish the children intentionally, the boys may regard their isolation from other children as a form of punishment. The mother and grandmother also tend to be highly intrusive and controlling. Overall, the children probably regard the women as intrusively affectionate, punishing, and demanding. In contrast, the two women are likely to see themselves as loving, not punishing, and not excessively demanding. This gap, as well as the women's inaccurate conception of child-rearing methods, seems to be the initial target for intervention.

Michigan Screening Profile of Parenting. This instrument is based on Steele's (1970) and Helfer and Kempe's (1968) idea that child abuse and emotional maltreatment are related to the parents' experience of emotional abuse as children, to the parents' exaggerated expectations of the child, and to the parents' lack of coping skills. It attempts to help us assess the degree of existing maltreatment and to predict the likelihood of future maltreatment, on the basis of the parents' own childhood and personality. In other words, the Screening Profile of Parenting evaluates the degree of risk created by the parents' social and emotional impoverishment.

The instrument was developed from clustering items derived from Steele (1970) and Helfer and Kempe (1968). Five main clusters emerged: (1) *relationships with parents*—the extent to which the parent felt close to and had affectionate relationships with his or her own parents ("My parents showed me love and warm feelings"); (2) *expectations of children*—the extent to which the parent expects the child to behave well ("Children should know what parents want them to do"); (3) *coping*—the parent's perceived ability to deal with stress ("I just feel like running away"); (4) *dealing with others*—the extent to which the parent feels accepted and loved by others ("I am very well liked"); (5) *emotional needs met*—the extent to which the parent feels emotional deprivation ("No one has ever really listened to me; I am always being criticized").

This instrument is filled out by parents and has been found to differentiate normal parents from high-risk or maltreating ones. For research purposes but *not* for individual diagnosis, the average internal consistency of its clusters is .65. However, if validated against other instruments and administered with them, this scale can be helpful in understanding current maltreatment and exploring parental risk factors.

If it is used as a *starting point* for clinical investigation, the Michigan Screening Profile of Parenting is a useful instrument for the assessment of high-risk families and psychologically maltreating parents.

Susan's mother (Case 1) seems to provide a high-risk environment for her daughter. Although more information is needed about her relationship with her own parents and her expectations from the infant, it seems that her ability to care for the baby is limited, that she lacks a social support network, and that her own needs are deprived. Susan's mother probably subjected her to the kind of emotional impoverishment identified by Helfer, Steele, and their colleagues. Intervention is likely to focus on coping skills, support networks, and the fulfillment of her needs—what Helfer calls "reparenting the parent."

Maternal Characteristics Scale. This scale measures the extent to which the mother's personality affects her maternal competence. Practitioners who are familiar with a family can fill out the scale after observing the mother and organizing their impressions of her personality and her behaviors toward the child. However, some expertise is required to interpret it. Polansky and his associates developed this scale from their studies of neglectful mothers (Polansky, Borgman, and De Saix, 1972; Polansky, De Saix, and Sharlin, 1972). Specifically, they found two major types of neglectful mothers: the apathetic-futile and the impulse ridden. The initial Maternal Characteristics Scale included 205 items; a revised version of the scale includes only 34 items. In both versions a practitioner determines whether a mother can be classified as one of the two major types. The first category, apathy-futility, includes *behavioral immobilization* (unable or refuses to do housework, impaired health, neglects cleanliness, shows physical aggression, lacks warmth) and *interpersonal detachment* (slips into daydreams, has inappropriate clothing, talks ambiguously, is indifferent, is uninterested in external events). The second category, childlike impulsivity, includes *impulsivity* (lacks persistence, plans unrealistically, flies into rages when frustrated, expresses feelings inappropriately) and *dependency* (whines when talks, clings to husband, shares her problems with the children, treats adults as if they were parents). The scale includes statements about these four personality categories. It is important to note that this is not a self-report instrument and that only a practitioner who is qualified and acquainted with a family can use it effectively as an assessment tool. Yet, when used correctly, it evaluates the mother's personality in terms of her adequacy in the maternal role. In doing so, it highlights important items on the intervention agenda.

A practitioner who knows Bobby's mother (Case 8) probably would rate her high on behavioral immobilization and on interpersonal detachment from the boy. She is also impulsive and dependent, especially during schizophrenic episodes. Thus, the evaluation of her personality places her maternal competence in doubt and stresses the need for intervention with her that will protect the child while an effort is made to determine the long-term prognosis for adequate parenthood.

Childhood Level of Living Scale. This scale measures the quality of the mother's child-rearing practices. It is aimed at evaluating both physical and cognitive-emotional aspects of child maltreatment (particularly neglect). The scale is based on the same studies that Polansky and his colleagues conducted to identify the psychosocial characteristics of neglectful mothers. It is also based on existing sociological knowledge about the special child care risk factors related to social class. Thus, the scale attempts to differentiate among lower-class maltreating mothers (separating low income from neglect). Although it was developed for use with four- and five-year-old children, it can be used to assess maltreatment of older and younger children as well.

The Childhood Level of Living Scale is composed of two parts. The first deals with the physical care of the child; the second deals with the emotional-cognitive care. The Physical Care scale includes such subscales as comfort, safety, state of repair of the house, hygienic conditions, feeding patterns, disease prevention, use of medical facilities, clothing, and sleeping arrangements. The Emotional-Cognitive Care scale includes such subscales as parental play with the child, promoting curiosity, consistency in encouraging superego development, level of disciplinary techniques, providing reliable role image, and evidences of affection.

The Childhood Level of Living Scale consists of 136 statements, to which a caseworker, or any other practitioner who is acquainted with the family, responds. Like the Maternal Characteristics Scale, this scale is not a mother's self-report but a practitioner's evaluation of a mother after observing her and the family, as well as interviewing them; and it operates consistently (the internal consistency of the Physical Care subscales is .95; for the Emotional-Cognitive Care subscales, .86). The Physical Care subscales were found to correlate significantly with the Emotional-Cognitive Care subscales (at $r = .75$, meaning that when parents provide inadequate physical care, they are also likely to provide inadequate emotional-cognitive care).

The Childhood Level of Living Scale, like the Maternal Characteristics Scale, reflects the central role played by mothers in child care. Both scales measure the mother's personality and her behavior with regard to child rearing and are capable of evaluating physically, emotionally, and cognitively maltreating mothers.

The practitioner who assesses Wanda's mother and her family (Case 13) finds that the mother has been neglecting and rejecting her responsibilities for the child's physical care. She does not care for the child's comfort, safety, health, or food over extended periods. (While the child was left with her grandmother, her needs were partially cared for, but the grandmother could not afford adequate sleeping, clothing, and health arrangements.) Similarly, the mother has taken no responsibility for Wanda's emotional-cognitive care, and the grandmother's own limitations make for low ratings on play with the child, promotion of curiosity, expression of affection, and provision of reliable role images.

Adult-Adolescent Parenting Inventory. Another instrument used to assess parent-child relationships and parenting patterns is Steven Bavolek's Adult-Adolescent Parenting Inventory (Bavolek, Kline, McLaughlin, and Publicover, 1979). The Parenting Inventory includes thirty-two items and has been developed specifically for the purpose of differentiating abusive and neglectful parents from others. It has the capability to assess (1) inappropriate developmental expectations of children, (2) lack of an empathic awareness of children's needs, (3) strong parental beliefs in the use of corporal punishment, and (4) reversing parent-child family roles. This scale might be useful for the purpose of assessing parent-adolescent relationships in maltreating families.

Assessing Children's Behavior and Personality

As mentioned earlier, psychologically maltreated infants, children, and adolescents tend to show evidence of psychosocial harm. Overall, they have behavioral problems, some emotional disturbance, and inappropriate social responses. More specifically, infants show irritability and, in extreme cases, "nonorganic failure to thrive"; in general, there is a lack of harmony in their relationships with the parents, accompanied by an anxious attachment to the parents. Children tend to be fearful and to have low self-esteem and feelings of inferiority. They either externalize or internalize their anxiety and aggression, and either avoid their parents or try to take care of the parents' needs. Similarly, adolescents tend to externalize or internalize their fears, their rebellious feelings, and their sense of injustice. They may become delinquent, truant, and emotionally disturbed.

The following infant, child, and adolescent assessment instruments are reviewed in this section: Bayley Scales of Infant Development (Bayley, 1969), Tennessee Self-Concept Scale (Fitts, 1965), State-Trait Anxiety Inventory (Spielberger, 1971; Spielberger, Gorsuch, and Lushene, 1970), Personality Assessment Questionnaire (Rohner, 1980; Rohner, Saavedra, and Granum, 1978), Child Behavior Checklist (Achenbach, 1978; Achenbach and Edelbrock, 1979), and Child Assessment Schedule (Hodges, 1984; Hodges and others, 1982a, 1982b). Resource 1, part 1, describes some additional instruments.

Bayley Scales of Infant Development. These scales provide a basis for evaluating the child's developmental status in the first two and a half years of life. Based on the assumption that motor, mental, and interactional abilities are highly interrelated, the scales assess the infant's cognitive and motor capacities as well as the infant's relationship with the parent. Infants do not have the understanding needed to follow the directions of an examiner, nor can they solve problems on request. Hence, in order to study them, we need to find another method. Infants respond to situations and tasks that capture their attention and interest. Bayley therefore attempted to provide stimuli that are attractive to infants.

The Bayley, which only a well-trained practitioner can administer, is composed of three scales: (1) The Mental Scale assesses sensory-perceptual acuities and discriminations; object permanence and memory; learning and problem-solving ability; vocalizations and verbal communication; and the ability to form generalizations and classifications, which is the basis of abstract thinking. (2) The Motor Scale provides a measure of body control, coordination of the large muscles, and finer manipulatory skills of the hands; it is directed toward behaviors reflecting motor coordination and skills and is not concerned with mental or intelligent functions. (3) The Infant Behavior Record helps to assess the child's orientations toward the environment, as expressed in attitudes, interests, emotions, energy, activity, and tendencies to approach or withdraw from stimulation.

These scales are known to be among the most reliable infants' tests and are useful in recording qualitatively significant aspects of the infant's observed behavior with a parent (or another adult) and with a variety of stimuli. They were standardized with tester-observer agreement of .89 and with test-retest reliability over one week of .76. The scales provide a basis for establishing a child's current status and thus the extent of any deviation from normal expectancy. In other words, with these scales one can assess developmental problems and even, to some extent, determine whether their causes are neurological, sensory, emotional, or environmental. In cases of psychological maltreatment the child's development is likely to be delayed. Thus, the Bayley Scales seem to be useful in assessing maltreated infants.

Frank (Case 3) was left with his grandparents and soon afterward started manifesting characteristics of delayed development. Because he is often left alone and is not exposed to stimuli, he is rated low on the Mental Scale. Further, because he has not been encouraged to develop motor skills, he appears nonnormative on the Motor Scale as well. Regarding his relationship with the environment, his listlessness and irritability point to a delayed interpersonal and emotional development. Perhaps his skin problems explain part of the delay in his development, but certainly the ignoring and rejecting environment plays a major role in it.

Tennessee Self-Concept Scale. This scale, which is used with children and adolescents, aims at assessing self-concept, self-acceptance, and perception of behaviors; it also aims to differentiate between normative and disturbed populations.

The Self-Concept Scale is based on the idea that the child or adolescent's self-concept influences behavioral patterns. The scale was developed from descriptive statements in other self-concept scales as well as from clients' statements about themselves. This process resulted in a 110-item self-administered scale.

There are two forms of the Self-Concept Scale: one aimed at counseling and the other at making clinical and research evaluations. The counseling form contains four major subscales: (1) *self-criticism* score: the extent to which the child or the adolescent tries to present a favorable picture of himself or herself or is pathologically undefended; (2) *positive* score: the extent to which one is satisfied with oneself and with one's behaviors (morally, socially, emotionally, and physically); (3) *variability* score: the degree of one's integrity, as measured by the extent to which self-concept changes among the different areas of evaluation; (4) *distribution* score: the extent to which one is certain about one's self-concept.

The clinical and research form of the Self-Concept Scale adds several subscales to the counseling form: (1) *true/false ratio:* a measure of response set (strong tendency to agree or disagree with the statements, regardless of their content); (2) *conflict* score: the extent to which one responds differently to items with the same underlying meaning, depending on whether they are written negatively or positively; (3) *general maladjustment, psychosis, personality disorders, neurosis, and personality integration* scores: measures that differentiate normative from nonnormative populations on key dimensions of personality.

Both forms of the Self-Concept Scale have been found valid for discriminating among different groups of children and adolescents according to their self-concept. (In technical terms, test-retest reliability over two weeks is .78 on the average.) Overall, this scale is considered capable of identifying the child's self-concept and self-satisfaction, as well as assessing various personality disturbances.

Teddy (Case 15) was isolated, rejected, and terrorized by his stepfather—so much so that he attempted suicide. He exhibits low self-esteem and has a poor self-concept; that is, he sees his physical, moral, social, and emotional self negatively and is not satisfied with himself. More information is needed about his self-criticism, variability, and distribution scores; yet it becomes clear that efforts to improve his self-concept should be part of intervention to assist Teddy.

State-Trait Anxiety Inventory. This inventory measures the extent to which the child or the adolescent is tense, nervous, worried, fearful, and troubled, both in general and at a particular moment. It is based on Spielberger's (1971) theory of state and trait anxiety. State anxiety is a transient experience of anxiety at a certain moment. It is one's emotional reaction to perceiving a specific situation as dangerous and frightening. Trait anxiety is one's proneness to being anxious. It is a stable personality characteristic that makes a person perceive many situations as threatening and have intense and disproportionate reactions to them.

Spielberger's inventory assesses both types of anxiety. The State Anxiety Scale is composed of twenty statements describing specific incidents; children or adolescents are asked to indicate the extent to which they feel calm, rested, and relaxed or upset, nervous, worried, and frightened at school, at home, with friends, and so on. The Trait Anxiety Scale contains twenty items concerning general states of mind; children are asked to indicate whether they "hardly ever," "sometimes," or "often" feel worried, unhappy, troubled, or fearful. It covers the same types of settings but focuses on the *level* of anxiety across settings.

The State-Trait Anxiety Inventory correlates with other anxiety measures and is relatively stable over time. Furthermore, children who are high on trait anxiety tend to have more frequent and severe increases in their state anxiety. Overall, this inventory is capable of evaluating the level of anxiety of maltreated children, both in general and in specific situations.

Jon's father (Case 6) terrorizes and ignores the child. As a result, Jon has been identified as tense at home and whining or aggressive at nursery school. Jon reports being worried, fearful, and unhappy in general (trait anxiety); he is particularly anxious when his father plays games with him or when there are guests at the house (state anxiety). Clearly, Jon's anxiety should be addressed in interventions with the family.

Depression and hopelessness often accompany high levels of anxiety. If depression seems to characterize a child or an adolescent, its extent and nature can be assessed as well.

Personality Assessment Questionnaire. This self-administered questionnaire assesses a variety of personality and behavioral dispositions of a child, an adolescent, or even a parent. The basis of this questionnaire is Rohner's (1980) parental acceptance-rejection theory, discussed earlier. Briefly, it claims that children who experience rejection (or any other form of psychological maltreatment) manifest aggression and hostility problems, dependency, low self-esteem, low self-adjustment, emotional instability, and negative world view. The three versions of the Personality Assessment Questionnaire (one eliciting the parent's perception of the child; another, the parent's view of self; the third, the child's view of self) can be used to evaluate the existence of these characteristics, whether in the child or in the parent.

The personality and behavioral dispositions evaluated are (1) hostility, aggression, passive aggression, and problems with the management of hostility and aggression ("I have trouble controlling my temper"); (2) dependence ("I like my friends to make a fuss over me when I am hurt or sick"); (3) self-esteem ("I wish I could have more respect for myself"); (4) self-adequacy ("I feel inept in many of the things I try to do"); (5) emotional responsiveness ("I feel distant and detached from most people"); (6) emotional stability ("Small setbacks upset me a lot"); (7) world view ("I view the universe as a threatening, dangerous place").

This scale is not as consistent as would be desirable for confident diagnostic use (the internal reliability of the child version ranges from .46 to .72, and the two adult versions are reliable at .73 to .85). However, the questionnaire can be useful in exploring personality types of maltreating parents and maltreated children. It can be utilized in beginning an exploration of behavior patterns of maltreated children and adolescents from both their own and their parents' perceptions.

Ann (Case 18) was terrorized by her father. Subsequently, she started talking in a strange voice, her posture became rigid, and she would sit mutely for hours and stare blankly. She is assessed as exhibiting passive aggression toward her father, having low self-esteem and feelings of inadequacy, being emotionally unstable and unresponsive, and viewing the world as a whole in negative terms. Overall, it is clear that she is poorly adjusted and has a negative view of herself and the world in general.

Child Behavior Checklist. This 118-item checklist evaluates the behavior problems and social competencies of children and adolescents as reported by themselves, their teachers, and their parents. The "behavior problems" portion permits classification as externalizing and internalizing. Achenbach (1978) developed the checklist by analyzing the responses of mental health clients to other checklists of behavior problems. It is a much-used instrument that has a good empirical reputation. The teacher's form (which also can be used by other adults) provides an objective assessment of the child's behavior in an environment outside the home. The self-report form elicits the child's view of self, which can be compared against that of the parents and teacher (or other adult) to see where there are agreements or divergences (see Garbarino, Schellenbach, and Sebes, 1986).

The responses to the checklist, when scored, result in a Child Behavior Profile. This profile describes the child according to the extent that he or she is socially competent, externalizing, and internalizing. Separate editions of the profile have been standardized for each sex, for the age groups six to eleven and twelve to sixteen.

The "social competence" part of the checklist contains three scales: an Activities Scale, a Social Scale, and a School Scale. The Activities Scale consists of scores for the amount and quality of the child's participation in sports; hobbies, activities, and games, other than sports; and jobs and chores. The Social Scale consists of scores for the child's membership and participation in organizations; number of friends and contacts with them; and behavior with others and alone. The School Scale consists of scores for the child's average performance in academic subjects; placement in a regular or special class; being promoted regularly or held back; and the presence or absence of school problems.

The second part of the checklist, the "behavioral problems" portion, is composed of two broad dimensions (internalizing and externalizing), each containing several specific clusters of problems. Internalizing includes anxious obsessive, somatic complaints, schizoid behavior, depressed withdrawal, being immature, and being uncommunicative. Externalizing includes being delinquent, aggressive, cruel, or hyperactive.

Significant differences between normal and disturbed children on all scales demonstrate the validity of the checklist. Research on its consistency and reliability is encouraging (test-retest reliability was found to be .89 on the average, and long-term average stability of the "behavior problems" part was .63).

In sum, the checklist can be administered to or self-administered by parents, teachers, and children or adolescents and can also be used to assess changes over time. The value of the profile lies in its efficient but comprehensive and meaningful description of children's behavior, its power to discriminate among children who may benefit from different kinds of help, and its sensitivity to detect changes and stabilities in children's behavior.

Jane (Case 5) was rejected and isolated by her family and became aggressive and acting out. She is assessed as externalizing more than internalizing her problems: being aggressive, hyperactive, and cruel. Some internalizing problems, such as immaturity and uncommunicativeness, also are evident. She is found to be low on the "social competence" measures: having no friends and lacking social skills. Overall, it seems that one needs to work both with her and with the family in order to reduce the extent to which she externalizes her problems and to increase her social competence so that she can profit from the compensatory influences of peers and nonparent adults.

Child Assessment Schedule. The Child Assessment Schedule provides a structured format for psychologically assessing a child. The instrument aims at assessing the child's personality through an interview with the child, along with observations by the interviewer. It is based on standard psychiatric diagnostic categories (diagnostic criteria in the American Psychiatric Association's *Diagnostic and Statistical Manual of Mental Disorders,* or *DSM-III*), as well as interview guides aimed at assessing adults' personalities and behavior problems (such guides appear in Spitzer, Endicott, Fleiss, and Cohen, 1970; and McKnew and others, 1979).

In the first section of the CAS, the interviewer records the child's responses to seventy-five questions about school, friends, activities and hobbies, family, fears and anxieties, worries, self-image, moods, somatic concerns, expression of anger, and thought disorders. In the second section, the interviewer records his or her observations on about sixty items, such as the child's behavior, the child's level of self-understanding, motor coordination, grooming, activity level, cognitive abilities, quality of verbalizations, and quality of the child's interpersonal interactions. In interpreting the CAS, the practitioner examines the various areas of functioning, in order to determine the types of problems the child has, and reviews the components related to cognitive functioning, in order to evaluate the extent to which the child is disturbed. Inter-rater reliability is good (ranging from .84 to .92), and a variety of groups of "problem children" were found to differ significantly on this instrument, meaning that it is both reliable and valid. Further, the instrument derives its content validity from *DSM-III*, which has widespread applicability.

Table 4. Instruments for Assessing Characteristics of the Maltreating Family and Parents and the Maltreated Child.

	Instrument	Purpose	Theoretical Basis	Examples of What Is Measured	Filled Out by:
Family Context	Family Environment Scale	Assess social climate in family	Ecological approach to human systems	Interpersonal relationships Personal growth Family structure	Each family member
	Family Adaptability and Cohesion Scale	Assess family's level of cohesion and adaptability	Systems framework of family relationships	Emotional bonds Sharing Roles Feedback	Each family member
	Interparental Conflict and Influence Scales	Assess content and frequency of arguments, relative power in decision making	Parental conflict and decision-making power	Finance Spouse characteristics Child-rearing practices Joint family activities	Each family member
Parental Factors and Parent-Child Interactions	Parental Acceptance-Rejection Questionnaire	Assess degree of parental acceptance or rejection	Parental acceptance-rejection theory	Warmth/affection Hostility Indifference Undifferentiated rejection	Each family member
	Children's Reports of Parental Behavior Inventory	Assess degree of parental love/hostility, autonomy/control, firm control/lax control	Relation of child's adjustment level to perception of parents	Sharing Affection Ignoring Intrusiveness Strictness	Each family member; mainly the child
	Bronfenbrenner's Parental Behavior Questionnaire	Assess parental loving, punishing, demanding	Relation of child's adjustment level to perception of parents	Nurturance Companionship Power Indulgence	Each family member; mainly the child
	Michigan Screening Profile of Parenting	Assess degree of existing maltreatment and predict further maltreatment	Child maltreatment is related to parental maltreatment as a child	Relationship with parents Expectations of children Coping skills	Parents

Instrument	Purpose	Theory Base	Dimensions	Completed by
Maternal Characteristics Scale	Assess how mother's personality affects maternal competence	Polansky's studies of neglectful mothers	Apathy-futility Childlike impulsivity	Practitioner
Childhood Level of Living Scale	Assess quality of mother's child-rearing practices	Polansky's studies of neglectful mothers	Physical care of child Emotional-cognitive care of child	Practitioner
Children's Behavior and Personality — Bayley Scales of Infant Development	Assess infant's development of motor, mental, and social skills	Infant development and the interrelatedness of motor, mental, and social abilities	Verbal communication Coordination of muscles Tendency to approach stimulation	Trained practitioner, rating the child
Tennessee Self-Concept Scale	Assess self-concept, self-acceptance, perception of own behavior	Theories of self-concept as influence on behavioral patterns	Self-criticism Positive self-perception Integrity across topics	Each family member; mainly the child
State-Trait Anxiety Inventory	Assess extent to which child is tense overall and at specific situations	State and trait theory of anxiety	Calmness Unhappiness Worry Fright	Each family member; mainly the child
Personality Assessment Questionnaire	Assess personality and behavioral dispositions	Rohner's acceptance-rejection theory	Hostility Dependence Self-esteem Emotional stability	Each family member
Child Behavior Checklist	Evaluate behavioral problems and competencies of child	General classifications of behavior problems	Participation in sports or activities Membership in organizations Grades in school Somatic complaints Hyperactivity	Each family member
Child Assessment Schedule	Assess child's personality and personality disorders	Standard psychiatric diagnostic criteria and general classifications of behavior problems	Fears Moods Thought disorders Self-understanding	Practitioner

In short, the Child Assessment Schedule, although it requires much effort and time from the interviewer in order to be effective as an evaluation instrument, has the potential to assess both the personality disorders and the behavior problems of a maltreated child and to serve as a guide for intervention through the interviewer's observations and impressions.

Cindy (Case 10) was described as a "Cinderella"—rejected and isolated by her family. She is fearful and anxious, and her low self-image renders her depressed and unhappy. Although more information is needed about her level of self-understanding and her cognitive and interpersonal capacities, Cindy appears to be internalizing and having some depressive disturbances.

Conclusion

Table 4 summarizes our discussion of instruments used in the assessment of psychological maltreatment. In reviewing the table, keep in mind that we view all these assessment techniques as tools for structuring exploration. It is the exploration that is important. Using these instruments may be impossible because of constraints imposed by inadequate resources, insufficient time or access, and low levels of professional expertise. Nonetheless, these instruments lay out an agenda for the practitioner. They provide a kind of map for assessment. If these instruments and the theory and research they reflect become incorporated in the practitioner's thinking about assessment, they have served a useful function. Such an accomplishment will bring to fruition our concept of practitioners as applied researchers as they go about the process of exploratory assessment.

ℵ 5 ℵ

Intervening to Reduce
Environmental Stresses
on the Family

Beyond the challenge of identifying and assessing psychological maltreatment, agencies and practitioners confront the challenge of providing effective interventions. They go forward to compensate for the consequences as well as to alleviate or reduce the social and personality problems that give rise to psychological maltreatment in the first place. As we indicated in Chapters Three and Four, the dimensions of psychological maltreatment include not only the parent-child dyad and the unique characteristics of both parties but also the family and environmental context of that dyad. Understanding the multidimensional nature of psychological maltreatment is crucial to the successful provision of treatment services. To provide adequate interventions, agencies and practitioners must be aware of the individual, family, and environmental contexts in which psychological maltreatment occurs and intervene wherever necessary to alter the dynamics that create and maintain an environment of psychological maltreatment. In this chapter we consider the agencies and individuals involved in service provision and examine strategies to alleviate and reduce environmental stresses that may contribute to psychological maltreatment. In Resource B we provide a list of national organizations that can provide assistance, information, and publications on child abuse or neglect. These resources can be used by practitioners and others who are responsible for responding to cases of psychological maltreatment.

105

Professionals and Their Roles

Child protective services are mandated by law in all fifty states (see Chapter Seven) to investigate allegations of abuse and/or neglect and provide services to families and children when maltreatment occurs. Most of the real "action," however, comes at the *county* level, where child welfare services are organized and delivered. We have *three thousand* child protective service systems (rather than fifty or one). For the last two decades, these services have focused primarily on intervening in cases of physical abuse and neglect and, more recently, sexual abuse. Though identified as one form of abuse/neglect in most state laws, psychological maltreatment (terminology varies from state to state, as we shall see in Chapter Seven) has not received the same programmatic *intervention* as physical and sexual abuse. As we saw in Chapter One, however, it is often cited as a protective service problem.

Within this legal framework, the role of the child welfare agency and worker varies from community to community and from state to state. In some communities child welfare workers investigate, develop treatment plans, and provide ongoing services to families in which psychological maltreatment has occurred. In other, usually larger, communities the child welfare worker acts as a case manager who develops treatment plans for families and monitors the delivery of services (such as counseling and day care) provided by other community agencies.

Shirley (Case 16) was referred to the child welfare agency by the principal of her school. The referral was made because Shirley had missed forty days of school. According to the principal, Shirley's father has no control over her. The child welfare worker investigated the case by talking with Shirley, her father, and the school personnel. The welfare worker concluded that Shirley and her father need counseling to resolve some of their relationship problems. Since they live in a small rural area, this service will be provided by another unit in the child welfare agency.

Despite the legal mandate of the child welfare system, not all children who are subjected to psychological maltreatment eventually receive services from this system, even in states that have good legal definitions. The definitional limitations of the laws (some definitions do not include psychological maltreatment; others interpret it narrowly) are compounded by the exigencies of day-to-day services, such as large caseloads, worker burnout, and poor coordination of services, to prevent many cases of psychological maltreatment from being dealt with as protective service cases. In some communities, even the system for reporting cases of psychological maltreatment may be ineffective, and thus referrals to the child protective service may be minimal. The reporting of such cases in a given community (and thus the status of psychological maltreatment as a formal protective service issue) will depend on whether a legal foundation (definition in the law) and a social foundation (responsive intervention by child protective services) exist. Where reporting is not reinforced by effective and responsive intervention, reporting declines (Garbarino, 1985). The law appears less significant as an influence on reporting than what practitioners perceive as the protective service agency's tendencies to respond (Alfaro, 1985).

Thus, since such cases do not always reach protective service agencies, professionals across the entire community intervene in cases of psychological maltreatment, primarily outside the child welfare system.

Severity also plays an important role in determining which agency will intervene in a given case. The list of those who can, should, and, perhaps in many communities, already do intervene in cases of psychological maltreatment (whether through referral by the child welfare agency or through direct intake of a case of psychological maltreatment) is long. For the purpose of this volume, we include as relevant groups child welfare workers, mental health workers, social workers in family and youth service agencies, medical professionals, psychologists, psychiatrists, child care workers, educators, and paraprofessionals. The common goals of all practitioners must be to eliminate the occurrence of psychological maltreatment and assist those who have been damaged, or are damaging, to rebuild and restructure their lives.

The most severe cases of psychological maltreatment are likely to fall within state definitions of "mental injury" and thus to become active child protective service cases. Moderate and mild

cases are much more likely to be served within the mental health/
counseling parent education mission of other agencies. This is
entirely appropriate from a practical standpoint; however, it may
technically violate legal mandates to report all cases and forms of
child maltreatment.

The range of services provided by these diverse groups is
shown in Figure 3. We depict these services in terms of the level of
intrusion into the family necessary to maintain the family as a
unit. We define intrusion as the degree to which agencies and
practitioners become involved in the day-to-day functioning of the
family in order to resolve and alleviate psychological maltreatment
and create an atmosphere conducive to healthy growth and
development. At the least intrusive end of the continuum are
services such as parent education or counseling that occur mainly
in an agency setting and on a time-limited basis. Moderate
intrusion includes a combination of services such as parent
education, parent-child counseling, or day care—in essence,
whatever combination of services is necessary to facilitate healthy
family functioning. At the intrusive end of the continuum is
Homebuilders (Kinney, Madsen, Fleming, and Haapala, 1977), a
group of therapists who "invade" the family for an extended
period of time (up to six weeks) and provide one-on-one and group
sessions to avert family crisis.

Placement of the child out of the home is also at the
intrusive end of the continuum. This occurs when interventions in
the home are not effective in resolving and alleviating psychological maltreatment. Though necessary in some cases, removal of the
child from the home is the least desirable intervention for children
who are abused and/or neglected (Goldstein, Freud, and Solnit,
1979).

Selecting Interventions

What influences our decisions about the goals and the
instruments of interventions? What factors in the environmental
context affect those decisions? We must look to several factors:
assessment, cooperation, and resource availability.

Figure 3. Range of Services Provided in Cases of Psychological
Maltreatment of Children.

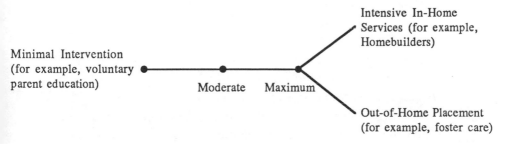

Assessment. A major factor in determining the type of intervention provided to a family and its members will be the characteristics of the environmental, family, and individual contexts in which psychological maltreatment has occurred. These characteristics are determined through the process of identification and exploratory assessment discussed in Chapters Three and Four. These processes determine the antecedents and consequences of psychological maltreatment and provide practitioners with information necessary to determine where and how to intervene effectively.

The assessment of Jon's family (Case 6) indicated that Jon's parents have very limited parenting skills and that Jon needs individual counseling to eliminate dysfunctional behavioral patterns as well as to enhance his future development. Thus, initially the treatment plan includes parent education classes for Jon's parents and counseling for Jon provided by a psychologist trained in play therapy techniques.

Family Cooperation. Another factor influencing the course of intervention is the willingness of family members involved in psychological maltreatment to participate in the process. By and large, many, if not most, families receiving services from the child welfare system or some other child service agency for psychological maltreatment have not volunteered for these services. Rather, they have been referred by professionals and others (such as neighbors or relatives) in the community. Even though legal mandate is designed to protect the welfare of children and to compel the family to take action in resolving its problem, a family may resent and object to the intrusion by an agency that is required to investigate and provide services. This resistance and negativity *may* reduce the effectiveness of services in alleviating psychological maltreatment; however, the fact that intervention faces involuntary "client" participation need not be crippling, as services to sexual abuse cases have demonstrated (Finkelhor, 1984).

Workers must recognize all this and develop a therapeutic style that reduces the negativistic nature of the act of intervening and, at the same time, creates a positive atmosphere whereby change and growth can occur. This is quite a challenge. Workers who are empathic, warm, and genuine may be able to reduce resistance and encourage families to cooperate (see Kadushin, 1980; Zuckerman, 1983). Beyond their interpersonal and clinical style, practitioners can look to less threatening areas for preliminary intervention. As we shall see when we examine stress-related interventions, focusing *initially* on concrete problems of family resources may pave the way for subsequent movement to more sensitive psychosocial issues of family dynamics (our topic in Chapter Six).

Cooperation is critical in the provision of services to families, since the effectiveness of those services will depend largely on the motivation and willingness of the family members involved.

Johnny's parents (Case 19) refused to cooperate with the school social worker and with the child welfare agency after his case was referred there. When the school social worker contacted them, the parents insisted that the only problem at issue here had to do with Johnny's behavior at school—his setting the school bathroom on fire. This, they maintained, was a problem between Johnny and school, since they had had nothing to do with it. Their response to the child welfare worker was equally resistive. The child welfare worker realized that her first task in working with Johnny and his parents was to decrease their resistance and develop a trusting relationship with them.

Agencies and Community Resources. The type of intervention provided to families and children depends on the resources available in agencies and in their communities. In an age when most community agencies are struggling to keep their institutional heads above fiscal water, service provision has been constrained by staff reductions and the elimination of programs. Indeed, even some of the basics (most notably, visiting nurse services) are being eroded in the current fiscal climate. Widespread implementation of expensive new services is virtually impossible without significant changes in social policy.

Under these conditions, agencies and practitioners are often limited in their ability to meet the needs of those involved in psychological maltreatment. Selecting an effective intervention is not simply based on what will best meet the needs of the client but, rather, depends on the minimal acceptability of the few available interventions to help families and children. To improve the net effect of the human services that are available, agencies as well as practitioners must be innovative in reallocating and piggybacking these resources.

Decision Making. Who will receive services? How will we decide? In many agencies and communities, practitioners, usually child welfare workers, balance assessment information, family cooperation, and resource availability against their own knowledge—knowledge based on experiences in working with families and on theoretical and empirical information regarding maltreatment and effective interventions—to develop treatment or service plans unique to a particular family and community (McDonnell and Associates, 1985). In some agencies multidisciplinary teams and agency-specific decision-making models are utilized to assist the practitioner in this decision-making process. In resource-poor situations, this decision making revolves around social triage—deciding who is "saveable" and who is a "lost cause."

Multidisciplinary child protection teams can be instrumental in determining appropriate and effective interventions. The basic team usually includes a social worker, a physician, a psychiatrist or psychologist, and a team coordinator or case manager (Kadushin, 1980, p. 222). The team uses the information gained through exploratory assessments to determine which of the available interventions would be most effective in meeting the needs of a particular family. The emphasis is on the collaboration of professionals, each with a unique perspective regarding services to families in which psychological maltreatment occurs. Thus, decision making is not limited to one individual but relies on a variety of experts who collaboratively decide on the best intervention plan. In many states multidisciplinary teams are legally mandated as integral parts of the service delivery system (Ziefert and Faller, 1981). Clearly, a community of practitioners can amplify the efforts of each and help reduce the stress associated with saving families involved in child maltreatment (Copans and others, 1979). The important thing to remember is that social isolation is as much a threat to the professional competence of practitioners as it is to the family well-being of parents and children (Whittaker, Garbarino, and Associates, 1983). Social support is the foundation for mental health *and* effective human services, whether one is a client or a provider.

An agency-specific decision-making model provides a structured framework through which practitioners can categorize and classify information about the family and its members in a systematic, logical fashion (McDonnell and Associates, 1985). For the most part, this model has been used to determine whether a child subjected to abuse and neglect should be removed from the home; however, it can also be used in determining what interventions should be provided to the family. The model organizes the information developed through exploratory assessment, categorizes that information, and assigns relative weights to the various pieces of information. Through this process strengths and weaknesses, motivation of family members, the severity of past behavior, and the current risk to the child are all factored into a final decision that guides interventions. In the most serious cases, particularly when intensive home-based services are unavailable, removal of the child from the home is warranted (see McDonnell and Associates, 1985, for more information on decision-making models).

To illustrate the selection of an intervention for a particular family, we use the following case example. For simplicity of presentation, we focus on the parents in this family. However, in an actual case, information on the maltreated child and other children in the family would be collected, assessed, and used in developing a treatment plan including parents and children.

Patty (Case 7) and her parents were referred to the local protective service agency by Patty's nursery school teacher. The teacher, as a mandated reporter, believed that the disciplinary techniques used by Patty's parents were psychologically harmful. Patty was also displaying psychosomatic complaints. Assessment of Patty's parents by means of the Inventory of Parental Behavior indicated that they were high on the scales measuring rejection, psychological control, and firm control. The parents also indicated to the caseworker that they had been physically abused as children. Further, the caseworker determined that the family was isolated from other families in the community. The caseworker presented this information to the multidisciplinary team (MDT), which recommended that the parents become involved in a parenting education group. Patty's parents, however, resisted receiving education as part of a group. Thus, in order to comply with the MDT as well as the parents' wishes, the caseworker referred the parents to a family service agency that provided parenting education to individual families.

Evaluating the Effectiveness of Interventions. Few interventions have been developed specifically for dealing with psychological maltreatment. Fewer still have been evaluated for their ability to resolve this problem. Thus, the interventions discussed in this volume—although not specifically developed for psychological maltreatment—are designed to alleviate environmental, family, or individual disturbances that contribute to psychological maltreatment. For example, intervening in the parent-child relationship can result from a variety of problems, of which psychological maltreatment is only one. However, as we argued in Chapter One, psychological maltreatment is the core issue in most cases of abuse and neglect. We can confidently assume that many of the techniques designed to deal with physical and sexual maltreatment are relevant here.

Our approach to program evaluation mirrors our attitude toward assessment. Thus, we recognize the need for practitioners to incorporate an applied research perspective into their own interventive efforts. Just as assessment must be explorative, so must interventions. Even when formal evaluation is impractical, an evaluative attitude toward programming is not. Practitioners would do well to build into their professional mind set a model of program evaluation. (For additional information on program evaluations, see Ahkisson and others, 1974; Austin and others, 1983; Maddus, Scriven, and Stufflebeam, 1983; McSweeny, Fremouw, and Hawkins, 1982; Patton, 1980; Rossi and Freeman, 1982.)

To facilitate our understanding of interventions and their relationship to the identification and assessment of psychological maltreatment, we present these interventions (in this chapter and in Chapter 6) in a manner congruent with the ecological-interactive framework established in Chapters Three and Four. Here we discuss (1) interventions aimed at reducing environmental stresses that may contribute to psychological maltreatment and (2) interventions reflecting active community (environmental) participation to prevent or alleviate maltreatment.

Interventions for Reducing Environmental Stress

As noted in Chapters Three and Four, environmental conditions may create an atmosphere conducive to psychological maltreatment. Some families are deficient in meeting the needs of individual members because the pressures they experience in coping with day-to-day existence leave little energy to provide a psychologically positive environment for their offspring and create intense negative reactions that poison parent-child relations. In intervening with these families, practitioners must be aware of the environmental conditions that contribute to psychological maltreatment and must provide interventions that will reduce or alleviate these stresses. These environmental conditions include lack of financial resources, unemployment, inadequate housing, lack of appropriate medical care, unavailability of services, and community isolation. For many families environmental stress is not a solitary negative influence, however, but rather a combination of multiple stresses that create a psychologically destructive environment.

In intervening with families stressed by limited financial resources, practitioners may need to refer the parents to the public welfare department and also may have to provide transportation and guidance in filling out applications and gathering information about financial assistance. Similarly, when unemployment has created financial hardship, practitioners can help locate educational or vocational training programs and may need to show parents where to look for jobs and how to fill out job applications and interview for positions. These supportive activities may become the basis for dealing with psychological maltreatment.

Rhonda's father (Case 9) had recently lost his job and was home every day. The protective service assessment indicated that Rhonda's father was greatly distressed over the loss of his job because he felt that he had no hope of future employment. The stress created by unemployment may have contributed to his abusive treatment of Rhonda. The caseworker's initial intervention was to locate a training program for Rhonda's father. The worker also helped him fill out applications and other necessary forms. With this source of stress alleviated, Rhonda's father might become better able to deal with and resolve his abusive actions. Furthermore, these activities provided a positive experience for the family in relation to the caseworker. As a result, greater trust and regard developed in their relationship, and the caseworker had an opportunity to engage the family in other, more psychological issues.

Stresses are not only the result of a simple lack of money. They are often the result of a family's inability to meet its needs adequately with the resources it has. Practitioners can bridge these gaps by locating services that can supply clothing, rooms, meals, and emergency assistance. The practitioner can assume a similar role in locating medical and nutritional services for families and their children. Families stressed by health problems may experience additional hardships because clinics are not easily accessible and/or they are unaware of doctors who accept medical assistance reimbursement forms. A practitioner may have to provide transportation to a clinic or locate a physician who will accept medical assistance reimbursement in order to remove this source of family stress. Once again, these supportive activities may provide the foundation for more psychologically oriented intervention. They can establish the practitioner as part of the family's social network.

Inadequate housing can also contribute to psychological maltreatment in families. The natural behavior of children confined to a small space can become intolerable and lead to inappropriate parental responses. Research on the social and developmental pyschology of crowding leads us to expect that relationships will improve when a family's physical space is improved (Wohlwill and Van Vliet, 1986). Vulnerability need not translate into harm if the environment is arranged to provide support rather than generate and exacerbate stress. The practitioner in these cases may be able to assist the family in securing low-rent housing, larger quarters, or rent subsidies.

Thus, the key to intervening in the environmental context lies in adequately assessing the family's needs and working with the family in alleviating or reducing resultant stresses. Practitioners must be aware that these families are often isolated from the mainstream of society and lack the resources and energy necessary to negotiate in their environment. Simply suggesting options may not be enough. Practitioners must assist the family through every step of the processes. This time-consuming endeavor may require gaining access to a cadre of "parent aides" who can invest large amounts of time in one family (a luxury not open to most professional practitioners).

Negotiating the transit system, arranging baby-sitting services, and dealing with social service agencies can be frustrating and discouraging experiences. These and similar negative experiences may have increased the family's isolation. By being supportive and providing guidance, practitioners can promote positive experiences and enhance the family's ability to negotiate successfully within its environment.

Practitioners should also be aware of how communities and agencies contribute to the isolation of some families. An agency or a clinic may be located too far away from a family in need of service, or the agency may refuse to serve families with certain types of problems, or the agency's personnel may not be trained to deal with cultural and ethnic minorities. In such instances practitioners may have to provide or arrange for transportation, or act as advocates for families, or attempt to alter conventional methods of intervention to compensate for the deficiencies of the system in relation to psychosocially needy families. As mentioned, a system that fails to recognize cultural and ethnic differences in the community can alienate a certain segment of the population (see Garbarino and Ebata, 1983). An understanding of cultural and ethnic differences is a critical factor in providing effective interventions. Practitioners who recognize these differences in world views, historical perspectives, relationship and interaction patterns, and identity formation can provide interventions that are culturally relevant and, therefore, beneficial in helping minority groups (Trankina, 1983). Services that are culturally relevant and/or bilingual can decrease a family's isolation and enable minority groups to utilize needed services.

Community Participation in Intervention

Whereas the preceding interventions were aimed at reducing stresses created by the environmental context, the following sampling of interventions reflects the active participation of communities (environmental context) in cases of psychological maltreatment. In this category we include preventive interventions and community-based out-of-home placements. In providing preventive interventions for high-risk parents, communities and agencies adopt a proactive, rather than reactive, stance toward psychological maltreatment. To do so requires extensive knowledge of the parental antecedents of psychological abuse, such as maternal age, addictive behaviors, and psychological problems, that have future implications for children. Intervention with these parents is based on theoretical formulations regarding the characteristics of potentially maltreating parents, as discussed in Chapter Three.

The prevention interventions in this chapter focus on the earliest possible points of intervention in the parent-child relationship, specifically those before and just after birth. Because development is greatly influenced by the nature of the parent-child relationship, interventions designed to enhance this relationship from the onset can have enduring benefits (Belsky, 1984; Belsky, Gilstrap, and Rovine, 1984).

Further, the role of the community is also more active in cases of psychological maltreatment when the child is separated from the family and placed in an alternative living arrangement in the community. The community and agencies within it become more intrusive in the lives of families and children. Rather than being a support system for families, they assume a substitute role in fulfilling those functions that the family was unwilling or unable to fulfill. Hence, the community and its agencies become significant contributors to the child's continued growth and development.

Preventive Interventions with High-Risk Families. As we saw in Chapters Three and Four, parental characteristics can place their children at high risk for psychological maltreatment. These characteristics are evident prior to the birth of the child or shortly thereafter. High-risk parents are likely to be low-income single mothers or teenage mothers. They tend to have low IQs and low socioeconomic status, have abused or neglected other children in the family, and were themselves maltreated as children. Interventions with these identified parents are directed to preventing furture abusive behavior. Such interventions can be provided in hospitals or prenatal clinics as well as in schools and family service agencies.

One such preventive program was developed by Olds, Henderson, Chamberlin, and Tatelbaum (1984). In this program comprehensive prenatal and postnatal care is provided to families by visiting home nurses. A home health visitor (a registered nurse) is assigned to the family during the pregnancy and continues through the first two years of life. Weekly visits eventually taper off to monthly visits. The nurses provide parent education in influences on fetal and infant development, encourage involvement of family members and friends in child care and support of the mother, and provide a linkage to other health and human services. The program emphasizes the development of an integrated complementary approach in order to improve the context for bearing and rearing children in socially disadvantaged families.

It has proved successful in creating a more positive mother-child relationship (among low-income, young, single-parent families).

A similar program, the Lay Home Visitor Program in Denver, uses lay therapists to work with parents (Alexander and Kempe, 1982; Sugar, 1984; Payne, 1984.) The program's goals are to reduce social isolation and increase the family's participation in the community, to encourage warm and stimulating interactions between parent and infant, to ensure optimal physical and nutritional status of the infant, and to help meet the mother's need for emotional support (Payne, 1984). The home visitor provides emotional support to the mother by being attentive and understanding. She also suggests techniques for infant care and models appropriate interactions with the infant. The visitor does not have a specific curriculum that she follows but is well informed on issues relevant to mothers. A second component of this program is a parent group consisting of six to eight mothers who meet to discuss parenting issues and to socialize.

Susan's mother, Linda (Case 1), has been referred to a lay home visitor program. By involving her in this program, the social worker feels that Linda's isolation and her feelings of being overwhelmed by the child may decrease and that her ability to parent her infant successfully will increase. The home visitor can also monitor the safety and welfare of the child.

Schmitt (1980) proposes increased physical contact in the delivery room and maternity ward to foster attachment between parents and infants who are in a high-risk category. In the delivery room, parents should be encouraged to hold the infant and spend the first hours of the baby's birth together. Rooming-in arrangements should be encouraged, and nurses should assume a supportive role with mothers in performing caretaking responsibilities. Altogether this package constitutes a "family-centered" approach to childbirth (Garbarino, 1980) and appears to be successful in reducing child maltreatment.

Children who are born prematurely are at particular risk for maltreatment. The special physical needs of the premature infant and the sometimes long-term separation while the infant's condition stabilizes seem to threaten the affective bond or synchronous harmony of a secure relationship with parents. In such cases parental visiting should be strongly encouraged, and parents should be allowed to assume a more intimate role by feeding or bathing the infant. By encouraging the mother (and father) to participate, medical personnel can help parents develop a nurturing relationship with their newborns and thus prevent the onset of psychological maltreatment (Schmitt, 1980).

Teenage mothers also are at high risk for developing abusive/neglectful parenting patterns. Programs have been developed in schools and hospitals to meet the needs of this special population. Sugar (1984) describes one comprehensive school program, the St. Paul Program (Alton, 1979). A clinic established in the school provides pre- and postnatal care. Family-planning courses provide information on prenatal care, human sexuality, and parents' roles and responsibilities. Social workers and other professionals attend to the emotional concerns of the teenage mothers. A day care center provides child care, including cognitive and emotional stimulation, while the adolescent parent completes high school.

Sugar (1984) also describes an in-hospital program for teenage mothers designed by E. Badger. In this program young mothers are taught techniques that can intensify their competence and satisfaction in rearing their children. Specifically, they are shown how to interact with the baby, respond to the infant's verbal behavior, encourage play, and teach developmental skills. In a follow-up program for the mother and infant after leaving the hospital, techniques for infant stimulation are provided as part of a group-oriented mother's training program. Weekly meetings provide mothers with the opportunity to learn parenting skills, gain information about child development, and deal with personal problems through suggestions, discussion, workshops, and filmstrips. The program emphasizes infant sensorimotor development, language, and cognitive growth. This program for mothers is designed to increase their satisfaction with the mothering role, their dignity and self-esteem as teachers of their infants, and their ability to deal with their own personal problems (Cataldo, 1983).

Frank's mother (Case 3) could have benefited from a program designed to help adolescent mothers. Unfortunately, in her community this type of program did not exist. Had Frank's mother been given support and information during her pregnancy and after Frank's birth, she might not have been overwhelmed by the parenting experience and might have been able and willing to parent Frank.

For the most part, programs for high-risk parents are multidisciplinary, providing for the physical, emotional, and intellectual needs of both the parent and the infant. The goals of such programs are to enhance the quality of life for parent and child as well as to prevent the development of patterns that can be psychologically damaging to the child.

Out-of-Home Placements. Removal of the child from the home is a drastic measure and is usually the intervention of last resort—that is, when maltreatment continues in the home, so that the child is placed at great risk. Foster homes and group homes are the most common types of out-of-home placements. However, in some cases institutional settings are considered appropriate. Placement of a child should be based on the characteristics of the child, the prognosis for the family, and the ability of a particular placement to meet these needs.

Foster home placements *in general* provide more intimate family-like settings than group home placements. Infants and young children are usually placed in foster homes, since their development is more dependent on individualized, intimate care by a mother figure.

Frank (Case 3) was placed in a foster home because the living arrangements with his grandparents had been psychologically damaging. He was placed with foster parents who have a great deal of experience with infants, particularly infants who have been abused and/or neglected.

Group home placements are usually most appropriate for adolescents because, among other reasons, foster parents willing to care for adolescents are scarce, the development of relationships between adolescents and foster parents is often difficult, and adolescents need peer interactions and the greater independence often provided in the group home setting (Kadushin, 1980). Supervised independent living arrangements may also be viable alternatives for mature and self-sufficient adolescents (Furrh, 1983; Mauzerall, 1983).

Ricky (Case 20) has been placed in a group home. The multidisciplinary team (MDT) felt that Ricky could begin to work out some of his problems in this setting. He is receiving individual, group, and family counseling. Arrangements also were made to include Ricky's parents in weekly counseling sessions at the group home. Since the group home is located in Ricky's school district, he can remain in the same school and maintain the relationships and support systems that have developed in that setting.

Therapeutic foster homes may be a reasonable alternative for children and adolescents who have been severely disturbed as a result of psychological maltreatment. Florida is one state that provides therapeutic foster home care (Friedman, 1983). These programs are community based, with the family as the major focus of treatment. Although the homes vary in the particular procedures they use, they do possess certain common features: (1) Foster parents are specifically recruited and trained to work with emotionally disturbed children. (2) Mental health workers with small caseloads work intensively with the family. (3) The foster parents receive financial, professional, and group support. (4) A limit of no more than two children per foster home increases the degree of individual attention.

Rhonda (Case 9) has been placed in a therapeutic foster home. The treatment plan developed by the child welfare agency indicated that Rhonda needs an intensive therapeutic environment, with individualized attention, to resolve her emotional and behavioral problems. The individualized attention provided by the therapeutic foster home may facilitate many changes in Rhonda's behavior and enable her to develop improved patterns of personal functioning.

Institutional care is another treatment possibility for children and youth who have been psychologically maltreated. In these settings intensive services are provided to older children and adolescents in a restricted environment. Children are placed in institutions when other forms of intervention have been unsuccessful or are considered inappropriate for meeting the child's needs (Kadushin, 1980).

Institutional placement can be short or long term. In short-term placement, the child is removed from the home and community for a time-limited period in order to provide intensive therapeutic treatment—for instance, in a psychiatric clinic or a drug/alcohol residential facility. Long-term placements are utilized when the child's emotional, mental, or physical disability prevents the child from living and coping adequately in the home or community.

Because of the severity of her symptoms, Ann (Case 18) has been placed in a thirty-day residential program where she will receive intensive individual, group, and family counseling. It is expected that Ann will benefit from being separated from her parents and allowed the space to resolve some of the complicated issues that confront her. Her suicide ideology also indicates that a short-term psychiatric clinic will be beneficial.

When used because in-home interventions have failed or because the child's problems cannot be resolved in the home environment, out-of-home placements can be instrumental in intervening with children and adolescents who have been damaged by psychological maltreatment. These and similar programs may help children and adolescents develop improved patterns of personal functioning that will enable them to lead psychologically healthy, productive lives.

Conclusion

In this chapter we have described the professionals and the agencies that are responsible for service provision and have discussed interventions in the environmental context. The professionals who provide services, the characteristics of families and children who receive services, family cooperation, and the decision-making process regarding treatment plans combine in a distinctive fashion for each community and agency. By understanding these factors and their role in shaping the course of intervention, practitioners, agencies, and communities can realistically assess their own capabilities for dealing successfully with psychological maltreatment.

Practitioners and agencies should consider several questions as they seek to understand the environmental context of psychological maltreatment. Which professionals and agencies in the community provide services to maltreated children and their families? How well do they meet this responsibility? What are your or your agency's strategies for dealing with resistant clients? How are decisions made regarding who receives treatment and what type of treatment? Are there guidelines for making such decisions? Do community or agency factors prevent adequate provision of services? Is there any way to reduce or eliminate these factors? Does the agency have an established method of evaluating the effectiveness of interventions? If not, what steps could be taken to develop an evaluation process?

☒ 6 ☒

Intervening to Resolve Problems Among Family Members

Successful intervention with children and families in which psychological maltreatment has occurred depends on the ability of the intervention to address the unique and special needs of a particular family and its members. The greater the range of services and practitioners who can intervene in cases of psychological maltreatment, the greater the chances of finding a good fit between client and intervention. Of greatest benefit are comprehensive interventions that address the multidimensional nature of psychological maltreatment—that is, the environmental, family, and individual levels. In all instances the goal of intervention is to alleviate psychological maltreatment and create psychologically positive environments conducive to the healthy growth and development of children.

Interventions in the Family

When exploratory assessments indicate that psychological maltreatment is a product of dysfunctional patterns of family interaction, interventions in the family context are crucial. Simple social support alone is not enough. The goals of these interventions are to resolve difficulties in interpersonal relationships and improve family functioning by creating an atmosphere that fosters positive psychological and emotional development. As we indicated in Chapter Three, dysfunction may occur in the marital relationship, the parent-child relationship, or the family system as a whole. Furthermore, inadequate parenting knowledge and skills as well as the social isolation of the family may create a context conducive to psychological maltreatment. The particular intervention used will depend on the assessment of family dynamics and the identification of the problematic level or levels of family functioning. Marital counseling, family therapy, parent-child interventions, parenting interventions, and interventions with socially isolated families may all be appropriate responses. These issues are germane to all families, not only those having characteristics that place them at high risk.

Practitioners in mental health agencies, family service agencies, and child welfare agencies as well as psychologists and psychiatrists can intervene in the family context. The type of intervention depends on the practitioner's training as well as the agency's resources. The existence of numerous therapeutic interventions having similar treatment goals provides a broad range of interventions available to many practitioners. In general, we strongly urge the use of comprehensive services that intervene on a variety of levels.

Marital Counseling. Psychological maltreatment may be a by-product of marital conflict when spousal conflict impairs the parent-child relationship. Thus, interventions designed to help couples resolve marital dysfunctions may alleviate the psychological maltreatment of children. When the marital relationship is improved and the consequent stresses of marital conflict are decreased, parents may be better able to meet the emotional and psychological needs of their children.

Counselors may use a wide variety of techniques for intervening in the marital relationship, depending on their training and expertise. In general, counseling techniques with couples utilize either a systems-transactional approach, a psychodynamic approach, a learning theory approach, or a mixture of these (Sager, 1981). In the systems-transactional approach (Gurman, 1978), the goal is to eliminate the dysfunctional transactions between husband and wife that are creating conflict and stress by using such techniques as restructuring or analyzing transactions, altering communication patterns, and using tasks to change behaviors. The psychodynamic approach (Greene, 1965) uses psychoanalytic techniques such as classical analysis, psychoanalytic psychotherapy, Gestalt therapy, and transactional analysis to resolve marital difficulties. A learning theory approach (Liberman, 1970) incorporates behavior modification and behavior therapy techniques such as the use of tasks and reinforcement to achieve changes in the marital relationship.

David's parents (Case 4) have a marital relationship characterized by lies, distrust, and infidelity. David's mother has isolated David from his father in order to prevent David from disclosing information about her extramarital affairs. David's father has ignored the boy ever since his wife told him that he might not be David's biological father. Their treatment of David appears to be a product of their dysfunctional marital relationship. The caseworker has referred them for marital counseling at a family service agency. Marital counseling may help them resolve their problems and develop more appropriate interaction and conflict resolution patterns. Consequently, their interactions with David may become more appropriate and psychologically healthy for David.

Family Therapy. Psychological maltreatment is often the result of family discord and problematic interpersonal relationships. Family therapy can be useful in reducing psychologically destructive family interaction patterns and inappropriate coping behaviors. The goal of family therapy is to enable the family to function in a healthy manner, providing emotional nurturance and support to all members.

As with marital therapy, many different types of family therapy interventions exist—among them, psychoanalytic family therapy, behavioral family therapy, communications family therapy, and structural family therapy (Nichols, 1984). The particular technique that practitioners will use in providing family therapy depends on their training and expertise.

Psychoanalytic family therapy (Ackerman, 1966; Boszormenyi-Nagy and Framo, 1965) focuses on improving family relationships by changing dysfunctional personality characteristics of family members through the use of psychodynamic techniques. Behavioral family therapy (O'Leary and Wilson, 1975) attempts to modify behavior patterns that contribute to family problems, using learning theory techniques such as shaping and reinforcement to create change. Communication family therapy (Haley, 1976; Satir, 1967) is based on the theoretical premise that dysfunctional family relationships are the result of poor communication patterns. Techniques that facilitate open, direct, assertive communication are utilized.

Structural family therapy focuses on changing the family structure (for example, the relationship between mother and daughter). The techniques used in this therapy are drawn largely from the work of Salvador Minuchin (Minuchin, 1974).

Johnny (Case 19) is constantly threatened by his father, unsupported by his mother, and in general dealt with more severely than his sister is. The caseworker's assessment indicates that there is little positive interaction among family members and that the processes of conflict resolution and decision making are inconsistent and chaotic. The family has been referred to a family therapist for counseling. As a result of family therapy, the family may adopt more appropriate interactional and coping patterns. These changes may provide a more positive home environment for Johnny.

Parent-Child Interventions. In cases of psychological maltreatment where the parent-child relationship is the root of the problem, direct intervention in that relationship is warranted. The goals of treatment are to eliminate dysfunctional interactive patterns and restore the relationship to a psychologically healthy level. A variety of professionals—including psychologists, child welfare workers, and family service workers—can be utilized to provide such interventions.

In such cases the parent-child dyad often has become "entrapped" in aversive exchanges and escalating negativity (Burgess and Richardson, 1984). Thus, interventions that utilize behavioral redirection with entrapped parents may succeed in eliminating psychological maltreatment. Gerald Patterson, John Reid, Robert Burgess, Rand Conger, Robert Wahler, and others have developed model programs to reduce negativity and establish positive exchanges.

Patterson's program (cited in Reid, Patterson, and Loeber, 1982) is designed to reduce the frequency of aversive parent-child interactions and increase the parents' skills in efficiently and nonviolently resolving discipline confrontations. Parents are trained in using a behavioral strategy to interpret their children's behavior and to modify maladaptive responses (Simpson, 1980). Parents are taught to conceptualize their children's maladaptive behavior in terms of specific observable behaviors, to monitor these behaviors, and to respond systematically to their occurrence with withdrawal of attention or mild punishment (such as time-outs or small chores). Further, parents are taught to encourage their children to adopt pro-social alternatives to the maladaptive behavior. Patterson and his colleagues have developed programmed textbooks to train parents to promote appropriate behavior and decrease inappropriate behavior in children.

Also worth mentioning here are the programs that incorporate advanced technology into the process of parental behavior modification. Richard Sanders and Ralph Welsh (Sanders and Welsh, 1965; Welsh, 1966) have used a device called "the bug in the ear" (now produced by Farrell Instruments). A mother wearing this hearing-aid communication device during interactions with the child that are observed by the therapist can receive feedback from the therapist on her behavior with the child.

At the age of nine, Ken (Case 12) has developed an explosive temper and displays aggressive behavior toward peers and adults. His parents attempt to control his behavior by using harsh disciplinary measures. The caseworker is using Patterson's program methods to modify parenting skills, to reduce aversive parent-child interactions, and to help Ken develop more appropriate behaviors.

"Filial" therapy (Guerney, 1983) is another treatment approach used to intervene in the parent-child relationship. It is a behavioral intervention for children under age twelve, using parents as primary therapists. This program has four main goals: (1) to enhance the parent-child (filial) relationship, (2) to reduce the child's symptoms, (3) to increase the child's competence and confidence, and (4) to improve the parents' child-rearing skills. Play is used as the medium for achieving these goals. The program is divided into five phases: an instruction phase (where parents learn to conduct play sessions), a practice phase (where parents practice skills under the therapist's supervision), a home-play phase (where parents use the skills learned in the laboratory setting at home), a generalization phase (where skills are generalized to other areas), and an evaluation and planning phase. Throughout these sessions, parents are trained to (1) be sensitive to their child's feelings and emotional needs, (2) communicate this sensitivity to the child, (3) permit the child age-appropriate and realistic self-direction, (4) recognize the need to set enforceable limits, (5) be sensitive to their own needs and communicate these needs, directly, promptly, and constructively, and (6) recognize their value as reinforcing agents (Guerney, 1976).

Jon (Case 6) has been psychologically maltreated by his father's techniques of ignoring and terrorizing. Jon is tense and tongue-tied at home; at nursery school he stutters, whines, and is aggressive toward the other children. The worker who investigated the case determined that the father's behavior is motivated by good intentions but that his knowledge of appropriate parenting techniques and age-appropriate expectations is very limited. The worker has referred the family to an agency that provides filial therapy. With increased parenting knowledge and improved parenting techniques, the relationship between Jon and his father may be greatly enhanced, and Jon's maladaptive behavior may decrease.

The Nurturing Program, developed by Bavolek and Comstock, as described by Bavolek (personal communication, 1985), is also designed to intervene with parents and children who are experiencing relationship difficulties. The program focuses on two levels of learning: the cognitive level (to learn new knowledge and skills) and the affective level (to experience positive healthy human interaction). Specific content areas include developmental expectations, empathy, behavior management, and self-awareness. Parents and children (ranging from two years to twelve years old) meet in separate groups two and a half hours a week for fifteen consecutive weeks. Parent trainers and child trainers use an established curriculum, which details goals, objectives, and activities for each of the fifteen sessions. Audiovisual materials (such as *Behavior Management*, a film explaining the principles of discipline, behavior management, and punishment), play materials (such as "Pair It," a card game in which matched pairs depict appropriate parent-child interaction), and group discussion are used to improve parent-child interactions.

Shirley (Case 16), her younger brother, and her father have been referred to the Nurturing Program, which is sponsored by the local Parents Anonymous group. Shirley's father, as a single parent, is having difficulty being a parent to Shirley and her brother. The Nurturing Program can help him improve his parenting skills, gain information about child development, and form a more nurturing relationship with Shirley and her brother. The children's group can help Shirley and her brother become more aware of themselves and their father as individuals and adapt to their father's new parenting techniques.

Patterson, Guerney, and Bavolek emphasize the active participation of both parent and child in improving the parent-child relationship. Improved parenting skills, as well as behavioral changes by the parent and the child, are integral components of these programs. When parents and children are not psychologically crippled by serious personality disorders and are motivated to change, these and similar programs can help them reduce negative interaction patterns by developing positive patterns of interaction and relationships characterized by nurturance and understanding. These interactions can be instrumental in reducing psychological maltreatment and creating family environments that are conducive to positive growth and development. Through this process parents learn to relate to their children in more appropriate ways and play an active role in decreasing the children's maladaptive behaviors. Thus, the quality of the parent-child relationship is enhanced, and the chances for psychological abuse are decreased.

Interventions with Infants and Parents. Interventions with infants who have been psychologically maltreated usually address infant-*mother* interaction, since in our society mothers usually are responsible for infant care. When assessment indicates that an infant is suffering from nonorganic failure to thrive or displays signs of developmental lag because the mother cannot nurture or stimulate the child, interventions to help the mother become more nurturant and more skillful in meeting the basic needs of the child are warranted.

Studies indicate that interventions in the home can greatly improve the quality of care for infants and provide the foundation for creating environments free from abuse and/or neglect (Dawson, Robinson, and Johnson, 1982; Fraiberg, 1980; Lally and Honig, 1975; Lally, 1984). Parent aides, lay therapists, and paraprofessionals called "Homemakers" can provide intensive direct services to mothers and infants in their homes. Lay therapists have been used successfully with infants suffering from nonorganic failure to thrive (Haynes, Cutler, Gray, and Kempe, 1984). Interveners can provide positive models of expressions of love, affection, and regard for the child; as a result, parents can learn to see the child as a valued person with needs and feelings. Practitioners can initiate discussions of what constitute realistic expectations about development and behavioral standards. They can also provide suggestions for handling difficult behavior and can compliment parents when they have successfully applied the techniques they have been taught.

The Neighborhood Support Systems for Infants project in Somerville, Massachusetts (cited in Payne, 1984), uses home visitors to intervene in the mother-infant relationship. Nonprofessional "core mothers" are trained as home visitors. These "core mothers" visit the home weekly and stay an hour to an hour and a half. During these visits the "core mother" tries to improve interaction between parents and infants by modeling, educating, and reinforcing parental strengths. Toys are used to stimulate and influence the relationship. The "core mother" can show the real mother how toys can be used to improve her relationship with the baby and to further the child's development. As part of their supportive function, "core mothers" also provide transportation to medical appointments and help the mother formulate questions to be discussed with the doctor.

Out-of-home programs have also been developed to intervene in dysfunctional infant-mother relationships. These programs have four goals: (1) to improve the infant-mother relationship, (2) to facilitate infant development, (3) to improve the mother's personal and parental functioning, and (4) to increase knowledge of parenting skills and child development.

The Milwaukee Project (cited in Cataldo, 1983) provides an infant stimulation program as well as a vocational, educational, affective, and home management training program for mothers. The infant program emphasizes cognitive-linguistic development in a planned environment. A paraprofessional teacher works with the infant, using a curriculum based on language development, problem solving, and achievement motivation. The teacher observes the child's abilities, develops tasks that are related to the areas of need, and constantly assesses the child's changing status. The maternal rehabilitation program emphasizes vocational-occupational training and the development of attitudes that lead to greater life success.

Finally, videotapes can be useful tools for intervening in dysfunctional infant-parent relationships (Lally, 1984). By actually viewing their interactions with their infants, parents may become aware of processes that they are unable to detect when interacting directly with the child. Professionals can help these parents understand their own and their child's behavior, so that they can eliminate dysfunctional interaction patterns in favor of more positive exchanges.

A practitioner working with Betty (Case 2) and her family could refer Betty's mother to a program similar to the Neighborhood Support Systems or the Milwaukee Project. The specific intervention would depend on agency and community resources. This intervention would enable Betty's mother to improve her parenting abilities and her personal functioning and to decrease her isolation.

Parenting Interventions. Parents who psychologically maltreat their children often lack the knowledge and the skills necessary to fulfill the parental role. Without such knowledge, parents act in ways that are psychologically damaging to their children. Thus, interventions designed to educate and modify parental skills can succeed in diminishing psychological maltreatment.

Patty (Case 7) is the victim of psychological maltreatment by parents who, as a method of discipline, have isolated and rejected her. The caseworker, in assessing this family, found that both parents had been physically abused as children. Their role models had used physical punishment and harsh disciplinary measures in raising them. Though strongly opposed to physical punishment, they are unable to discipline Patty without resorting to psychologically damaging enforcement measures. As a result of this investigation, however, they have begun to recognize the consequences of their actions. Consequently, the caseworker has referred them to the child welfare agency's parent education program.

Similar to other interventions discussed in this chapter, parent education and training can be provided in a variety of settings by a range of practitioners. The particular form of intervention depends on the age of the child(ren) and the intellectual abilities of the parent as well as the cultural and environmental context in which the family lives. Thorough assessment can determine the appropriate interventions.

Currently, many models of parent education programs exist and are used successfully in many communities throughout the nation. The goals of these systematic, conceptually based programs are to provide information, increase awareness, and teach practical skills to parents. Such programs usually are conducted weekly for a few hours over several weeks. The format includes presentation of specific ideas, group discussion, sharing or processing of ideas and experiences, and some skill-building activities (Fine, 1980).

Despite similar formats, the theoretical bases of these programs differ significantly. Some programs emphasize the use of behavioral modification techniques in parenting, while others emphasize communication techniques as important parenting skills. Still others emphasize the need for parents to possess information about developmental needs and changes.

Although packaged programs may be an efficient, effective way to provide parents with skills and knowledge that heretofore have been lacking, such programs are not appropriate for all parents. Practitioners often must modify and restructure these programs, or even develop their own programs, to meet the special needs of the parents and families they are helping. As mentioned, the intellectual abilities of the parents as well as the ages and developmental stages of the children need to be considered. For example, the knowledge and skills needed by parents of adolescents differ considerably from those needed by parents of infants. Thus, for parent education to be effective, practitioners should make every effort to provide age-appropriate information. Moreover, for some parents group interventions are not appropriate, since these parents regard a group experience as threatening and stressful. They might respond better to an initial one-to-one relationship, which may serve as a bridge to group sessions.

Many practitioners—including child welfare workers, family service workers, parent aides, community public health nurses, and "Homemakers"—can provide parenting education on a one-to-one basis, usually in the home. These practitioners can adapt the content from group formats; the interactions are most effective, however, when they provide information on an informal basis, discussing parental responsibilities and modeling appropriate adult-child relationships by interacting with the children in the home. The strength of the one-to-one approach lies in seizing specific opportunities as they arise in parent-child encounters.

Homemakers are paraprofessionals who intervene in the family in order to strengthen and support the family in its role of caring for and nurturing children. The specific duties of the Homemaker depend on the needs of the family. When the parents' lack of parenting skills has resulted in psychological maltreatment of their children, the Homemaker can provide information to parents through a structured educational format or more informally through guided conversation in which practical questions of child care are discussed. Since Homemakers often spend considerable time in the family setting, their interactions with the children as well as the parents can be useful in modifying parental behavior. By observing and interacting with the Homemakers, parents can improve interpersonal relationship skills, coping abilities, and child care and management skills. Further, the supportive, nurturing relationship with the Homemaker may improve the parents' feelings of worth and self-esteeem (Faller, 1981; Kadushin, 1980; Mayhall and Norgard, 1983).

Community public health nurses also can provide parenting information and skills training to families in which psychological maltreatment is present. By working with parents in solving normal childhood problems and understanding child development, nurses can suggest specific techniques to parents for physically, nutritionally, and emotionally caring for the children (Mayhall and Norgard, 1983). At the beginning of such interventions, the nurses mainly provide role modeling, showing parents how to express feelings, display warmth and affection, deal with anger, play with children, and set limits in a manner that is not rejecting. Beyond the initial stages, other teaching methods may then be used to help parents learn parenting skills, basics about child development, and methods of disciplining (Anderson, 1980; see also Faller, 1981).

The caseworker assigned to Rhonda's family (Case 9) determined that the home environment is very chaotic and that the family has many problems in addition to the current sexual abuse problem. The mother has little knowledge of parenting techniques and child development. Her coping patterns are inappropriate. Further, the mother, who was an orphan, never developed a positive nurturing relationship with an adult. The caseworker has recommended that Rhonda's mother be provided with Homemaker services, community public health services, or parent aide services.

Despite the strong impact that community public nurses, Homemaker services, and parent aide services can have in helping families in which psychological maltreatment occurs, the cost of such services may restrict their use to only the most serious cases. The narrowing of mission of visiting nurses is already a national (and disturbing) trend. In recognition of current fiscal limitations as well as the increasing numbers of families in need of such interventions, many communities make use of volunteers to provide parent education.

Parent aides or lay therapists are volunteers who work closely with families over an extended period of time. These volunteers are sponsored by various agencies and are supervised by professionals. Parent aides fulfill functions similar to those of Homemakers. They model appropriate parental behaviors and provide direct information to parents regarding child care and child management. Their very presence in the home may relieve some of the overwhelming stress and isolation that parents often feel in caring for their children (Alexander and Kempe, 1982; Faller, 1981; Mayhall and Norgard, 1983).

A pilot project in Pittsburgh utilizes foster grandparents in a similar role. The program, the Action Foster Grandparent Program directed by the Lutheran Services Society, places older adults in homes with emotionally needy children. The grandparents model nurturant behavior, parent the parent, and demonstrate learning and play techniques that stimulate child development. The grandparents often coach the parents in direct child management as well as share personal parenting experiences (Arch, 1978).

Interventions with Socially Isolated Families. Families in which psychological maltreatment occurs are often isolated not only from the formal systems and institutions of society but also from the informal supportive networks of family, neighbors, and friends. Further, the informal networks that do exist may have negative influences on these families. Interventions designed to decrease isolation and increase social connectedness—for example, group interventions or visits by parent aides, Homemakers, home health visitors, or community public health nurses—can enable the family to provide a positive and healthy growth environment for children. In some families child welfare caseworkers can provide similar social support, although the family's perception of these workers as part of the enforcement system often prevents a positive, trusting relationship from developing (Alexander and Kempe, 1982; Faller, 1981; Mayhall and Norgard, 1983).

By being warm, accepting, and supportive, home visitors can create an atmosphere that fosters the development of trusting interpersonal relationships. By modeling these behaviors, parents can begin to develop positive patterns of interaction with others beyond the family unit, as well as adopt improved strategies to cope with their environment. The home visitor can provide an invaluable service simply by being a concerned caring individual.

Similarly, parenting education groups can provide positive experiences for those who are isolated and who lack the ability to trust others. According to Justice and Justice (1976), group interactions allow such parents to have different and positive experiences with other people. Groups foster competent parenting not only by providing information but also by providing emotional support and a nonthreatening social environment conducive to growth and change (Belsky and Vondra, forthcoming). Two good examples of group interventions for isolated parents are drop-in centers and Parents Anonymous groups. Both these interventions utilize volunteers.

Family Focus (Weissbourd, forthcoming) and the Michigan Drop-In Center (Fried and Holt, 1980) use volunteers and professionals to provide early-childhood and parental education as well as a parental respite. Family Focus centers are open long hours and offer a wide and exciting variety of experiences. The Michigan center is open for three hours two to three days a week and provides activities for children from infancy to kindergarten. During the last hour of each drop-in session, parents are invited to participate in a sharing period. In addition to social visiting and recipe exchange, parents are encouraged to discuss their anxieties and concerns about toilet training, aggression, sibling rivalry, and other family issues in a comfortable, nonthreatening setting. Family Focus programs also provide opportunities to share experiences on these family issues, but in a context with greater professional leadership and with broader resources.

David (Case 4) and his mother were referred to a Family Focus program. The caseworker in his investigation determined that David's mother has no support system in the community. Her family lives miles away, and she has no friends with whom she can share personal or parental problems. The Family Focus program can give David and his mother an opportunity to socialize and improve their interpersonal relationship. As noted earlier, David's mother and father are also receiving marital counseling. The caseworker feels that the resolution of this family's problems will be enhanced by utilizing both of these interventions.

Parents Anonymous (PA) is a voluntary self-help support group that meets every week. When these groups sustain themselves (with professional support), they can be a powerful positive intervention (Lieber and Baker, 1977). But when they do not meet the challenges of institutional maintenance, they can drain enormous amounts of professional energy with uncertain therapeutic payoff.

This program provides an accepting, caring atmosphere where parents who are experiencing difficulties in fulfilling their parental role can find support and guidance in their attempts to change dysfunctional behaviors. In weekly group meetings parents are encouraged to be completely honest about their relationships with their children and accept suggestions from others for resolving problems. This process also fosters the development of personal characteristics such as self-esteem, self-confidence, and respectability, which are critical elements in fulfilling the parental role. In addition to the group meetings, a parental support system is available via telephone contact for those experiencing overwhelming stress and in need of immediate support and advice.

The caseworker referred Ricky's parents (Case 20) to Parents Anonymous. She believed that they could benefit from a supportive self-help group because they had isolated themselves from the community and, despite the harshness of their parenting techniques, were cooperative and genuinely concerned about being good parents.

Isolated families also can be helped in a day care setting. By encouraging and promoting parent participation, day care programs can provide an atmosphere conducive to increased parental socialization. Moreover, the child care worker may provide the only adult relationship a parent has (Friedman, Sale, and Weinstein, 1984) and may be instrumental in decreasing the isolation a parent experiences. In addition, day care workers often can connect families with other needed services (Friedman and Friedman, 1982).

Bobby (Case 8) came to the attention of the child protective service agency through a referral by the day care center. However, prior to this referral, the day care center had had little contact with Bobby's mother. After talking with the child welfare worker, the staff of the center began making an effort to include her in day care activities and to support her on an individual basis. This personal contact with the day care center may help to alleviate the mother's isolation and improve the home environment.

Intervention with Individuals

A person-oriented intervention may be a necessary complement to a relationship-oriented intervention when a parent or a child has a personality disturbance that must be corrected before the family can profit from a relationship-oriented intervention or before the child can, if necessary, function outside the family (in foster care or residential institutions, for example).

Parental Characteristics. When exploratory assessment indicates that parental personality problems are largely responsible for psychological maltreatment, interventions designed to alleviate dysfunctional behaviors and increase personal competence are beneficial, not only to the parent but to the child as well. Many parents cannot fulfill their parental role because of their own psychological, emotional, or intellectual deficiencies and therefore require individual therapy to meet their own primary personal needs before they can become adequate parents.

Individuals whose personal characteristics—such as low self-esteem, feelings of futility or apathy, impulsiveness, and insecurity—have impaired personal and parental functioning may benefit greatly from a supportive, nurturing therapeutic relationship (Polansky, Chalmers, Buttenweiser, and Williams, 1981). Often these parents have never fully participated in a warm, nurturing relationship and thus have severely diminished ability to develop such relationships with their children. Workers in a variety of settings with diverse backgrounds can provide the basis for positive growth by establishing an atmosphere of respect, acceptance, support, and nurturance while simultaneously teaching mature adult behavior and appropriate parenting skills.

Helfer (Helfer and Kempe, 1980) calls this process "reparenting the parent."

Breton (1981) suggests that practitioners working with abusive/neglectful families can be most helpful by resocializing the parents. Parents who maltreat their children often are emotionally and socially deprived, evidence unmet emotional needs, and are unable to ask for help. The worker's relationship with the parents, which may be long term, should focus on meeting their immediate needs in a nurturing, noncritical manner. By providing the support and guidance necessary for decision making and goal setting, workers can enable parents to cope better with their environment and to control events in their lives. Further, practitioners in this role also provide information to increase the parent's knowledge of child development, child management, problem solving, and stress reduction.

In a program called "Crash Course in Childhood for Adults" designed by R.E. Helfer and R. Esba (cited in Fried and Holt, 1980), professionals teach specific interaction skills to parents who never learned these skills or learned them poorly during the critical childhood period. Parents are assigned tasks and problem-solving exercises to practice interaction skills. These exercises focus on understanding oneself and one's interactions with others. Such a program may take three to twelve months to reach its goal and can be a prerequisite for parenting education courses.

Teddy's mother (Case 15) not only has problems in fulfilling her parental role but has personal problems that have impaired her functioning. She has never had the opportunity to develop a warm, nurturing relationship with anyone and thus has great difficulty relating to her son. Realizing that Teddy's mother must resolve her own problems if she is to help Teddy, the practitioner has arranged to meet with Teddy's mother on a weekly basis.

Abusive or neglectful parents who are addicted to drugs or alcohol or who have psychiatric problems other than substance abuse will need individual counseling focused on their problems to help them develop responsible, nurturing responses to their children.

Concluding that drug and alcohol abuse has impaired their parental and personal functioning, the caseworker has referred Elsa's parents (Case 17) for drug/alcohol abuse counseling.

Bobby's mother (Case 8) was diagnosed as paranoid schizophrenic but terminated mental health services against her doctor's wishes. As a precondition for continued custody of the child, the caseworker has referred her back to treatment and begun a trial period of close supervision of the family to determine whether the situation can be stabilized and improved or whether Bobby should be placed outside the home to protect his best interests.

Interventions with Infants. Interventions with infants on an individual basis are rare. The main focus of interventions with infants is the parent (mother)-infant relationship. However, one viable alternative for intervening with infants is in a day care setting.

A model program developed by J. Gonzalez-Mena and D. Eyer (cited in Cataldo, 1983) focuses on the physical, cognitive, and psychological development of infants. The primary emphasis is on psychological development. A small ratio of staff to infants allows infants to develop an intimate nurturant relationship with an adult. Positive socialization experiences with a caring adult can lead to healthy psychological development. Within this context, physical and cognitive development are facilitated through the use of age-appropriate activities and toys.

Frank (Case 3) has been referred to a program similar to the Gonzales-Mena and Eyer program. Through adult nurturance and stimulation, this program can restore Frank to normal development and help him overcome the developmental and emotional setbacks he has encountered as a result of his mother's and grandparents' treatment.

Interventions with Children. Interventions ranging from day care to volunteer efforts can help children overcome behavioral, cognitive, emotional, and interpersonal deficits created by psychological maltreatment. Professionalized day care centers can provide cognitive, interpersonal, and motor experiences to compensate for the home environment. Workers serve as alternative role models and give nurturance and structure to children who do not receive these precious commodities in their own homes (Mayhall and Norgard, 1983). Further, children can improve their social competence through interactions with day care workers and other children. The day care setting can be a primary resource for improving self-esteem, interpersonal relationships, and socially appropriate behavior patterns. Likewise, when it is offered by individuals particularly adept at compensatory nurturing, small-scale family day care can be beneficial for children who have suffered psychological maltreatment. The benefits a child can gain from the nurturance and guidance of a responsive adult in a small-scale setting are numerous. A warm, stimulating, structured environment can contribute greatly to psychological growth and provide an opportunity to counterbalance a cold, dehumanizing home environment.

The psychologist who assessed the children in Betty's family (Case 2) has recommended day care or family day care for Betty's three-year-old sister. Such an intervention could provide this child with a developmentally stimulating environment and the opportunity to interact with appropriate adult role models. It would also relieve Betty's mother of some of her child care responsibilities. This is a second form of intervention with Betty's family, since Betty and her mother are also involved in the Neighborhood Support Systems for Infants program.

For children experiencing more severe consequences of psychological maltreatment, therapeutic day care may be warranted (Mayhall and Norgard, 1983). Such programs can meet the needs of children who have difficulty in developing positive relationships with others, expressing themselves, and resolving anger, fear, or other issues. The Virginia Frank Child Development Center in Chicago offers one such program, "a specialized therapeutic nursery and kindergarten for children three to five years of age who are showing signs of emotional and behavioral problems" (Kadushin, 1980).

Jane (Case 5) has developed serious emotional problems, probably because she has been rejected and isolated by her parents. She and her parents have been referred to a therapeutic day care center that provides intensive services to emotionally disturbed children, as well as family therapy and parenting education to their parents.

A variety of counseling techniques can be used with children who have been maltreated. Psychologists, psychiatrists, social workers, and caseworkers can select counseling methods that best meet the unique needs of the children with whom they work.

Play therapy may be an appropriate treatment option. According to Whittaker (1974), play therapy uses the child's play situation as both locus and focus of therapeutic behavior change. Children who possess low self-esteem, experience depression, display aggression toward others, or have severe behavior management problems can benefit from play therapy (Mayhall and Norgard, 1983). In the safety and security of the play situation, children can express their feelings and resolve their conflicts.

A variation of play therapy, developed by V. Brody, C. Fendeson, and S. Stephenson, is "developmental play" (cited in Gumaer, 1984). This is a highly structured play program for children experiencing emotional, social, or learning deficiencies. The children are paired with trained adult partners who, through play activities, help them develop intense interpersonal relationships that involve deep levels of commitment, caring, and acceptance. The program assists children in overcoming personal difficulties through the development of positive, loving interactions with significant adults who also serve as models for relating to others.

To help Bobby (Case 8) resolve his anxiety and fear and develop a positive one-to-one relationship with an adult, his caseworker has referred him to a child guidance clinic for play therapy. He is also involved in a day care program that can meet some of his emotional needs. Thus, play therapy may further strengthen Bobby's chances of developing a psychologically healthy personality.

Behavioral counseling—the use of behavioral concepts and techniques to alter behavior—may also be effective with children who have been psychologically maltreated (Gumaer, 1984). Through behavioral counseling, children who have acquired maladaptive behavioral patterns as a result of psychological maltreatment may be assisted in developing more appropriate, less dysfunctional behavioral patterns.

Mark (Case 11) has been referred to a children's service center for behavioral counseling. This referral is based on Mark's personality and his aggressive behavior. The techniques of behavioral counseling may help Mark to modify his aggressive behavior and develop more appropriate behavioral responses.

Social skills training—the teaching of specific skills to enhance interpersonal relationships—can be effective for children who are socially isolated and withdrawn (Hops, 1982). Children who are psychologically abused often lack the social competence to form positive peer relationships and therefore are often further victimized by peers, who reject, isolate, and ignore them. They need to learn how to "break the ice" with their peers, how to act positively with other children, and how to manage conflict constructively (Stocking and Arezzo, 1979).

In one type of social skills program, children are exposed to individual "models" who demonstrate desired skills. Children learn by observing and then imitating what they have seen (Hops, 1982). A second type of program utilizes modeling and reinforces children for appropriate behavior while ignoring inappropriate behavior (Hops, 1982). Another technique used in social skills training is coaching. An adult instructor coaches the child in a specific social skill, and the child is then paired with a peer to practice the new skill (Hops, 1982). In other programs individuals are taught a set of general problem-solving skills useful for interpersonal adjustment (Hops, 1982).

Mark's brother, Bill (Case 11), is a socially isolated and withdrawn child. He lacks the competence to form positive relationships with his peers and is often ignored and frequently teased by them. The caseworker recognized Bill's social limitations and referred him to a psychologist who uses social skills training, so that the psychological maltreatment at home does not deprive him of the benefits of social experience outside the home.

As we noted in previous sections of the chapter, volunteers can be an invaluable resource for helping parents and children who are involved in psychological maltreatment. Volunteers can help meet the child's need for a positive nurturing relationship with at least one adult as a foundation for healthy psychological growth and development. Perhaps the best-known program of this type is the Big Brother/Big Sister program, which gives children an opportunity to develop meaningful relationships with appropriate role models. A big brother or big sister can provide nurturance, structure, and guidance to a child whose parents are unwilling or unable to do so. Such an intervention may improve a child's self-esteem and enable the child to develop positive social interactions as well as trust and feelings of acceptance. The Big Brother/Big Sister program carries with it the risk that, after establishing such a relationship, the big brother or big sister will lose interest—thereby producing a sense of loss in the child and reinforcing the child's feelings of rejection and worthlessness. If one can ensure against this risk, however, the program can contribute greatly to tipping the balance in favor of healthy emotional growth.

Wanda (Case 13) has never had the opportunity to develop a positive relationship with an appropriate female role model. Although her grandmother is loving and nurturant, the great age difference has been problematic. Activities and interaction with a younger adult woman can be beneficial in helping Wanda. Therefore, her caseworker has referred her to a Big Brother/Big Sister program, where she will be matched with a big sister.

Interventions with Adolescents. Adolescent responses to maltreatment range from depression to aggression to juvenile delinquency to suicide. Despite this range of responses, most emotionally maltreated adolescents feel worthless, unloved, and inadequate. Thus, professionals working with youth—youth services workers, mental health clinicians, child welfare workers, clergy, or school personnel—should help youth control their destructive behavioral responses while, at the same time, to improve their self-concept, social competence, and interpersonal relationships. As with most of the interventions discussed in this chapter, warmth, acceptance, and nurturance by practitioners in a growth-inducing environment are often the most significant factors in assisting these troubled youth.

Individual therapy with a worker who is accepting, supportive, and nurturing may improve an adolescent's self-esteem as well as provide a model for developing social competence and interpersonal relationships (Garbarino and Associates, 1985). The development of a strong therapeutic relationship depends on the therapist's ability to be nonjudgmental, sensitive, and caring while simultaneously assisting the youth in making behavioral and attitudinal changes (Garbarino and Associates, 1985). Individual counseling can be psychoanalytically based or can utilize behavioral and social skill techniques similar to those used with younger children.

Elsa (Case 17) has been referred to a youth services bureau for individual counseling. A supportive nurturing counselor can be a more adequate role model for Elsa than her alcoholic father or her drug-addicted mother is able to be. The counselor should be able to help Elsa cope with her chaotic home environment and develop a more positive self-concept.

Adolescents who have severe emotional problems, such as anorexia nervosa and suicidal tendencies, require more intensive treatment—either therapy provided by psychiatrists and psychologists or, in some instances, residential treatment. Likewise, adolescents who have substance abuse problems require specialized treatment, either through an outpatient drug/alcohol treatment facility or through an inpatient program.

Ricky (Case 20) is receiving treatment in a residential program. The decision to place Ricky in this short-term treatment environment was based on his suicide attempt and on his deteriorating emotional state. Assessment indicated that Ricky could benefit from being separated from his parents and could also benefit from the intensive treatment program. This program would include group, individual, and family counseling.

The importance of peers to the developing adolescent makes group intervention a promising vehicle for helping psychologically maltreated adolescents. Groups can facilitate socialization, self-awareness, and personal growth and foster the development of sensitivity to others (Mayhall and Norgard, 1983). The group process with adolescents can often be enhanced by the inclusion of recreational activities, which provide an arena for personal interaction as well as cooperative problem solving and decision making.

One example of a group intervention is the Youth Helping Youth Program, which helps abused adolescents gain interpersonal and social skills (Lonnborg, Fischbach, and Bickerstaff, 1981). The goal of the program is to provide a supportive atmosphere in which abused adolescents learn, for example, to develop self-esteem, to recognize and understand their own feelings and those of others, and to respond to criticism (Garbarino and Associates, 1985).

Johnny (Case 19), in addition to receiving family counseling, has been referred to a Youth Helping Youth Program. In the past he has had little opportunity to interact with his peers and thus is socially unskilled. A supportive group experience could help Johnny acquire social skills as well as increased self-esteem, improved coping patterns, and problem-solving abilities. The combination of family therapy and peer-group involvement may greatly enhance Johnny's personal development.

Comprehensive Interventions

As we have stated previously, psychological maltreatment is a multidimensional problem. Accordingly, the most effective approaches to intervening with children and families will be those that are comprehensive, able to address the problem on several levels. In most cases comprehensive services can be provided only through the coordination of multiple *agencies* (rather than individuals within agencies) that offer specialized services. However, several model programs now provide comprehensive services to families within one setting. These programs are designed to intervene with all forms of child abuse or neglect.

One such model is the Family Services Program (Dougherty, 1983). It has three main objectives: increased self-esteem for the parents; a positive growth-enhancing experience for the children; and improved relationships between parents and children, leading to better individuation and increased self-reliance. The program consists of a discussion group, a task mastery activities group, a parenting program, a therapeutic nursery, and a low-cost lunch. Individual therapy and family therapy are also available within the scope of the program. Further, transportation is provided to those who need it. The program is based on the concept that parents who abuse or neglect their children were themselves deprived of security, nurturance, guidance, and encouragement from their own parents. By providing these missing links, the program attempts to compensate parents as well as children for earlier deprivation.

The discussion group and task mastery activities group allow mothers to develop competence in social skills and to improve their self-concept by mastering certain tasks. The parenting program allows parents to review their parenting role as well as learn about child development and child management. The therapeutic nursery addresses the needs of the child in a loosely structured, accepting environment. The nursery staff maintains a consistent, reliable, and loving atmosphere in which the children experience continuous positive regard.

Another model program is the Family Stress Center, located in Concord, California (Payne, 1984). The center provides support to families through comprehensive, interrelated services that focus on both children and families. Direct therapeutic services to children are provided through the Time Out Nursery, a stimulating and nurturing environment that offers respite care to parents, and the Child Enrichment Program, a nursery program for toddlers of thirteen to forty months and their parents. Children are assisted with developmental tasks while parents spend time observing and participating in the learning experience. Parents may participate in parent programs while the children attend the nursery program. The parent education program gives parents the opportunity to share mutual concerns, study child development, and learn techniques for handling family stress. Parent aides are also available to lend support in times of stress. They spend a minimum of four hours a week interacting with their clients through home visits or telephone conversations. The counseling component of the program offers crisis intervention as well as family, group, and marital counseling. Support groups are also part of the program.

A third model program is offered by the Blosser Home for Children (Wood, 1981), where parents and children live together in a supervised, supportive environment with service delivery by a multidisciplinary team. The goal is threefold: (1) to remedy harmful parent-child interaction by teaching nonhurtful child discipline and facilitating parent-child bonding; (2) to help parents with personal and interpersonal problems; (3) to remedy child behaviors that result from parental abuse or neglect and that may promote parental anger, leading to abuse. For parents, life skill classes, individual counseling sessions, quality time with each child, and adult basic education classes are structured parts of their days. Each child spends half of the day in the day care facility, which is located in the building. This facility is used to help children develop socialization skills and to provide additional stimulation.

A comprehensive approach to treatment has been recommended for Betty's family (Case 2). Because of the many complex problems of this family, an intensive, comprehensive program of services is warranted. The exact type of program is contingent on community and agency resources. A program focusing on the mother's personal needs, her parental needs, and the needs of the child can help this family develop a more positive, psychologically healthy environment that will benefit all members of the family.

By recognizing the needs and limitations of the victims as well as the perpetrators, such programs can provide a strong foundation to diminish and eliminate psychological maltreatment. Further, a broad ecological approach rather than a limited approach should increase the likelihood of successful therapeutic intervention.

Figure 4. Interventions for Families and Individuals.

Interventions	Practitioners											Primary Client								Others Who Benefit Indirectly from Intervention							
	Child welfare workers	Mental health workers	Social workers/counselors in family/youth agencies	Medical professionals	Psychologists	Psychiatrists	Child care workers	Educators	Paraprofessionals	Volunteers	Clergy	Mother	Father	Foster parents/other caretakers	Infant	Early childhood	School age	Adolescent	Family as a unit	Mother	Father	Foster parents/other caretakers	Infant	Early childhood	School age	Adolescent	Family as a unit
Environmental Context																											
Supportive Services	X	X	X				X	X	X	X	X	X	X	X								X	X	X	X		X
High Risk																											
Home Health Visitor			X									X			X												X
Lay Home Visitors										X		X			X												X
Teenage Mothers: School Programs		X	X	X			X	X	X	X		X	X		X												X
In-Hospital Programs				X								X			X												X
Follow-up Group			X									X			X												X
Family Context Marital Counseling	X	X	X		X	X						X	X									X	X	X	X		X
Family Therapy	X	X	X		X	X											X	X	X								X
Parent-Child Interventions Patterson Program	X	X	X		X	X						X	X			X	X										X
Filial Therapy	X	X	X		X	X						X	X			X	X										X
Nurturing Program	X	X	X		X	X		X	X	X	X	X	X			X	X										X
Infant-Parent Interventions Home Interventions	X	X	X						X	X		X			X												X
Neighborhood Support System for Infants									X	X		X			X												X
Out-of-Home: Milwaukee Project			X				X					X			X												X

Figure 4. Interventions for Families and Individuals, Cont'd.

Interventions	Practitioners											Primary Client								Others Who Benefit Indirectly from Intervention							
	Child welfare workers	Mental health workers	Social workers/counselors in family/youth agencies	Medical professionals	Psychologists	Psychiatrists	Child care workers	Educators	Paraprofessionals	Volunteers	Clergy	Mother	Father	Foster parents/other caretakers	Infant	Early childhood	School age	Adolescent	Family as a unit	Mother	Father	Foster parents/other caretakers	Infant	Early childhood	School age	Adolescent	Family as a unit
Parenting	X	X	X	X				X	X	X	X	X	X										X	X	X	X	X
Individual	X	X	X	X				X	X	X	X	X	X										X	X	X	X	X
Group	X	X	X	X				X	X	X	X	X	X										X	X	X	X	X
In Home — Homemakers									X			X	X	X	X	X	X	X	X								X
Community Public Health Nurses			X									X											X	X	X		X
Parent Aides									X	X		X	X	X									X	X	X	X	X
Foster Grandparents										X		X	X	X									X	X	X	X	X
Social Isolation	X	X	X	X			X	X	X	X	X	X	X						X				X	X	X	X	X
Parent Aides									X	X		X	X	X									X	X	X	X	X
Homemakers									X			X	X	X									X	X	X	X	X
Home Health Visitors									X			X	X	X									X	X	X	X	X
Community Public Health Workers			X						X			X	X										X	X	X	X	X
Group — Parent Education	X	X	X	X				X	X	X	X	X	X										X	X	X	X	X
Drop-In Centers								X	X			X				X	X										X
Parents Anonymous									X			X	X										X	X	X	X	X

Figure 4. Interventions for Families and Individuals, Cont'd.

Interventions	Practitioners											Primary Client								Others Who Benefit Indirectly from Intervention							
	Child welfare workers	Mental health workers	Social workers/counselors in family/youth agencies	Medical professionals	Psychologists	Psychiatrists	Child care workers	Educators	Paraprofessionals	Volunteers	Clergy	Mother	Father	Foster parents/other caretakers	Infant	Early childhood	School age	Adolescent	Family as a unit	Mother	Father	Foster parents/other caretakers	Infant	Early childhood	School age	Adolescent	Family as a unit
Parent																											
Individual Counseling	X	X	X		X	X					X	X	X	X									X	X	X	X	X
Reparenting	X	X	X						X	X		X	X										X	X	X	X	X
Crash Course in Childhood for Adults	X	X	X		X							X	X									X	X	X	X	X	X
Child																											
Day Care							X								X	X	X			X							X
Family Day Care															X	X	X			X	X						X
Therapeutic Day Care																	X			X	X						X
Play Therapy	X	X	X		X	X										X	X			X	X						X
Developmental Play Therapy	X	X	X		X	X										X	X			X	X						X
Individual Counseling	X	X	X		X	X											X			X	X						X
Behavioral Counseling	X	X	X		X	X										X	X	X		X	X						X
Social Skills Training	X	X	X		X	X										X	X	X		X	X						X
Big Brother/Big Sister										X							X	X		X	X						X
Groups	X	X	X					X	X	X								X		X	X						X
Youth Helping Youth Program	X	X	X					X	X	X								X		X	X						X
Comprehensive Programs																											
Family Services			X		X		X					X	X	X	X	X	X	X	X								X
Family Stress Center			X		X		X					X	X	X	X	X	X	X	X								X
Blosser Homes			X		X		X					X	X	X	X	X	X	X	X								X

Conclusion

We have adopted an ecological-interactive approach to psychological maltreatment. Thus, interventions are presented in the same manner. In order to provide a more succinct presentation of these interventions, we have summarized them in Figure 4 as a conclusion. In the next chapter, we will address the issue of community action to create a social climate that can prevent psychological maltreatment.

We must end this chapter on intervention with the recognition that much of what we do is a matter of faith. At its worst, intervention can do harm. Often, it is just "whistling in the wind." And sometimes it even helps people. Few follow-up studies of routine intervention exist. Most tell us to expect positive change only to the degree that we make major *positive* changes in the core relationships of a child's life. It is easy to be destructive; building a better life is a tougher proposition. One key to doing so is intervention in the *community* to reorganize the social environment in an enduring fashion. Community action is an important piece of the puzzle.

﷽ 7 ﷽

Intervening to Mobilize
Community Resources

One of our premises is that the social environment is closely related to the climate existing within a family. As we have already mentioned, the patterns of interaction in a family, together with its members' mutual perceptions, are influenced by the surrounding environmental conditions and, in turn, have an impact on those conditions. When a family is successful in adapting to the social environment, we say that a family-environment fit exists. If the environment fails to adjust to a family's needs or if the family's adaptation to the environment is violated, the family-environment fit deteriorates or generates negative characteristics. One potential manifestation of this deterioration is the psychological maltreatment of children.

In this chapter we deal with one aspect of a family's environment, the community in which it lives. As a geographical and social system, and as a combination of social units responsible for local functions, the community serves as a connection between families and the larger society. It is also the vehicle through which socialization, social control, social participation, mutual help, and allocation of material goods occur (Warren, 1978). When a community serves these functions, families prosper psychologically; when it does not, a climate of social risk arises.

In Chapter Five we described the community characteristics that foster maltreatment: poverty, unemployment, poor housing, crime, unavailability of services, and deficiencies in the naturally corrective and supportive influences of pro-social systems. Indeed, socioeconomic (family income), demographic (transience, number

155

of single-parent households, number of mothers with young children working outside the home), and attitudinal factors (negative feelings about neighboring and neighborhood) are reliable predictors of rates of child abuse and neglect at the community level (Garbarino, 1976; Garbarino and Crouter, 1978). Furthermore, child maltreatment is related to juvenile delinquency (Garbarino, Schellenbach, and Sebes, 1986), teenage pregnancy, crime, and mental illness (Bateson, 1972; Bronfenbrenner, Moen, and Garbarino, 1984). These relationships demonstrate not only that community-level factors are predictors of maltreatment but also that maltreatment serves as a predictor of several other community-level phenomena, such as crime. Overall, maltreatment and certain characteristics of a community, such as those listed above, seem to be closely interrelated.

This interrelatedness is evident in a set of studies of attitudes toward communities and maltreating families. Garbarino and Sherman (1980) studied attitudinal differences between two communities with similar demographic and socioeconomic characteristics but disparate rates of child maltreatment. They found that members of the community with lower rates of maltreatment regarded the community as supportive, helpful, and encouraging, whereas those in the other community had less positive attitudes. In a complementary study, Polansky and Gaudin (1983) found that community members tend to distance themselves from parents who appear to be neglecting their children; moreover, neglectful or abusive parents perceive the community as nonsupportive and seek to distance themselves from it. Thus, not only is the community experienced as nonsupportive when cases of maltreatment exist, but the families themselves further decrease the support received by distancing themselves.

A circular negative relationship seems to exist between maltreating families and their community. High-risk communities do not adequately connect families with the broader society, nor do they promote socialization, social control, social participation, mutual help, or the allocation of material goods. High-risk families exacerbate this vicious cycle of negativity and isolation. To break this cycle of destructive family-community relationships, and to encourage the community to assume a more responsible and responsive role toward families, we need to intervene on the community level: first, to stop the social amplification of high risk and maltreatment; and, second, to utilize the community resources on behalf of intervention with families. These two modes of community-level interventions constitute the major issues in this chapter.

How do we choose a community intervention model that has the potential to achieve these goals? In general, there are three approaches to community intervention, or community organization. These approaches, though not mutually exclusive, are oriented toward different theories of social intervention. The first, "community development," presupposes that community change may be pursued through broad participation from a wide spectrum of people in the community as a whole. The second, "social planning," emphasizes the process of rational problem solving by establishing community leaders responding to a substantive and clearly defined social problem. The third approach, "social action," presupposes a disadvantaged segment of the community that needs to be organized in order to demand increased resources or social justice (Anderson, 1981; Rothman, 1979). Table 5 summarizes the three approaches: their goals, the dimensions of intervention they emphasize, the change strategies they recommend, the roles of the worker, and the roles of the participants.

As mentioned earlier, in this chapter we present a model of community intervention that attempts to offer ways to stop the social amplification of maltreatment and motivate the community to provide family intervention programs. Since these are the goals, the basic assumption of this model is that knowledge of the community, clear definition and understanding of its problem of maltreatment, careful and gradual planning of intervention, and participation of community members in activities are the critical components of a successful intervention. From this point of view, therefore, the most appropriate intervention models are those that emerge from the "community development" and "social planning" approaches. In this chapter we combine the general premises of these two approaches and integrate them with a

Table 5. Approaches to Community Intervention.

Characteristic	Community Development Approach[a]	Social-Planning Approach[b]	Social Action Approach[c]
Goals			
Self-help	H	L	M
Problem solving	M	H	L
Reallocation of power	M	L	H
Process	H	L	M
Task	L	H	M
Main Dimensions			
Anomie/alienation	H	L	M
Interpersonal relationships	H	L	L
Democratic problem-solving capacities	H	L	M
Social problems	M	H	M
Disadvantaged populations	L	M	H
Social injustice	M	M	H
Change Strategies			
Broad-based participation in problem definition	H	M	L
Intergroup communication	H	L	M
Small-group discussion	H	L	L
Building consensus	H	M	L
Fact gathering for rational decision making	M	H	M
Conflict intensification	L	M	H
Crystallization of issues	M	L	H
Organization of people against targets	L	L	H
Confrontation	M	L	H
Direct action	L	L	H
Negotiation	M	L	H
Worker's Roles			
Enabler-catalyst	H	L	M
Coordinator	H	M	L
Teacher of problem-solving skills	H	L	M
Teacher of ethical values	H	L	L
Fact gatherer and analyst	M	H	M
Program implementer	L	H	H
Facilitator	H	M	L
Activist-advocate	M	L	H

Table 5. Approaches to Community Intervention, Cont'd.

Characteristic	Community Development Approach[a]	Social-Planning Approach[b]	Social Action Approach[c]
Agitator	L	L	H
Broker	M	L	H
Negotiator	M	L	H
Partisan	L	L	H
Participants' Roles			
Citizens	H	M	L
Consumers	M	H	M
Victims	L	L	H

H = high emphasis; M = moderate emphasis; L = low emphasis.

[a]For more information about this approach, see Biddle and Biddle, 1965; Grosser, 1976; Russ, 1967.

[b]For more information about this approach, see Kahn, 1969; Morris and Binstock, 1966; Perlman and Gurin, 1972; Warren, 1971.

[c]For more information about this approach, see Alinsky, 1972; Thursz, 1966.

Source: From *Social Work Methods and Process* by Joseph Anderson, © 1981 by Wadsworth, Inc. Reprinted by permission of the publisher.

systems model for community work. (For further discussion of the integration of community development, social planning, and the systems model, see Brager and Specht, 1973; Cox, Erlich, Rothman, and Tropman, 1979.)

The process of intervening with the community is described here as a process model, tracing step by step the activities that are likely to prove helpful.

Initiating and Maintaining Community Intervention

Community intervention is a six-step process of initiation and maintenance. More specifically, the steps are (1) building a community profile and assessing the needs of its members, (2) organizing a task force, (3) educating practitioners and the public, (4) facilitating community consensus and planning intervention, (5) conducting community intervention and education, (6) maintaining community intervention.

Building Community Profile and Assessing Members'
Needs. A community's profile consists of its particular history (for
example, patterns of immigration and emigration), geography
(rural, suburban, or urban), economy (industrial or farming),
government (policies and laws), and characteristics of its residents
(ethnicity, socioeconomic status). The resulting profile provides a
way to look at the community as a context for the lives of the
individuals and families who live there. For example, the zoning
laws administered by the local government may affect families'
housing options. The amount and diversity of employment
opportunities may affect the level of income and financial security
of families (Garbarino and Associates, 1982). Both may ultimately
influence the etiology of maltreatment and the prognosis for case-
by-case intervention.

This profile also captures the norms and values held by the
members of the community. For example, a community may value
education. In that community citizens would be active in the
parent-teacher organization and the school board, and the quality
of education received by the children would reflect this activity and
concern. Similarly, a community has norms for parenting that are
reflected in local policies, the functioning of organizations, and
social programs. Those norms are a crucial element in the
construction of the community profile.

Also important in building a community profile is an
assessment of needs, both for the community as a whole and for its
individual members (see, for example, Bell, Sundel, Aponte, and
Murrel, 1976; Glampson, Scott, and Thomas, 1977; Hargreaves,
Attkisson, Siegel, and McIntyre, 1974; Neuber and Associates, 1980;
United Way of America, 1982). In other words, part of building a
community profile is understanding what services the community
offers and what services it does not offer, and how those that are
offered operate, all in light of the community members' perceptions of their needs. In today's world the danger of "reinventing
the wheel" is always great, and an assessment of existing resources
is essential.

In order to construct a community profile with respect to
child maltreatment, the practitioner should take the following
steps:

1. Observe the physical appearance of the community as well as interactions among people in it at different times during the day.
2. Read literature about the community, including materials written *by* community members.
3. Obtain information about existing social services: the resources offered, the service goals, and the level of use.
4. Talk with key persons in the community (and knowledgeable outsiders) about their concerns, their wishes, their view of the quality and scope of services, what they think ought to be changed, and how they think action should be taken.
5. Participate in activities and social programs operating in the community.

This process is likely to answer such questions as: What is the community's economy? What are the sociodemographic characteristics of its members? What are the principal problems identified? Are there any problems not recognized? To what extent are needs answered? What are the norms regarding child rearing? What is the scope and severity of child maltreatment? To what extent is child maltreatment a problem *perceived* by community members? Are they ready to work on it? This stage is likely to result in an overall identification of community problems and needs, some of which have to do directly with child maltreatment.

Organizing a Task Force. Once the practitioner knows the community and has developed some preliminary ideas about goals and modes of intervention, efforts can begin to utilize existing social resources. The starting point is to organize a task force, either from within an existing child welfare organization or by developing a separate committee, if there is no such organization in the community. Organizing the task force from within an existing child abuse organization is preferable. Identifying this organization will be easy in communities that already have child abuse and neglect organizations, many of which are affiliated with the National Committee for Prevention of Child Abuse (see Resource C for a list of NCPCA chapters). A special task force for dealing with psychological maltreatment of children can be formed in this organization, with the worker a full member of it.

The key community persons, previously identified, should participate in this task force if its activities are to gain community approval.

If the local child welfare organization resists the idea of expanding its focus to include psychological maltreatment, or if there is no existing organization, the next step for the worker and the community leaders is to form a task force on their own. The location and affiliation of the task force may determine issues such as funding, bureaucratic structure, pace of work, and accountability required from the task force. The key point is that the task force have its own agenda, regardless of the organization in which it resides.

Once the task force is organized, its members must arrive at a consensus concerning the definition and scope of psychological maltreatment in their community. Then, through meetings with other community members and representatives of local organizations, they should seek to make their consensus a community consensus. For example, they may conclude that the most important characteristic of maltreatment is, as in Erin's case (Case 14), the terrorizing nature of a high-crime neighborhood, in which case community safety issues might be the logical vehicle in initiating programming.

The next step is to develop an action plan for the task force. First, the general goals (for example, "To educate the community about psychological maltreatment") should be stated. Second, the task force should formulate specific objectives in terms of observable changes and outcomes. Again, these goals and objectives must eventually become integrated into the particular community. Community "ownership" is a primary goal. A good example of general goals appears in the description of the Coordinated Child Abuse Program of the Greater Lehigh Valley (Polansky and Gaudin, 1976). These are some of that program's goals:

> To prevent the abuse of children by effecting psychological changes in parents and responsible adults.
> To enhance children's development.

To modify the home environment so as to lessen stresses that may precipitate abuse.

To improve the effectiveness of the program's training component.

To conduct research that will add to the understanding of both the etiology of abuse and the effectiveness of different treatment modalities.

To further educate the community in order to create a more favorable climate for positive family change.

The mission statement of "Home Start," one of the services offered by the Greater Lehigh Valley Program, can serve as an example of more specific objectives:

To provide parents with general knowledge of early-childhood development.

To assist parents in developing skills in observing their child's growth and development.

To aid parents in setting realistic individual goals for each child.

To help parents in planning activities and methods to work toward these goals.

At this point, when the task force has an understanding of the problem and has articulated its goals and objectives, it can begin to plan its activities. To achieve citizen participation in these programs and to increase the likelihood of their success, the task force has first to raise community awareness of the problem and gain a broader basis of agreement and support for the planned intervention. With the tentative plan of intervention in mind, the task force's members must educate the public about psychological maltreatment of children. Simultaneously, practitioners in the community should also be educated about maltreatment and trained to handle the increased caseload likely to result from increased public awareness of the problem.

Educating Practitioners and the Public. Using the previously collected information about social service organizations in the community, the task force can set up a training program for social workers, child welfare workers, day care personnel, teachers, school guidance counselors, nurses, or any other local professionals who work with children and their families. The training program itself can follow the sequence of this book: increasing competence to define and identify cases of maltreatment, assess them, and plan and implement interventions.

In all likelihood, the training program will be organized and conducted by members of the task force. However, guest speakers can be used to enrich the content and scope of the training: a psychologist or psychiatrist to discuss the assessment or consequences of psychological maltreatment; a lawyer presenting whatever reporting regulations the state has instituted (for example, who is required to report suspected cases and to whom to report them); and a physician or a schoolteacher describing the symptoms that maltreated children manifest.

In general, the best way to provide the training is through workshops in which psychological maltreatment is illustrated and analyzed through case studies, audiovisual materials, role plays, and discussions. The exact mode of conducting the training must be determined by the nature of the participating practitioners and the specific community. This volume can, of course, serve as a resource, as can videotapes prepared by Garbarino and Merrow (available through the Erikson Institute in Chicago).

If training takes place before the public information project is launched, practitioners can help to design and implement that project. Its goal is to increase community awareness of the problem of psychological maltreatment and its characteristics, thereby increasing both current reporting and future participation in social service programs. Helpful guidelines for carrying out such a project were issued by Florida's Division of Family Services in 1976 after successful completion of a public information campaign about child abuse. We follow those guidelines in proposing an agenda for public education on psychological maltreatment.

1. *Determine the scope and focus of the project.* Who is the intended audience (general public, maltreating parents, or some other group)? How much does the public already know about

psychological maltreatment of children? Are any social services already dealing with it? What are the current social attitudes regarding maltreatment, reporting, and intervention? What values currently held by community members can be used to intervene with maltreatment?

2. *Formulate specific, measurable goals for the project.* The following goals are examples: to increase public knowledge of maltreatment; to increase sensitivity to identifying children who might be victims of maltreatment; to change attitudes toward children in general and parenting in particular; to develop an understanding of the relationship between community characteristics, familial behavior, and child maltreatment; to reach specific minorities with any of these messages; to activate private and public initiative to deal with the problem of maltreatment; to increase reporting; to build public support for improved social services; and to stimulate formation of self-help groups.

3. *Plan and evaluate the content of the project.* The content of the public information project should be composed of two parts. The first explains what the phenomenon of maltreatment involves, how it can be identified or observed, and why it is wrong. This explanation should be presented simply and clearly, not stigmatizing the parents but, rather, conveying the message that psychological maltreatment is a response to personal and environmental stress—one that is ultimately dangerous, however, both to parents and to children. The best approach, in all likelihood, is to know in advance (from the stage of information collection about the community) what the community especially values and to use those values as an incentive to act against maltreatment. For example, if the community places a special value on education, it can be shown how maltreatment reduces children's capabilities for learning. If the community particularly values obedience, the point can be made that early obedience from fear often results in later resentment, rejection, and rebellion.

In the second part of the project, the task force explains the process of reporting and the intervention that follows; and the task force members can describe the programs they have in mind, ask for comments and other suggestions, and evaluate the likelihood of participation. It is important not to offer more services than can be delivered and to keep the offer in proportion to the scope and severity of maltreatment in the community.

4. *Plan the implementation of the project.* The task force should target three major modes of information dissemination. First is the public media. Short public service messages, presented on local television or radio or printed in a local newspaper, can portray the phenomenon and explain what can be done about it, perhaps giving emergency numbers to call. Second, posters can be displayed in public places and child-related settings (such as day care centers, preschools, and clinics), or pamphlets can be distributed or materials mailed directly to families in the community (perhaps to all new parents or all parents of kindergartners). The third mode is more personal and involves speaking to parents in workplaces, talking to teachers and children at school, or organizing public meetings for all who want to participate. In general, it is important to match the mode of dissemination with the content of the information as well as with the characteristics of the population.

5. *Provide means to evaluate the project.* Even the most simple evaluation of the project's effectiveness will aid the future intervention and programs. For a simple evaluation, task force members ask people whether they think the project was worthwhile and how it could have been improved. Or the cost of the project can be compared with other available mechanisms of increasing public awareness. A formal evaluation with objective measures will provide more valid results, of course; and these results can then be reported to funding sources, so that future funding might be obtained. Although we are aware of the numerous difficulties involved in carrying through a formal evaluation, we encourage a task force to attempt at least a simple one, given its importance and worth.

Overall, this project should keep its focus on psychological maltreatment of children if it is to achieve its goals. There is the temptation to include more topics ("We are doing such a big project anyway"); yet losing focus means losing public attention. It is also important for the task force to be realistic about what the project can achieve and to be patient in moving toward its goals. However, at the end of the public information project, the community members are likely to seek ways to deal with maltreatment; and the task force, with the practitioners, should be ready to intervene. Furthermore, the task force and the practitioners should know what social programs they want to carry through and how, and be ready for the final stages of planning and executing them.

Securing Community Consensus and Planning Interven-tion. Following completion of the awareness stage, during which time public awareness of psychological maltreatment of children has increased, some agreement among the community members should have been reached concerning the nature of the phenomenon in their community and the appropriate ways of dealing with it. The task force must fully understand the components of this agreement, whether they are explicit or implicit. For example, one common implicit agreement among the community's professionals may be that they are going to report only what will be considered, according to their criteria, a serious case and that they will try to deal with less critical cases on their own. Informal discussions and formal analyses of responses to critical incidents or case studies can reveal the nature of such implicit understandings. Revealing these agreements, and organizing interventions and social programs according to them, is likely to elicit community support for those programs and hence increase their potential effectiveness. The task force, in turn, is advised to facilitate these agreements and work on developing others, so that it will have a wide and supportive basis for its programs.

Agreements such as "We are concerned mainly with the terrorizing aspect of maltreatment" or "We want to learn to raise our children so that all of us will be happy"—together with the community's values, needs, and wishes—can serve as a guide for the final planning of social intervention programs. This final planning might broaden the base of involvement to enhance community support.

What is the task force's programmatic agenda? Parent education programs, the creation of social support networks, coping-with-stress programs, awareness enhancement for teachers, and teaching children to know when they are maltreated are all possibilities. The process through which this agenda is set is crucial (perhaps more important than which of several worthwhile endeavors is chosen). The second aspect of planning has to do with the delivery of services. Depending on the practitioners who were gathered for that purpose, two types of teams are likely: an interagency team composed of practitioners from the various social agencies or a hospital-based mental health team. The main advantage of the first is the opportunity to coordinate available services and avoid duplication of services. The Lehigh Valley program, mentioned previously, is a good example of coordination of services. In this program two counties joined efforts and resources to deal with child abuse. A special coordinator position was created in order to tie together the various components of the program and offer children and families the particular services they need the most. An interagency team has a wide basis to make decisions about children and can also be responsible for offering specialized services, as has been done in sexual abuse treatment programs.

In sum, once the grounds are prepared for carrying out community intervention with psychological maltreatment, the task force announces where to report, where individual intervention is done and by whom, where and when the programs will occur, and what they will be like.

Conducting Community Intervention and Evaluation. At this point the practitioners start doing individual interventions and also working with the people who choose to participate in the social programs. Simultaneously, the role of the task force changes from raising public awareness and organizing the network for intervention to monitoring and supervising the intervention process. It is important to start as planned and follow the outline that was presented to the public, so that an atmosphere of trust and reliability can develop. Further, some misconceptions of a program can emerge—false or unreal expectations or other ambiguities regarding purposes and activities. The practitioners are advised to clarify and explain the program and its goals so as to make the service and the expectations from it compatible.

Contacts with journalists and government officials are crucial for this sort of "trouble shooting." Yet, if some of the participants' ideas (or other community members' ideas) seem plausible, the program can be adjusted accordingly. Additional components can be added to the programs upon participants' requests, or more paraprofessionals and volunteers from the community itself can be added as a resource to a program. Overall, the programs should be structured and purposeful, yet flexible enough to accommodate to participants' wishes and expectations.

During the course of the programs, changes are likely to take place, whether these entail increased reporting or an apparent shift in community standards of child care. For example, the participants may come to realize that their major need is to learn parenting skills; or the accepted definition of psychological maltreatment may expand beyond terrorizing to include rejecting, isolating, and ignoring. The programs, as well as the individual interventions, should be sensitive to these changes and adjust their activities and attitudes accordingly. To increase sensitivity, the task force and the practitioners should maintain ongoing contact with the people in the community, asking them for opinions, wishes, and ideas. It is important that the programs consistently meet the changing needs, values, and agreements of the community, and thus they should always be tuned in to the participants in them. A growing body of research tells us that a science of community-based organizations is emerging, and issues of reliable purposeful-ness, flexibility, and realistic goal setting are crucial (Wandesman, 1985). Wandesman reports that the community groups most likely to survive are those which have a clear purpose that changes as goals are met, which can absorb a diverse and changing mix of individuals, and which do not bite off more than they can chew.

This practice of consistently updating the program is a form of evaluation. If a more organized evaluation is planned, this is the point to outline its details and carry it through. The evaluation can include distributing questionnaires to programs' participants, comparing reporting rates, or analyzing the cost of the programs relative to their benefits. As previously mentioned, such an evaluation is useful for the continuation of these programs, as well as for initiating new ones.

Maintaining Community Intervention. Once programs and interventions have been initiated, and some changes start to emerge, the task force and the practitioners must maintain what has been achieved and facilitate additional changes. They can do so by working in two directions. First, they should continue running the programs in light of the changing community needs, wishes, and agreements. Second, they should begin to shift responsibilities to the community itself, conveying the message that it has enough strengths to take care of its own.

Community members should recognize a shift toward a more preventive social environment and take responsibility for maintaining it (although impoverished communities or neighborhoods will need ongoing resources supplied from outside). Community members may volunteer to address new needs that have emerged in one of the programs; or the worker who formed the task force can become a consultant to it, leaving the task force itself composed entirely of community members. The members would then decide whether to rotate participation in the task force, whether to form subcommittees according to needs, and how to respond in general to psychological maltreatment of children in the community.

The specific form of organizing the community should match its special characteristics to the demands of program maintenance. However, communication must not disappear as the transition takes place. The link to professional expertise is crucial, be it in telephone contact or a consultation to a drop-in center run by community members. This follow-up is important to maintain community-based programming *and* to justify and promote efforts to utilize community resources in family-level interventions.

Community Involvement in Family-Level Interventions and Prevention

The organized community is a resource in efforts to enhance family-level interventions. A community committed to the elimination of psychological maltreatment creates a supportive environment for those providing and utilizing family-level interventions. Community resources can be tapped to support the activities of agencies in the community. These activities include fund raising, linking well-functioning families with maltreating ones, and using community members as volunteers. Further, a supportive community can reduce attitudinal and system barriers that often prevent those in need of help from asking for it and also can provide a mechanism by which others in the community can report incidents of maltreatment in families that are unwilling or unable to ask for help.

An organized and aware community is also prepared to make progress in preventing psychological maltreatment of children. Prevention means anticipating the needs of families, stimulating positive patterns of child care, and offering the services of social support systems early on, before maltreatment emerges as a pattern (Hermalin and Weirich, 1983; Kempe, 1976, 1978; Lally, 1984; Nagi, 1977; Soumenkoff and others, 1982). Thus, in order to deal with the prevention of psychological maltreatment of children, we need to tackle the factors related to it on the community, family, and individual levels, factors described in Chapter Three.

Community organization around practical issues can contribute to prevention by reducing social isolation. For example, programs to improve housing, start community gardens, or create recycling projects can also enhance social support networks. These social supports can reduce stress, increase a family's capability to cope with it, and thereby lower the likelihood of maltreatment (Barrera and Balls, 1983; Cohen and McKay, 1984; Gottlieb, 1981; Howze and Kotch, 1984). Thus, addressing the community's need for all forms of development can have preventive value, even if there is little in the initial formulation of these needs that relates to psychological maltreatment. Almost any program that can strengthen the social and individual capacities of community members will have preventive value and will enhance the following preventive strategies.

Improving Family's Attitude Toward Social Services, People, and Society. Programs such as home visitors or meetings with parents at schools or in day care centers can help make the family more receptive of its environment. Some communities have home visitors on a limited basis for all women who have had babies; again, the program is not unique to abuse/neglect.

Enhancing the Family's Emotional Climate. Families whose climate is characterized by tension, threat, or aggressiveness, coupled with problems in relationships and in communication, are at high risk for psychological maltreatment (Caffo, Guaraldi, Magnani, and Tassi, 1982). For those families preventive programs aimed at teaching communication skills, developing empathic skills, working on marital relationships, enhancing parent-infant bonds in childbirth classes or hospital maternity programs, or promoting parent-child relationships are needed. For example, the Parent Cooperation Preschool Program (Spokane, Washington) uses preschools as laboratories for parents to try out parenting skills they have learned; Advance (San Antonio, Texas) combines parent education and children's activities; and Parents in Touch (Indianapolis public schools) links home and school. Preventive programs in this area may also provide a one-day festival in which all the activities entail positive parent-child interactions, as in the Kid Connection (Mifflin County, Pennsylvania).

Increasing Parenting Knowledge. Parents who lack sufficient knowledge of child development and thus have unreal expectations of the children; who undermine their child's physical and/or psychological needs; or who make inappropriate responses to the child (infantilizing, being inconsistent) also are at risk for psychological maltreatment. In order to prevent maltreatment, programs such as parent education in child development, parenting skills programs, drop-in nurseries or day care centers, and parent support groups can be helpful.

Preventive programs that deal with the parent as a person, and with the child as an individual, can also be worthwhile. Parents who have been maltreated as children, who are abusing drugs and alcohol, who are mentally or physically ill, who are mentally retarded, or who consistently create stress around them are more likely to maltreat their children than other parents are. Thus, preventive programs should be targeted at them. In addition, parents who have difficulties in coping with the demands of everyday life, who have low self-esteem, and who are dissatisfied with their lives as individuals are at risk for child maltreatment. In order to prevent child maltreatment, programs should attempt to reach these parent populations. Further, whether they are parent education programs, communication skills programs, or programs aimed at promoting parent-child relationships, they should also attempt to increase the parents' coping skills, raise their self-esteem, and help them search for ways to make their lives more satisfactory.

As mentioned earlier, children may contribute to their own maltreatment. When they are exceptionally nonnormative in developmental status or exhibit high-risk personality traits (such as extreme passivity, dependence, shyness, aggressiveness, or violence), they are more likely to be maltreated than other children. Thus, nursery schools, day care centers, kindergartens, and schools should be sensitive to exceptional children who are in them and work with those children toward greater sociability. For example, a teacher could be guided to work with a child in a way that would decrease the child's passivity and shyness. Simultaneously, if work can be done with the parents to accept their children as they are, maltreatment from another angle may be prevented.

Relating Prevention to Comprehensive Intervention. In sum, it seems that prevention of psychological maltreatment of children is an important aspect of the whole cycle of intervening in child care and parenting. The prevention of maltreatment is most appropriate after the community has been organized around the theme of "supporting families and protecting children." Overall, we view prevention as part of the circle of comprehensive intevention: organizing the community to work on maltreatment → providing individual interventions and social programs → maintaining change and increasing the community's self-responsibility → developing preventive programs → organizing the community still further. In other words, preventive programs can be implemented together with therapeutic intervention to prevent the occurrence of new cases and to halt further deterioration of existing cases.

National Organizations and State Laws

The circle of community organization, individual interventions, social programs, and prevention of psychological maltreatment of children is embedded within the larger, national context of caring. This context is crystallized in the private sector by the National Committee for the Prevention of Child Abuse and through its local chapters and in the public sector by federal and state legislative and executive actions.

   National Committee for the Prevention of Child Abuse and Local Chapters. Community intervention in the reduction and prevention of child maltreatment has long been recognized by the National Committee for the Prevention of Child Abuse (NCPCA) as an essential ingredient in the national effort to prevent child abuse and neglect. Community and state organizations help to determine the national agenda regarding prevention and also support and strengthen the national commitment. Conversely, the National Committee supports and assists local and state chapters and coalitions in their efforts to prevent child maltreatment. Among other functions, the National Committee promotes public awareness through media campaigns and publications. The state-level organizations attempt to secure legislative and financial support. Local organizations promote programs designed to meet community needs in preventing child maltreatment.

   The link between the National Committee's national office and individual communities is accomplished through community chapters or coalitions. Coalitions in local communities are made up of volunteers who are concerned about the problem of child abuse and neglect and want to do something about it. Not all communities have local chapters, however (see Resource C). New local initiatives are needed.

   The Kansas Committee for the Prevention of Child Abuse, a leader in the development of local coalitions and chapters, provides the following guidelines for developing local chapters: (1) an emphasis on prevention; (2) utilization of volunteers as the most important resource in child abuse prevention programs; (3) a representative board of directors, including businesspeople, professionals, and community leaders; (4) bylaws; (5) local control over funding, policy, and programs; (6) a shared common mission with and active participation in the national network; and (7) utilization of technical assistance from the NCPCA staff. In addition, if a task force has been previously organized as part of a community intervention program, a local chapter can be developed on its basis. If all the local chapters in a state follow these guidelines, a strong statewide network of coalitions will result.

These guidelines recognize the need for local autonomy in developing programs for preventing child maltreatment. They also recognize the need for a collaborative effort among national, state, and local organizations to prevent child abuse and neglect. Local coalitions are encouraged to develop programs and agendas that reflect their own community needs; at the same time, they are expected to support state and national organizations. Such unity of purpose can greatly strengthen the commitment to prevent child abuse and neglect at all levels.

Legislative and Executive Actions. Legislative actions greatly influence the role of communities, agencies, and practitioners in intervening in and preventing child maltreatment. Two legislative actions especially pertinent to psychological maltreatment are (1) the status of psychological maltreatment as a legal entity and (2) the availability of funds for intervention and prevention programs.

Although all states have laws regarding child abuse/neglect, not all laws identify psychological maltreatment as a form of abuse/neglect. Where they do, the laws provide definitions of maltreatment and identify the agencies responsible for child protective services. These legal definitions guide practitioners, agencies, and communities in identifying abuse/neglect and provide the legal sanction for intervening in these cases. Hence, the legal status of psychological maltreatment varies, and this variability influences the response of communities, agencies, and practitioners to psychological maltreatment.

As reviewed by Corson (1983), state laws concerning maltreatment fall into six categories, which are summarized in Table 6.

Twenty-three states include reference to "mental injury" in their definition of abuse/neglect but do not define mental injury. Only four states define the term "mental injury." Nevada, for instance, defines it as "a substantial injury to the intellectual or psychological capacity of a child as evidenced by an observable and substantial impairment of his ability to function within his

Table 6. Use of the Terms "Mental," "Psychological," and
"Emotional" in State Statutes.

Terminology	*States*
Include "mental injury" or similar term but do not define it	Ala., Alaska, Ark., Calif., D.C., Fla., Ga., Hawaii, Kans., Ky., La., Mass., Maine, Mich., Mo., Mont., N.C., N.Dak., N.J., N.Mex., Ohio, Okla., Texas, Utah, Va., W.Va.
Define "mental injury"	Nev., R.I., S.C., Wyo.
Define emotional abuse/neglect by child's behavior	Ariz., Conn., N.H., Pa.
Include impairment of emotional health through physical injury or use "mental," "psychological," and "emotional" only when referring to health	Del., Ill., Ind., Iowa, Md., Minn., Miss., Nebr., N.Y., Tenn., Wash.
Do not use "mental," "psychological," or "emotional" in their definition of maltreatment	Colo., Idaho, Oreg., S.Dak., Vt., Wis.

Source: Based on information provided by Corson, 1983.

normal range of performance or behavior" (Nev. Rev. Stat. sec.
20C.5011(2) (1986 Nev. Stats. 1844)). Four states define emotional
abuse/neglect by the child's behavior, including such terms as
"severe anxiety," "depression," "withdrawal," "symptoms of
emotional problems generally recognized to result from consistent
mistreatment or neglect." Delaware, Illinois, Mississippi, and New
York define emotional maltreatment only as a consequence·of
physical injury. Seven states include mental injury or harm as a
consequence of negligent actions by parents or others. Eight states
do not include terms reflecting psychological maltreatment.

Thus, we can assume that responses by community agencies
and practitioners will display the same variability as the state laws
that guide these responses. Furthermore, not only will the laws in
and of themselves shape the response to psychological maltreatment, but the interpretation of these laws by the executive branch
through regulations, and by the judiciary through disposition of

cases, will also influence community, agency, and practitioner activities.

To illustrate how the laws influence judiciary, community, agency, and practitioner activities, we examine the California law regarding psychological maltreatment and its enforcement through the judicial system. The California law (Cal. Welf. and Inst. Code sec. 18951(e) (*West's Annotated California Code*, 1980) defines abuse/neglect as a harm or threatened harm to a child's health or welfare and includes "mental injury" or a comparable phrase as a cause of such harm (Corson, 1983).

Two cases will exemplify the interpretation of this law. In the first case, *In re Carrie*, the court ruled that the children should be removed from their mother because of her emotional instability. Although the children's financial and physical needs were well met by the mother and they were not physically abused, the court ruled that the mother's extreme emotional instability, characterized by fear of persecution and harassment, prevented her from providing her children with a healthy home environment. In another case, *In re Biggs*, a four-year-old girl was made a dependent of the court because, in the court's view, the parents' allowing her to witness acts of cruelty that they inflicted on her seven-year-old brother constituted emotional neglect (M. McManmon, personal communication, 1986).

These cases demonstrate the varying interpretations of the law and of "mental injury" in cases of psychological maltreatment. These are two cases within the same state; other states and communities may have interpreted this law in a different manner, and as a result the children in these cases would have received different treatment.

Thus, the status of psychological maltreatment as a legal entity and the interpretation of that status by the judicial system provide the broad framework within which communities, agencies, and practitioners work to intervene in and prevent psychological maltreatment. Because these laws define psychological maltreatment in broad, general terms, and because they are subject to interpretation by executive agencies and the judiciary, communities, agencies, and practitioners must arrive at a consensus about the dimensions of psychological maltreatment. A well-developed consensus will not only help agencies, and practitioners identify psychological abuse but will also focus intervention and prevention efforts. Furthermore, in communities where psychological maltreatment is not recognized as a legal entity, consensus regarding the dimensions of psychological maltreatment can provide a foundation for efforts (by local chapters of NCPCA and other community agencies) to advocate for laws directed at psychological maltreatment.

Legislative acts include initiatives to redirect the allocation of resources aimed at prevention. One such funding initiative is the Children's Trust Fund, used specifically for programs concerned with preventing child maltreatment. To date, more than thirty states have enacted legislation to create a Children's Trust Fund. The funds are maintained by surcharges put on marriage licenses, birth certificates, and divorce filings or by tax checkoffs. The critical element is that prevention funds do not have to compete for year-by-year funding with treatment programs. Innovative efforts to prevent psychological maltreatment can look to the trust funds for guidance and start-up support.

Thus, laws about maltreatment of children influence both the decisions regarding specific cases and programs and the general allocation of financial resources to intervene with the phenomenon. Together with NCPCA they form the national context for dealing with psychological maltreatment of children.

Conclusion

It is clear in this chapter that the prevention and remediation of psychological maltreatment are not only individual and family responsibilities: they are responsibilities shared by all of us. The impact of any individual effort is greatly diminished in communities where a commitment to prevention and intervention is lacking. Undoubtedly, the task of organizing communities is great, but it is not impossible, as we have illustrated in this chapter. In a cost-benefit sense, the gains to communities that adopt an active role in developing a coordinated, comprehensive approach to reducing psychological maltreatment will be measured in the healthy growth and development of their children.

8

Identifying Psychological Maltreatment Outside the Home

At the end of 1983, about 400,000 children and youth were living in group residential homes in the United States and approximately the same number in foster homes (Campbell-Smith, 1983). Most of these children and youth are there mainly because their parents cannot or will not care for them appropriately. Only a small proportion of the children in out-of-home care are there because of their own personality disturbances (Gil, 1982). Regardless of the reasons for placement, these children deserve to be raised by caring adults in a nurturing environment and in a manner that meets their developmental needs. In reality, however, out-of-home facilities often are large and overcrowded and therefore not conducive to normal personality development (Moos, 1975; Paulus, Cox, McCain, and Chandler, 1975); and staffs often are overworked, underpaid, and burned out and therefore tend not to satisfy the children's needs fully (Durkin, 1982a; Mercer, 1982; Shaughnessy, 1984). Officials responsible for the institutional care of children receive complaints about the quality of care at a rate in excess of forty per thousand (Rindfleisch and Rabb, 1984). The real numbers probably exceed this estimate of maltreatment and "client dissatisfaction."

Clearly, maltreatment of children exists in residential out-of-home care and in schools, day care centers, child welfare agency shelters for children, and detention centers. Hence, in this chapter the term "out-of-home care" refers to all such organizations. In some respects maltreatment in any of these organizations is similar to maltreatment in the family as discussed throughout this book, in that an adult caregiver behaves in ways that violate norms so as to harm the child (Agathonos, 1983; Durkin, 1982a). Whether within or outside the home, the adult often is overstressed and inadequately supported (Durkin, 1982a). Yet, in many respects, the dynamic differences between out-of-home care and family care may imply differences in the nature of the maltreatment.

Maltreatment in out-of-home care occurs in the context of much more formally defined relationships, embodied in program-related, institutional, bureaucratic, and fiscal roles. Thus, there is no necessary connection between a caregiver's personal feelings toward a particular child and the treatment of that child. In other words, maltreatment can occur "impersonally" in the context of role overload or of too many children demanding the worker's attention simultaneously (Hosie, 1979). Furthermore, children in care are often difficult to raise and handle because they have behavior problems and/or special needs and often tend to irritate and frustrate workers (Durkin, 1982a). In addition, staff-child relationships are open to closer scrutiny by other children and by staff (Hosie, 1979). Finally, some caregiver behaviors considered illegitimate at home may be allowed in residential facilities in the name of treatment.

Defining Maltreatment in Out-of-Home Care

Maltreatment in out-of-home care involves the five forms of psychological maltreatment introduced in Chapter One, as well as a range of behaviors and conditions linked to institutionalization that undermine child development. We begin with a general conception of maltreatment as "acts of omission or commission" by a caregiver which are "judged by a mixture of community values and professional expertise to be inappropriate and damaging" (Garbarino and Gilliam, 1980, p. 7) and which, in the case of psychological maltreatment, can be classified as rejecting, isolating, terrorizing, ignoring, or corrupting the child (see Chapter One). Beyond this we recognize several other formulations, each of which derives from a model of what is possible, desirable, and tolerable in institutional care.

Gil (1975, 1977) regards as institutional maltreatment any policies that "inhibit, or insufficiently promote, the development of children, or that deprive children [of], or fail to provide them with, material, emotional, and symbolic means needed for their optimal development." The San Francisco Child Abuse Council defines institutional maltreatment as "any system, program policy, procedure, or individual interaction with a child in placement that abuses, neglects, or is detrimental to the child's health, safety, or emotional and physical well-being, or in any way exploits or violates the child's basic rights" (cited in Gil, 1982, p. 8). Others, such as Kunkel (1983) and Thomas (1982), include in their definitions acts of omission or commission that are committed or permitted to occur by responsible adults and are harmful to the child.

In light of these general definitions, we define the broader domain of maltreatment in out-of-home care as acts of omission, commission, or permission (acts perpetrated or promoted by the child welfare system, child care policies, a child care organization, a specific program, or a specific procedure) that violate the goals of out-of-home care, thereby harming the child. A situation would be considered harmful if it (1) endangers the protection, security, and/or safety of the child; (2) prevents the child from obtaining basic care and satisfying basic physical and emotional needs; (3) places obstacles in the way of the child's development or severely restricts the developmental opportunities available to the child; or (4) prevents the child from participating in the special care and treatment that he or she needs for adequate developmental progress. This conception of developmentally harmful institutional settings provides a context for our concern with psychological maltreatment in its five forms.

In this chapter we deal with psychological maltreatment as it occurs in places such as residential centers, group homes, institutions for delinquents, hospitals, long-term shelters, detention homes, centers for mentally retarded children, centers for developmentally disabled or otherwise handicapped children, foster homes, treatment centers, child care agencies, child welfare departments, schools, preschools, and day care centers.

Classifying Maltreatment in Out-of-Home Care

Physical and psychological maltreatment of children in out-of-home care emerges from three sources: staff, program, and system problems.

Staff may resort to maltreatment when they are unprepared and untrained to deal with difficult children, inadequately supervised, overwhelmed by the demands of their job, and under stress; and when they feel powerless in the organization, cannot express their frustration to the administrators, feel that they cannot adequately control the children, and lack support or rewards (Durkin, 1982a; Gil, 1982; Gil and Baxter, 1979; Thomas, 1982).

Programs or facilities may promote maltreatment when they are below normally accepted standards, lack standards for the control of children (and therefore permit peer abuse or staff provocation), lack a comprehensive custody and intervention plan, and follow policies emphasizing the children's adjustment to the institution rather than their own individual growth. Further, facilities that are isolated, overcrowded, and underdeveloped; that lack resources; and that seem always to be in a crisis tend to foster maltreatment (Agathonos, 1983; Chase, 1975; Gil, 1982; Mercer, 1982).

Systems for child and youth care that cannot guarantee safety to children and that put children in situations inimical to development are a source of maltreatment. These systems indirectly foster maltreatment when they do not make enough efforts to return children to their families, label children as "different" for the rest of their lives, keep transferring children among institutions and foster homes, are satisfied with vague placement guidelines, offer only minimal consultation and assistance to workers and foster parents, and remove children from their homes without any efforts to intervene with the family (Chase, 1975; Gil, 1977, 1982; Oswin, 1979).

These three sources of maltreatment engage children and youth in:

Psychological Maltreatment:
  Rejecting: failing to meet the child's basic physical needs or needs that are specific to a given child (inadequate diet

or exercise, inappropriate medical care, insufficient regard for specific activities a child must do in order to improve).

Isolation: cutting children off from normal life and from their family and home community or from other children in the facility (the absence of open area in the institution, preventing children's participation in activities outside the facility, restricting family visits and phone calls, locking children up as punishment).

Terrorizing: creating an atmosphere of fear by verbal and nonverbal methods (yelling at and cursing children, forcing children to comply with authority in order to gain "privileges" that are actually their rights, threatening, constantly punishing, enforcing strict rules, using public ridicule and shaming, constantly criticizing, and name calling).

Ignoring: psychological unavailability (disregarding children's wishes and interests, not trying to get special therapies that children need, being emotionally detached, seldom talking and playing with the children, only pretending to be listening to children).

Corrupting: "mis-socializing" children either directly or by a lack of efforts to socialize them (exploiting children, unreasonably employing children in maintenance jobs, behaving in questionable moral or legal ways, encouraging children to violate norms, ignoring times that children behave asocially).

Physical and Sexual Abuse:

Physical abuse: direct and indirect worker behaviors that physically harm the child (hitting, using force, spilling hot water on child), as well as failure to intervene when other children aggress against a child.

Sexual abuse and misuse: direct sexual exploitation of children by staff or failure to handle sexual activities of the children themselves appropriately (having sexual relationships with residents, dating residents, giving adolescents insufficient sex information, denying or ignoring sexual activities that occur among residents).

Developmentally Harmful Conditions:

Misusing intervention or custody methods available to the worker: using allowed procedures either in an inappropriate situation or in an inappropriate manner (discharging a child to a more restrictive institution without just cause, maintaining the child in the institution, overmedicating children to control them, overfeeding children to prevent activity).

Promoting conformity and deindividuation: failure to recognize the uniqueness of each child (ignoring children's specific needs, inhibiting critical and responsible individual living, inhibiting spontaneity and creativity, ignoring children's hobbies, not providing proper educational and recreational environment).

Lacking appreciation of children as persons: perceiving children's nature as bad and distrusting children in general (always looking for behavior misconducts, disbelieving children, not keeping promises or lying to children, deceiving children, tape-recording children without their permission, having unreal expectations of the children).*

These ten threats to development in out-of-home care are by no means mutually exclusive. A child may suffer the effects of several simultaneously or sequentially, and a single worker's behavior may fall into more than one category. However, this classification system seems to capture the range of behaviors in out-of-home care that threaten development. Each of these behaviors has its roots in one or more institutional problems (staff, program, system) but is implemented in a situationally specific manner by a specific individual. For example, a worker who uses

*This categorization of maltreatment in out-of-home care is based on existing classifications, such as Rabb and Rindfleisch's (1985), and on examples of maltreatment that appear in Campbell-Smith (1983); Chase (1975); Drotman and Goldstein (1977); Krugman and Krugman (1984); Paulson (1983); Savells (1983); Shaughnessy (1984); and Thomas (1982).

overmedication of children as a control mechanism might do it as a consequence of personal frustration, the lack of clear institutional guidelines regarding medication and control, an emphasis on maintaining the status quo in the overall child welfare system, or a desire to prevent disclosure of sexual abuse. It is important to understand these sources in order to perform an accurate assessment and intervene effectively. The following five case examples clarify all this in more concrete terms and serve as analogues to the family cases presented in Chapter Two.

1. At the middle school where Mr. Dorn teaches, he has a reputation for being able to make anyone, even the toughest boy, cry in front of the class. He tongue-lashes almost all his students. His subject for twenty-five years has been math, but even the few "whizzes" who have come to his classes, confident of their immunity from verbal abuse because of their ability, are subject to his sarcasm. When such students have the right answer, he says that they guessed it, tries to confuse them, and calls them names. When they are wrong, he ridicules them, claiming that they cannot possibly succeed. Girls, in his opinion, are no good for anything. Roy and John, two of his best students, felt that they had a rapport with Mr. Dorn, for he had been teaching them chess after class. When he humiliated them in their turn, saying, among other things, that their brains were too slow and that they would never get beyond ninth grade, they felt extremely hurt and puzzled. The school counselor reported that they started doubting their intellectual abilities and the trustworthiness of adults.

2. A group of about thirty boys, most of them about fourteen years old, decided to have some fun amidst the boring life of their residential center. That night some of them broke into the kitchen and took all the sweets and fruits they could find; others took white sheets and scared the younger children in the institution, and still others opened all the sprinklers, so that when staff members (who lived in a different building) went out to see why the young children were screaming, they were drenched with water. When these boys were later identified, they were not allowed to go home on weekend leaves for two months and were forbidden to use the telephone. Furthermore, all the children in the residential center were invited to watch when each of these boys was forced to announce that he was "a complete failure in all respects." During that year the boys were employed in the kitchen, as well as in other maintenance jobs, and were constantly

reminded that this was the result of their night of misbehavior. Gradually, some of these boys started skipping school, others tried to run away from the institution, and still others were frequently seen walking aimlessly around the grounds of the facility.

3. In a residential center for emotionally disturbed children, a behavior modification program was instituted. The children had to act like nondisturbed children in order to gain points, and they lost many points for every minor deviation from normative behavior. When they had no more points to be taken off, yet still behaved "inappropriately" (according to staff's perception), they were locked up in isolation, often being forgotten there until the next morning's count. The staff were so busy calculating points that they often forgot to give children their medicine or to attend to their special needs. Recreational activities and educational games with the children were never observed in that facility. The only treatment that the children received targeted compliance with institutional regulations.

4. Observations of about sixty to seventy preschools in New York between 1976 and 1981 revealed that teachers were covertly and overtly maltreating the children (Paulson, 1983). The following covert forms of maltreatment were noted: insisting that children learn to be independent but, at the same time, reinforcing dependent behavior; overemphasizing the acquisition of academic skills; relying excessively on packaged educational materials and failing to use materials that have an intrinsic interest to children; showing a lack of enthusiasm for working with children; and behaving inconsistently. Overt forms of maltreatment included verbal attacks on children; withholding affection; physical coercion consisting in pulling, pushing, shoving, and isolating; and manifesting a dislike of particular children while being excessively attached to others.

5. Krugman and Krugman (1984) studied maltreatment in a single classroom dominated by a psychologically abusive teacher. This teacher used verbal put-downs and harassed children; physically punished some children to scare others; labeled, screamed at, and threatened children; used homework as punishment; made unrealistic demands on children; manifested inconsistent behavior toward children; and allowed children to hurt each other. During school hours the children were quiet and well behaved, hoping to lessen the extent of maltreatment. Outside the classroom they showed the symptoms of school avoidance or school phobia. They worried excessively about their performance, expressed fear of teachers, exhibited somatic complaints, cried about school, developed a negative perception of school and

education, lowered their self-image, and manifested withdrawal and depressive symptoms, and their overall social functioning decreased in general. Hyman (1985) has called this pattern "educator induced-posttraumatic stress syndrome" and has argued that it is a definite category for the mental health system. With appropriate intervention and a change of the teacher, most of the children's symptoms disappeared.

These cases illustrate the nature and range of developmental threat in out-of-home facilities. Each contains a measure of psychological maltreatment. Before professionals can intervene effectively in such cases of maltreatment, they must develop practical strategies for identifying the maltreating behaviors.

Identifying Maltreatment in Out-of-Home Care

As with maltreatment in the family, identification of developmental threat includes both the behaviors that staff members exhibit and the consequent symptoms that children manifest. In addition, it includes the characteristics of staff members, programs, and systems. We hold an ecological-interactive view of the phenomenon and thus look at worker-child interaction in the context of the child's characteristics, the worker's characteristics, the program's (organization's, institution's) characteristics, and the characteristics of the child welfare system. We also look at worker-child interaction in the context of the child's family, the child's home community, and the community that surrounds the facility.

Children's Characteristics. Are some children more likely to be maltreated than others? In general, we can suppose that severely maltreated children manifest severe behavior problems. Children who come from severely deprived socioeconomic contexts and who lack a social support network in their home community are more likely to be institutionalized and are more vulnerable to maltreatment (Drotman and Goldstein, 1977). Children who belong to minority groups or who are socially deviant or handicapped are maltreated more than others (Agathonos, 1983; Drotman and Goldstein, 1977). Others at high risk for maltreatment are slow,

unhappy, sickly, acting-out, or attention-seeking children, those
who require more effort and attention from caregivers (Durkin,
1982a). For example, the children in the residential center that
employed aversive behavior modification techniques (Case 3) were
severely disturbed and could not perform the everyday tasks
required of them. As a result of the program, they were punished
more often and did not receive even the minimal affection they
needed. Another example is cited by Reppuci and Sanders (1977).
They found that acting-out residents were often transferred back
and forth from one unit to another, were continuously referred to
maximum security and treatment units, and were released from the
institution as soon as possible. It does appear, then, that children
who are harder to handle and require more of the workers'
attention are more likely to be maltreated. Overall, we can say that
children whose behavior characteristics decrease the worker's self-
appreciation as professionals are more likely to be maltreated than
others (Scheinfeld, 1985). Having said all this, however, we must
not leave the impression that only troubled children are mistreated
in institutions or that social competence is an effective buffer in all
cases.

   Workers' Characteristics. Workers who tend to maltreat
children in out-of-home care lack full professional competence
(and thus appear to be similar to maltreating parents), work under
inappropriate conditions, have unhealthy relationships with their
administrators, and/or work under continuous stress. These
conditions are conducive to the occurrence of maltreatment and, in
turn, are strengthened once maltreatment occurs. Institutional
maltreatment is self-reinforcing. Once started, it tends to stimulate
more.

   1. *Incompetent workers.* Like incompetent parents, incompetent workers are unaware of children's needs, lack understanding
of children, and have unrealistic expectations (Agathonos, 1983;
Gil and Baxter, 1979; Thomas, 1982). Furthermore, they tend to
become angry with the children because of the children's problems, failing to understand that these problems are a consequence
of these children's life circumstances (Krugman and Krugman,
1984). Like parents, workers may hold incorrect conceptions of

child development and lack the skills needed to cope effectively with socially deviant and difficult children.

2. *Inappropriate work conditions.* Maltreatment in out-of-home care is also associated with inappropriate work circumstances. The workers usually are overworked and underpaid and lack opportunities for career development. Often they are inexperienced or are unable to ask for or receive help in dealing with the children. Supervision, training, and consultation are rare, and workers feel isolated and in need of support services. These conditions foster low staff morale, which exacerbates poor work conditions and prepares the ground for maltreatment (Durkin, 1982a; Gil and Baxter, 1979; Hosie, 1979; Krause, 1974; Mercer, 1982; Shaughnessy, 1984). Indeed, excellent training and supervision may well be the best way to prevent institutional maltreatment in all forms (Whittaker, forthcoming).

3. *Unhealthy relationships with administrators.* Workers who resentfully comply with orders, whose needs are neglected by the organization, who do not participate in decision-making processes, who are not listened to, and who are remote from the administration of the facility tend to feel helpless, powerless, and alienated. They feel that they do not have a sufficient back-up to their activities and consequently are afraid of losing control over children. In such situations the only way they find to maintain some control over the children, as well as to foster a sense of their own personal significance, is through the use of power and force (Etzioni, 1961, 1975; Thomas, 1982).

4. *Stress.* Workers who are subjected to frequent or chronic stress are especially vulnerable to maltreating the children for whom they are responsible. Frustration that cannot be expressed and is not dealt with reduces the workers' motivation and patience. Whether the sources of the stress involve organizational policies, "untreatable" or extremely difficult children, or a worker's personal problems, they contribute to the incidence of maltreatment (Gil, 1977; Hirschbach, 1982; Shaughnessy, 1984; Thomas, 1982).

For example, the teacher in Krugman and Krugman's (1984) study (Case 5) might have had insufficient understanding of children. He was isolated from effective supervisory support and was frustrated and burned out. In such conditions minor irregular events are likely to foster maltreatment.

Programs' Characteristics. Programs, institutions, or organizations make their own contribution to the occurrence of maltreatment. The general situation of the organization—for instance, its isolation from the children's home community— might foster the conditions that generate maltreatment. Conditions within the facility may enhance it; and the organizational procedures may be inappropriate, thereby causing the maltreatment of children. As with worker characteristics, each of these conditions strengthens the occurrence of maltreatment and, in turn, is strengthened by it, thus creating a closed circle of maltreatment.

Some factors that contribute to maltreatment are associated with the general situation of the institution. In institutions isolated from the children's home community, so that the staff and the children have no ties to the regular life and activities of the community, the risk for maltreatment increases (Solomons, Abel, and Apley, 1981). Centers that are large and contain many units, subunits, and workers tend to maintain only minimal coordination. They thus enhance the likelihood that a child will be continually transferred or will not get appropriate services, since one unit may assume that another unit is responsible for those services. In addition, institutions that are in chronic crisis (for instance, financially) tend to be preoccupied with organizational maintenance and therefore are insensitive to children (Agathonos, 1983). Finally, behavior modification programs that include elements of "aversive therapy" are, by the nature of their ideology and practices, more likely to foster maltreatment than other programs (Wooden, 1976).

Another set of factors consists of conditions within the facility. Institutions that have minimal resources and personnel, as well as poor and overcrowded physical conditions, are often unable to implement intervention programs appropriately and can hardly maintain the children in satisfactory conditions (Gil and Baxter, 1979; Mercer, 1982; Shaughnessy, 1984). Organizations that have high turnover rates of staff and children and make numerous referrals to other organizations also tend to have high rates of runaways and high failure rates (Hosie, 1979; Shaughnessy, 1984). Further, in places where few rewards and opportunities for career development are available to workers, frustration and dissatisfaction are likely to emerge, laying the groundwork for maltreatment. Overall, poor, unstable, and unsatisfactory institutional conditions generate and sustain maltreatment.

Finally, maltreatment may be related to inappropriate organizational procedures. An institution that lacks sound employee-screening procedures; that does not enforce licensure and other quality controls for its staff; that is satisfied with limited accountability, where no one specific worker is ever responsible for events; and that does not offer enough appropriate supervision and consultation tends to promote maltreatment indirectly. When an institution of this kind places conflicting demands on its workers, the likelihood of maltreatment increases. Institutions that have ambiguous intervention policies or that lack programmatic clarity or sufficient funding also promote maltreatment (Durkin, 1982a; Gil and Baxter, 1979; Mercer, 1982; Thomas, 1982).

For example, the residential center in Case 2 is isolated from the children's home community, preventing their parents from protesting against the forms of punishment instituted. It is a large center that needs more maintenance staff and that has no clear policy regarding who can be employed in maintenance jobs. Furthermore, high staff turnover prevented the staff from understanding the circumstances that prompted the children's activities that night. In general, an unclear understanding of how to intervene with misbehaving children, linked to system problems, has led to maltreatment.

Systems' Characteristics. Child and youth care systems that cannot guarantee safety and developmental opportunities to children provide the broadest context for understanding maltreatment in out-of-home care. They foster maltreatment in the preplacement, placement, stay, and release stages of the child's institutional career. Social policies that are unable to protect children from poverty, undernourishment, and inadequate education place these children at developmental risks. After labeling them deficient, some child and youth care systems prematurely place children in out-of-home institutions without investing enough effort toward successful retention at home. Thus, vague guidelines on placement and deemphasis on home-based intervention with the family indirectly promote institutional maltreatment (Chase, 1975; Drotman and Goldstein, 1977; Gil, 1982). In addition, during the child's stay in any out-of-home arrangement, maltreatment is encouraged by child and youth care policies that emphasize narrowly defined academic achievement rather than personal development, that create a gap between the actual developmental circumstances and the optimal ones, that continually transfer children among institutions, that do not provide sufficient support for foster parents or other workers, and that maintain the institutionalized children in an inferior and powerless societal position, thus letting their social-physical conditions be ignored (Chase, 1975; Drotman and Goldstein, 1977; Gil, 1977; Savells, 1983). Such a system tends to place its children in double binds: it tells them that ultimately they will return to their families and parents, but it also tells them that their parents are failures and that there is little hope for their families. This double bind is especially strong when children are encouraged to call their foster or house parents "Mom" and "Dad," knowing that soon they will be in another foster family or residential institution (Fortin and Reed, 1984).

Child and youth care systems may also maltreat children through their release procedures. On the one hand, the system tends to maintain children in care without making efforts either toward permanency planning or toward family reunion. On the other hand, it may release them without appropriate follow-up services or without the needed preparation to cope with life (Gil, 1982; Whittaker, Garbarino, and Associates, 1983).

Workers' Behaviors. Rabb and Rindfleisch (1985) have examined institutional maltreatment on the basis of the following eight categories: (1) physical maltreatment; (2) sexual maltreatment; (3) failure to provide for physical needs; (4) failure to supervise—to provide guidance, structure, and discipline; (5) emotional maltreatment; (6) questionable moral behavior; (7) harmful restraint and control; and (8) deception, inconsistency, and unrealistic expectations. When asked to evaluate these categories, workers rated all as serious. Overmedication and overcontrol, harsh and shaming punishment, sexual maltreatment, failure to give medicine, and indirect physical harm (such as pushing a child when near stairs) were rated as particularly serious. Yet few incidents of these types were actually reported to protective authorities. These results testify to the need for aggressive efforts to elicit information from *inside* institutions that "care" for children.

Children's Responses. To a large extent, the behaviors, attitudes, perceptions, and emotions of children subjected to institutional maltreatment are similar to those manifested by children who are maltreated by their families.

Infants who are maltreated by day care workers, by babysitters, or by staff in other settings are likely to show irritability, resistance, or avoidance of that caregiver, inadequate social responses, and anxiety. In serious cases the infant may even exhibit nonorganic failure to thrive, accompanied by apathy, passivity, and emotional withdrawal. Infants will manifest disturbed behaviors with the parents and other adults as they generalize from the maltreating caregiver. They tend to cry often and to be unresponsive to, resist, or avoid contact with adults. Despite widespread concern about the behaviors of maltreated infants in out-of-home care, we have little research beyond the classic studies of infant deprivation conducted by Spitz (1945, 1946; Spitz and Cobliner, 1965). Infants suffer when they are removed from home and treated in an emotionally detached manner (Bowlby, 1973); given rote, depersonalized care (Provence and Lipton, 1962); or cared for erratically by several caregivers (Sagi and others, 1984). Even when physically treated well, these infants are more likely than others to show problems in social relations during infancy and to suffer from immediate and long-term developmental difficulties. On this basis we might conclude that maltreated infants in out-of-home care are even more likely than maltreated infants at home to manifest disturbed symptoms.

Children who are subjected to institutional maltreatment are likely to feel unloved, unwanted, inferior, and inadequate, in much the same manner as children who are psychologically maltreated by their parents. They are likely to develop a negative view of the world and perceive it as hostile to them. This may be a direct consequence of the maltreatment. Yet it may also result from recognizing that their families really did not want them or from acknowledging a label of deviance. These children are more likely than others to lose their trust in people and to become wary and suspicious (Erikson, 1963), viewing caregivers and other people as strange, unpredictable, and untrustworthy. With increasingly lower self-esteem (resulting from the caregivers' behaviors), these children tend also to become anxious, aggressive, or hostile. Anxiety and aggressiveness may be turned outward or inward. When the aggression is turned inward, these children can be identified through their self-destructiveness, depression, passivity, withdrawal, shyness, or restricted communication with others. When it is turned outward, they can be identified through their overactivity, destructiveness, violence, or difficulties with self-control. The child who tends to feel different from other children as a result of placement alone can only feel even more different and inferior when being maltreated.

When coupled with this basic fear of and mistrust in people and the environment, when coupled with low self-esteem and perhaps even self-doubts, institutional maltreatment can lead children to develop exceptional patterns of behavior and communication. They may show dependency with anger; approach-avoidance behavior; noncompliance, overactivity, and destructiveness; or indifference and submissiveness. Children in out-of-home care especially tend to feel separate and apart, humiliated and ashamed, and wicked or inadequate (Kunkel, 1983; Thomas, 1982). They are more likely than other children to have difficulties in forming relationships with adults or with children and tend to have unstable and short friendships (Hirschbach, 1982; Kunkel, 1983). What is often observed in out-of-home care is that children who have been maltreated manifest strange and bizarre behaviors. They will sit motionless, staring at the floor, or they will develop habits of self-stimulation. They may have extreme difficulty controlling themselves and coping with stressful situations. Thus, they are often identifiable by their self-destructiveness or aggression against others, on the one hand, and withdrawal and alienation, on the other (Hirschbach, 1982; Oswin, 1979).

Children's lives in out-of-home care are relatively public (and thus open to observation), in contrast to being "behind closed doors," as in the family. As a result, whereas children who are maltreated by their parents may believe that they deserve it, children who are maltreated in out-of-home care may view themselves and their experiences quite differently. In other words, they may believe that they do not deserve to be maltreated. Whether it is because they have experienced some good relationships in the past, because they see other children treated more appropriately, or because they experience different treatment at the hands of successive caregivers, we suspect that children in institutional settings are likely to protest against the maltreatment if allowed to do so.

Adolescents who are maltreated by youth workers, teachers, or any other professional tend to feel rejected and uncared for. They may feel worthless as a consequence, or they may believe that adults will never understand their worth. When adolescents feel inadequate and unworthy, they often behave in an immature and childish manner. They may prefer to be alone most of the time and may engage in solitary activities, or they may avoid only their own caregivers and peers and join groups of younger children. Or if they feel undervalued by important adults, they may look for ways to prove their worth and maintain their self-esteem; these adolescents often seek out others who feel the same way and create a subculture within the organization (or institution). As a group, they will establish close bonds and, together, may run away or become truant, delinquent, or substance abusive—often in open rebellion against authority figures—and at times deliberately destructive. The potential for the development of emotional disturbance and instability is great among all types of maltreated adolescents, who may develop somatic, sleeping, eating, or other disturbances or become depressed and attempt suicide as a "strategy" for responding.

Our discussion of infant, child, and adolescent maltreatment in out-of-home care has dealt mainly with the relationship of the resident with a caregiver. Yet, as we stated previously, the children themselves may maltreat another child, a circumstance that is nevertheless under staff responsibility. The type, scope, and severity of behavior problems that a child will manifest depend on (1) the severity and persistence of the maltreatment, (2) the existence of supporting/comforting factors, and (3) the nature of the child's initial problems. These behavior problems tend to elicit condemnation and rejection even from caring adults, a phenomenon that may exacerbate maltreatment and its consequences.

Maltreatment in out-of-home care may be identified when a child is consistently, severely, and generally distressed in the presence of a particular caregiver or other children. But we must be careful to differentiate the consequences of maltreatment from the maltreated child's original problems (for which he or she was initially placed). For example, we must differentiate between a child who manifests behavior problems as a result of being maltreated and a child whose behavior problems are caused by his or her initial personality disturbance. In other words, infants, children, or adolescents may manifest identical disturbed behaviors as a result of maltreatment or as a result of preexisting personality problems. Therefore, before any intervention can take place, the identification of irregular behavior patterns that lead one to suspect maltreatment should be followed by systematic information collection and assessment.

Collecting Information

To gain a better understanding of the situation, we need to gather information about both the context and the child. More specifically, we need to examine the characteristics of the child that might contribute to maltreatment as well as result from it. We also need to explore the setting provided by family and home community, staff in the out-of-home placement, other professionals in contact with the maltreated child, and the systematic characteristics of the program or organization.

It is advisable to start by observing the facility and the children. Are the children handicapped and thus especially vulnerable? Do they seem malnourished and uncared for? Is the facility remote from the children's home community and isolated from any other community? Does it seem too large, overcrowded, and with poor physical conditions? Does the facility need more resources and staff? These observations can give a general idea of possible characteristics that can foster maltreatment. They also can suggest what information is still needed and from whom to collect it.

Approaching the administration might be the next step for the purpose of gaining an overview of the facility and of the extent to which children are likely to be maltreated in it. As a way of eliciting their beliefs about workers' compliance and participation and about rearing children, on can ask the directors about their administration ideology. They can also be asked about turnover (of staff and children), referral rates, failure, and runaway rates. Further questions can deal with the existence and quality of screening procedures, accountability requirements, and licensure. One can also ask about placement, transfer, and release procedures. These questions should help one comprehend the extent to which maltreatment is occurring. Yet administrators—or any other worker, for that matter—may not be explicit about maltreatment even if they know that it occurs (Rabb and Rindfleisch, 1985). Furthermore, they are likely to do their best to hide it. Consequently, one is advised to be careful and indirect when trying to gather information from the directors of a facility.

Information about the child, staff, and institution can be obtained from all staff members who work with that child (for example, teachers and counselors), from staff members who are indirectly related to that child (for example, supervisors and consultants to the staff), and especially from the direct caregivers (for example, child care workers and youth workers). These staff members can be asked questions such as these: Is this child different from others (handicaps, behavior problems)? Is this difference central in the child's life? How and to what extent is the family contributing to the child's difficulties or helping the child cope with them? Is there a support network in the child's home community? In the case of infants, workers should also be asked about the adequacy of social responses, any resistance or avoidance of caregivers, and the level of irritability and anxiety. When focusing on children, one should ask about the child's apparent attitude toward the world, behaviors and emotions among peers, behaviors manifested with the worker, level of self-esteem, passivity and withdrawal versus overactivity and violent acts, strange behaviors, rejection of workers, and, generally, tendency to trust or distrust people. With regard to adolescents, the questions should deal with the extent to which the youngsters seem rejected and uncared for, exhibit childish and immature behaviors, reject or avoid staff, have good relationships with peers, belong to youth gangs involved in truancy and substance abuse, and manifest behavior problems.

Staff should also be asked about their work in the organization: Do they *feel* skillful in working with children? Do they think they understand the children and their problems? Have they observed incidents of maltreatment? Are their working conditions inappropiate (overwork, underpay, no professional help, availability of training, supervision, and support services)? What are their relationships with the administration (comply with orders, not listened to, no participation in decision making, feel helpless)? What about the level of stress in daily working conditions? Do they feel burned out? Do the workers believe that the facility is in a chronic crisis? Does the organization operate ethically? Is their work appreciated? What is the quality of the supervision and consultation? Do they feel that they operate under conflicting demands? What should be changed if they are to work better with the children?

The child and the family can serve as additional resources for understanding maltreatment in the out-of-home setting. Initial information should deal with family history and with characteristics of the child, the family, and the home community. Questions can be asked about the child's behaviors and attitudes, the number of friends the child has, the activities that the family members enjoy together, what each likes and dislikes about the other family members. It is also worthwhile to ask family members to describe their attitudes toward the community in which they live. The intent here is to gain some understanding of the extent to which the child, the family, and the community might be contributing to or working against the maltreatment. Specifically, questions about the child's behavior and attitudes should address the kinds of problematic behaviors that appear as a consequence of maltreatment, as described in the section on identification.

After collecting information by observing the staff and children in the facility and talking with administrators, staff members, the family, and the child, one should have some sense of the probability of maltreatment as well as its nature. More specifically, one should be able to form hypotheses about the maltreatment (for example, whether or not it is primarily psychological); about the child's characteristics that might be contributing to the problem; and about worker, program, and system characteristics that might be linked to maltreatment. This information can be helpful in determining what assessments are needed before intervention can proceed.

❉ 9 ❉

Preventing Psychological
Maltreatment Outside the Home
Assessment and
Intervention Strategies

In making an exploratory assessment of maltreatment in out-of-home care, we try to clarify the dynamics among the contributing child, staff, and program-related factors. We also try to determine how the maltreatment has affected the child, so that we can consider possible interventions. Thus, as in Chapter Four, where the target was the family, assessment here becomes the bridge from identification and information collection to intervention. Here, as in Chapter Four, we adopt the perspective of an applied researcher in dealing with issues of assessment. The key is to bring to bear a truly exploratory approach, one that opens doors for understanding intervention.

Assessing the Program and the Facility

In addition to gathering data about the child welfare organization, we can look for existing formal or informal evaluations of the program and staff. These evaluations may shed light on the current situation. In addition to such idiosyncratic evaluations, some more standard assessments should prove useful as a basis for comparison. Commonly used for this purpose are the Work Environment Scale (Moos and Insel, 1974) and the Ward Atmosphere Scale (Moos, 1974). (For sources through which these instruments can be obtained, see Resource A, Part 3.) Both scales are based on an ecological approach to human service systems and thus are consistent with our perspective. They link physical and social aspects of the work or treatment environment to the professional functioning of workers in it. The scales were developed by Moos as part of a package of instruments to measure the psychosocial environment of psychiatric hospitals (Moos, 1974), community-based psychiatric treatment settings (Moos and Otto, 1972), correctional institutions (Moos, 1975), and sheltered care settings (Lemke and Moos, 1981).

Work Environment Scale. This scale measures the quality of worker-worker and worker-administrator relationships as a function of the organizational context. It is composed of three basic dimensions.

1. *Relationship*: the extent to which staff members are involved with and tend to support each other. Subscales used to measure this dimension are an involvement subscale (extent of staff's active participation in the facility), a cohesion subscale (the degree to which there are close personal relations among staff), and a staff support subscale (level of encouragement and support of workers by other workers and by supervisors).
2. *Personal Development*: the extent to which the environment affords opportunities for staff growth and development. Includes an independence subscale (amount of encouragement for autonomous work) and a task orientation subscale (amount of emphasis on getting job done effectively and quickly).
3. *System Maintenance and Change*: the extent to which the environment is well organized, clearly known, and open to change. Includes a work pressure subscale (expectations from staff with respect to time limitations), a staff clarity subscale (level of understanding of how the facility operates), a control subscale (amount of regulation of workers' activities by agency rules and strict supervision), and a comfort subscale (conditions of physical surroundings).

Moos and Insel (1974) report that this scale is internally consistent and reliable. It is similar to the Family Environment Scale (discussed in Chapter Four) in that its subscales are conceptually and statistically independent of one another, thus enabling each to measure a distinct aspect of the work environment. The scale is widely used and is helpful in understanding the work environment of an organization in general and its potential role as a catalyst for maltreatment in particular. It is also useful in determining what aspects of the work environment can serve as an aid to intervention.

Ward Atmosphere Scale. This scale measures the quality of worker-client relationships and interactions as they are influenced by organizational and professional roles. Like the other Moos scale, it is composed of three dimensions.

1. *Relationship*: the extent to which clients are involved with and supported by other clients and agency staff. Includes a support subscale (encouragement and support to clients), a spontaneity subscale (encourage clients to express themselves), and an involvement subscale.
2. *Personal Development*: the extent to which the environment affords opportunities for client growth and development in accordance with the treatment program. Includes an autonomy subscale (level of encouragement of clients for independence and decision making), a practical orientation subscale (level of encouragement of clients to be concerned with personal problems and feelings), a personal problem orientation subscale (level of encouragement of clients to discuss their personal problems and feelings), and an anger and aggression subscale (level of encouragement of clients to express frustration and anger).
3. *System Maintenance and Change*: the extent to which the environment is well organized, clearly known, and open to change. Includes an order and organization subscale (level of organization and planning of program), a clarity subscale (extent of clarity of goal expectations and agency procedures), and a staff control subscale.

This scale, too, was found to be internally consistent and reliable. When coupled with the Work Environment Scale, it helps provide an understanding of an organization's treatment environment and its relation to the work environment. In addition, it contributes to an understanding of aspects that promote or inhibit maltreatment.

The work and treatment environments in the schools studied by Krugman and Krugman (1984) (see Case 5 in Chapter Eight) appear inadequate on several dimensions of these two scales. The teaching environment (including staff and staff-administration relations) probably would be scored low on teacher support and involvement. Task orientation probably is high, whereas independence is low—a combination likely to provoke frustration among teachers. In addition, work pressures and controls are high, but staff clarity and comfort are low. The treatment environment (in this case teacher-child interaction) is likely to be scored low on support and spontaneity and too high on practical orientation. Order and organization probably are high, whereas innovation is low. All these aspects of the treatment environment create conditions that facilitate maltreatment.

Assessing Workers' Competence and Professional Conditions

Several measures are available for evaluating workers' treatment of children. Taken together, these measures can give a comprehensive description of what workers do, how they do it, and whether they could have done it better. Each answer has specific implications for cases of maltreatment. (For sources through which the instruments discussed in this section can be obtained, see Resource A, Part 3.)

Competence Test. Defined from an ecological perspective, competence is an attribute of the transaction between a person and the environment (Maluccio, 1981). Its components, then, are the workers' capacities, skills, and motivation in relation to environmental demands and opportunities. In order to evaluate staff competence, we look first at staff members' capacities and skills. We can do so by observing them at work, by presenting them with case material and asking for their responses, or by simulating situations in which they function as workers. When conducted by someone who is clinically skillful and knowledgeable, as well as experienced in staff evaluations, this exploration can lead to a useful assessment of the quality of the staff's work. Exploring the institution as a work environment is essential in understanding it as a child care environment (just as understanding a family as a household tells us much about it as parent-child relationships).

Worker motivation is a second critical domain for assessment. The purpose is to determine the mix of extrinsic and intrinsic motivation (Deci, 1975): whether the worker is motivated primarily by financial need for a job, a wish to satisfy someone, a wish to be cared for by the children, a need for a place to live, or an interest in and passion for the work, a need to be engaged with challenges in order to feel competent and self-determining, and a feeling of mission. We assume that the more intrinsic the motivation, the less the likelihood of maltreatment.

Task Analysis. When it comes to institutional care, we must always be wary of rationalization of maltreatment through the application of professional jargon. One way of tackling this problem is through task analysis. This technique helps to determine the discrepancy between what the workers are doing and what they think they should be doing. Staff are asked to keep a daily record of their activities and the length of time spent in each activity. During transitions from one type of work to another, the worker notes how much time the previous activity took and what the new activity entails. Such a list by a residential child care worker may read something like: 8:00-8:30, arrive and chat with other workers; 8:30-9:00, check children's rooms; 9:00-10:00, see a parent; 10:00-12:00, sit in office doing nothing; 10:20-10:45, telephone calls. Beside each activity the worker is asked to write what he or she thinks *should* have been done during that time. The analysis highlights discrepancies between what *is* and what *should* be.

This method is useful on several counts: it focuses workers' attention on the way they allot their time on the job; it offers them the opportunity to think about what they should have been doing; and it increases their awareness of any gaps between what they actually did and what they should have been doing. The mere act of monitoring the time and the activities tends to motivate individual workers to increase their effectiveness and efficiency. Furthermore, at the end of several weeks or months, the activity records from all the workers in an organization can be aggregated and analyzed to determine how much time is devoted (on the average) to particular activities in that facility. The analysis also suggests desired directions for change. Although the initial reaction to task analysis tends to be "too time consuming and complex to do it," it can and does work, both for individual workers and for the organization as a whole.

Needs Assessment. The assessment of workers' needs should complement efforts at task analysis because it gives a better understanding of the staff's everyday work. While task analysis highlights what workers do and want to be doing, needs assessment indicates what they need in order to do the job as they think they should. The needs assessment, in this case, can be done both objectively and subjectively. Objectively, the workers' conditions can be compared against some standard of acceptable conditions. Thus, one can assess phenomena such as the appropriateness of the content of in-service training programs, the number of hours of supervision that workers get, the resources available to each worker, or the number of children per worker. Comparison with an objective standard points at some recommended changes. Subjectively, the workers can be asked to list their needs in such domains as knowledge and skills, resources, supervision and training, coordination, and overall work relationships. Discrepancies suggest heightened risk of maltreatment.

Quality of Supervision. A questionnaire developed by Munson (1983) assesses the worker's evaluation of supervisors in three basic areas of supervision: education, support, and administration. It seeks to integrate these functions with dynamic considerations of style, structure, authority, and autonomy. Munson's questionnaire assumes that, to be effective, supervision must be offered regularly and must be structured, consistent, case oriented, and open to evaluation (Munson, 1983). Thus, the questionnaire contains items about the quality of learning from the supervisor, the support workers receive from the supervisor, the supervisor's effectiveness as an administrator, the supervisor's attitudes toward the workers, staff satisfaction from supervision, and the structuredness, regularity, consistency, and case orientation of the supervision sessions.

This questionnaire is useful in evaluating each individual worker's supervisory situation and needs, as well as the overall status of supervision in a facility. It describes the current supervisory situation, enables workers to assess their expectations from supervision, broadens workers' understanding of what supervision can include, points to needed changes, and, above all, helps to evaluate the link between the quality and extent of supervision and the risk for maltreatment in out-of-home care.

Burnout Questionnaire. Staff burnout increases the risk for maltreatment. Much as an overstressed parent is at heightened risk, so a depleted, exhausted professional caregiver is a danger to children (Freudenberger, 1977). Burnout reflects a situation where workers feel that they are hardly able to cope with everyday tasks, let alone handle emergencies. Burned-out workers feel emotionally exhausted, anxious, or even depressed. They believe that their work is useless; they feel "tired of it all," "fed up," and "at the end of their rope." Where does burnout come from? From work overload, insufficient challenges and rewards on the job, role ambiguity and conflict, poor interpersonal relations on the job, or any other person-inhibiting factors (Maslach, 1976; Maslach and Jackson, 1981). Burnout is evidenced by several behavioral indicators:

> *Interactional indicators*: loss of interest in children, inattentiveness, impatience and anger with children, misinterpreting children's behaviors, and avoiding interaction with staff and children.
>
> *Psychological indicators*: general depression and withdrawal, anger, cynical attitudes toward children and their families, negative attitudes toward administrators, rapid mood changes, suspiciousness and feelings of isolation, and expressions of uncaring attitudes toward others.
>
> *Physical indicators*: fatigue, tiredness, headaches, or other physical symptoms that depend on the particular individual and the kind of stress (Munson, 1983).

The burnout questionnaire, developed by Munson (1983), is designed to assess the causes of the phenomenon, attitudes and feelings of the individual who experiences it, and its behavioral indicators. It is used widely (for example, see Meier, Guttmann, and Eisikovitz, 1984). Most important, it helps illuminate the links between burned-out workers and child maltreatment. What is more, it can highlight avenues for intervention.

Overall, the utility of a competence test, task analysis, needs assessment, asessment of the quality of supervision, or burnout evaluation lies in its ability to detect vulnerability in individual workers, the staff in general, or the system as a whole. For example, the preschool teachers in Case 4 (Chapter Eight) lack skills for dealing with young children. They have low intrinsic motivation and feel that they need more resources and consultation in order to do their job well. Furthermore, we can hypothesize that there is a large gap between what they are doing and what they expect to be doing and that they are dissatisfied with the little supervision that they receive. We are also likely to find that they are experiencing job burnout as a consequence of overwork and that, all in all, they have come to dislike their jobs. Given these conditions, the likelihood is substantial that the everyday challenges of managing young children will trigger maltreatment. Suransky's (1982) account of psychological maltreatment in a for-profit child care center highlights precisely this dynamic.

Assessing Children's Responses and Worker-Child Relations

Children's responses to maltreatment in out-of-home care resemble the responses of children who have been maltreated in the home. Therefore, the assessment instruments discussed in Chapter Four can be applied to maltreatment in out-of-home care. Once again, we view these instruments and their use as a vehicle for exploration. Exploration is the basis for intervention—if not on a case-by-case basis, then as a vehicle for improving global competence, as a learning experience to enrich case-by-case assessment and management. Exploratory assessment is thus an appropriate investment, even for those practitioners who must proceed to "eyeball" or "fly by the seat of their pants" on a day-to-day, case-by-case basis in the field. (For sources through which the instruments discussed in this section can be obtained, see Resource A, Part 2.)

Staff members as well as children can fill out the Parental Acceptance-Rejection Questionnaire (Rohner and Rohner, 1980), which reveals perceptions of workers' treatment of the children in terms of warmth/affection, hostility/aggression, indifference/neglect, and undifferentiated rejection, from both staff and child perspectives. The questionnaire is especially sensitive to the level of hostility, neglectfulness, and rejection among staff. The Children's Reports of Parental Behavior Inventory (Schaefer, 1965a, 1965b) can also evaluate attitudes of workers in out-of-home care. Here the children rate the child care worker or teacher on dimensions of love/hostility, autonomy/control, and firm control/lax control. When administered to the workers, it measures their own perceptions of their behaviors with the children. Bronfenbrenner's Parental Behavior Questionnaire (Devereux, Bronfenbrenner, and Suci, 1962; Siegelman, 1965) can be used to assess a worker's behavior in terms of loving, punishing, and demanding. Children, too, can fill out this questionnaire to evaluate caregivers, teachers, or any other staff member. The value of these three questionnaires lies in their capacity for assessing maltreatment, both from a worker's point of view and from the child's.

The Maternal Characteristics Scale and the Childhood Level of Living Scale can be used as well (Polansky, Borgman, and De Saix, 1972; Polansky, De Saix, and Sharlin, 1972; Polansky and Pollane, 1975). These scales can be completed by a supervisor or consultant who is familiar with the foster parent, the child care worker, or the youth worker. The Maternal Characteristics Scale will assess the degree of apathy-futility (behavioral immobilization and interpersonal detachment) and child-like impulsivity (dependence and impulsiveness) observed in the staff member. The Childhood Level of Living Scale will evaluate general child-rearing practices: the quality of physical care and the quality of the emotional-cognitive care given to the child.

Infants suspected of having been maltreated can be assessed by the Bayley Scales of Infant Development (Bayley, 1969) in the first two and a half years of their lives, or by the Strange Situation Procedure (Ainsworth, Blehar, Waters, and Wall, 1978) when they are a year old or older. Children's and adolescents' responses to maltreatment can be assessed by the Tennessee Self-Concept Scale (Fitts, 1965), the State-Trait Anxiety Inventory (Spielberger, 1971; Spielberger, Gorsuch, and Lushene, 1970), the Personality Assessment Questionnaire (Rohner, 1980; Rohner, Saavedra, and Granum, 1978), the Child Behavior Checklist (Achenbach, 1978; Achenbach and Edelbrock, 1979), or the Child Assessment Schedule (Hodges, 1984; Hodges and others, 1982a, 1982b).

Some of the children in out-of-home care are maltreated because their conditions are "untreatable" (Hirschbach, 1982), yet the workers desperately try to help them improve. If a child has been subjected to severe early deprivation, has a character disorder, has lived in many temporary placements, and shows no change after extensive intervention, the challenge of producing significant improvement in personality and behavior is enormous (Hirschbach, 1982). Workers who continue to expect improvement through intervention with such a child may be setting themselves up for frustration and disappointment. These unmet expectations may set the state for maltreatment if, because of their disappointment, the workers begin to blame the victim.

Mr. Dorn (Case 1, Chapter Eight) would appear hostile and rejecting, both from his point of view and from the children's. He is likely to emerge as overcontrolling children in class, punishing, and unreasonably demanding, as well as low on love and warmth. The children—especially John and Roy, who appreciated him at first but were then psychologically abused by him—would almost certainly rate him more critically than he would rate himself. Roy and John would probably appear as having average self-esteem, since the maltreatment has not been occurring for a long period, but their anxiety level would be unusually high. Over time, they could score above average on hostility, aggression, and emotional instability. Perhaps one boy might begin externalizing his reactions and misbehave with other teachers; the other might internalize his reactions and begin to report somatic complaints. Exploratory assessment would generate some plans for intervention.

Intervening with Cases of Maltreatment in Out-of-Home Care

Before describing possible avenues of intervention in cases of out-of-home maltreatment, we need to consider the goals of such intervention and its relation to the goals and practices of the facility where maltreatment has occurred. Here we are asking whether the goals and nature of intervention should be different for schools, residential centers, day care centers, and foster homes. In a sense, all interventions with maltreatment aim at eliminating the maltreatment and improving the child's situation. Yet a "good" situation for a child will be defined very differently, depending on whether the child is at home, in an institution, or in a foster home. For example, in intervening with a teacher at a school, we can readily provide alternatives for the children while we proceed to retrain or dismiss the offender. In intervening with foster parents, we would work on child-rearing skills but might be less likely to recommend marital therapy than if they were the biological parents of the child. In a residential center, a child care worker should be taught to manage children in groups and to share authority with co-workers. All these represent program-specific interventions beyond the general elimination of maltreatment.

In other words, once maltreatment in out-of-home care has been identified and assessed, we need to answer six questions:

1. What are the workers' behaviors that we must eliminate?
2. Which system, program, worker, child, and family characteristics must we change? What can we change within the limits of existing resources and regulations?
3. What are the specific goals of intervention beyond the elimination of maltreatment?
4. Who will be the target of intervention? (Worker? Child? Program?)
5. Who will supervise and conduct the intervention?
6. What should be the content and procedures of the intervention?

Data obtained in the identification and assessment stages provide answers to the first four questions and serve as a guide for planning and executing the intervention. As indicated in our examples, we are likely to know at the end of the assessment stage which worker behaviors need to be eliminated (isolation, terrorizing, ignoring, and the like); what characteristics of the system, program, worker, and child need to be and can be changed (for instance, working conditions or relationships with administrators); what the specific goals of the intervention are (for instance, that workers acquire more child-rearing skills or that teachers use more teaching methods); and who will be the target of the intervention.

The fifth question (who will conduct the intervention?) is a sensitive one. If supervisors are asked to do the intervention, they can work with the maltreating worker or with the maltreated child but may be inappropriate agents of change for the program as a whole. If the case is especially severe (for example, if sexual abuse has precipitated a suicide attempt), perhaps an outside specialist should be asked to do the intervention. If, however, the central intervention target is the program, the best catalyst for change may be the concerted efforts of all staff members. Staff can change the program itself or suggest a more general policy change that will, as a consequence, change the program. Obviously, the question of who is to intervene is not only a sensitive but a complicated one. The choice of intervention agent must be specific to each institution and to each case of maltreatment. Consequently, we cannot offer explicit rules concerning who should be selected and in what circumstances. All we can offer is a number of questions that need to be considered when one is choosing an intervention agent:

a. Should that person be from within the facility or from outside? What are the advantages and limitations of each?

b. Should a single intervention agent or a group of persons be selected?

c. Should change occur "from the bottom up" or "from the top down"?

d.   What should be the qualifications and skills of the intervention agent?

When these questions are considered in light of the responses provided for the four previous questions (workers' behaviors to be eliminated, program's characteristics to be changed, goals of intervention, and intervention target), the fifth question, regarding supervision, becomes easier to answer. For example, if the goal is to eliminate excessive conformity and deindividuation in a residential center, to initiate changes in the staff's working conditions, to teach the staff techniques of promoting children's growth, and to work mainly with the staff itself, the best solution may be to have a current supervisor work with staff or to bring in a specialist from another agency.

The sixth and final question, how to plan and conduct the intervention, is the topic of the following sections. We consider the processes of intervention that may be employed with the child and family, the staff, the program, and the system as a whole. We often refer to a specific facility or intervention agent, emphasizing that each interventive action is program specific. The order of the intervention targets just cited is intentional: it is often advisable to intervene first with the child (and the family if needed and possible), then or at the same time with the staff, then or at the same time with the program, and only at the end with the overall system.

Intervening with Children and Their Families. The first target for intervention in cases of maltreatment in out-of-home care should be the child who has been subjected to maltreatment. If at all possible, one also should work with the child's parents, so that the child is given indirect support and, if he or she should return home at a later date, a more nurturant environment. The first decision to make concerning intervention with the child is whether it should be part of a broader intervention plan. If separate, it should be goal and problem oriented, and also time limited, so to keep maltreatment in a focused, "normalized" perspective (Thomas, 1982).

The goals for the intervention are to help the child gain back trust in people and in the world; to reduce the symptoms of emotional disturbance, such as violence, withdrawal, or destructiveness; to improve communication, interpersonal skills, and social skills; and to help the child modify any behaviors that may have contributed to the maltreatment. In broad terms, the goal is to promote competence in the child and to help overcome anxiety, negativity, and distrust about self and others (Durkin, 1982b; Kunkel, 1983). When we are dealing with infants, there seem to be two options: either intervene with the caregiver or refer the infant to another facility, perhaps a facility that offers the Gonzales-Mena and Eyer program (see Chapter Six) or a similar program that emphasizes nurturant adult-infant relationships.

The same two options—working with the caregiver or making a new placement—are available when the maltreated youngster is a child. But here we also have to intervene directly with the child and, if possible, with the family. When the option of a new placement is chosen, the new day care facility, school, residential center, or foster home must be able to provide developmental compensation for the previous environment, and its workers must be able to deal effectively with a child who has been maltreated and is manifesting any number of behavioral disturbances. However, the goal of reducing multiple placements argues for an initial effort to improve the quality of care within the existing placement. Multiple placements are themselves often psychologically abusive.

Interventions with the child may involve play therapy, developmental play, behavioral counseling, social skills training, and supplementary caregivers or role models (as already discussed in Chapter Six). In addition, the practitioner who intervenes with children should help them modify behaviors—such as uncontrolled activity, talking back, and attention seeking—that are likely to stimulate maltreatment. In work with older children, the other children in the facility can serve as "peer helpers" and help the child regain trust in the social surroundings. Whatever intervention is chosen, it should be coordinated or integrated with any other ongoing interventions involving the target child.

Interventions with adolescents can be carried out individually or in groups. Individual counseling can be behavioral, psychodynamic, or social-cognitive, depending on the adolescent's problems and the practitioner's clinical orientation. Groups of youth are often most helpful, since other youth who have the same problems can serve also as helpers and pave the way for the maltreated adolescent to trust adults again. Group work with adolescents has been found most conducive to interpersonal and social development, especially when these youth live together (see Ohlsen, 1977).

At a minimum, families of maltreated children and youth should be aware of the incident and of any current or planned intervention involving their child. They should know that they have a right to participate in planning and to refuse the intervention (Gil and Baxter, 1979). They should also be encouraged to participate in the child's treatment. When the maltreatment has occurred in school or day care, from which the child returns home every day, parental involvement in the intervention is vital. These families need guidance in how to respond to the child in their everyday interactions. The parents should be alerted that their child might begin to behave strangely (for instance, isolating herself in her room and refusing to come to meals) and that they should place limits on this behavior (by gently insisting that she appear for meals and encouraging her to join in other family activities). They also should be informed that the child may feel threatened or frightened by their normal behavior toward her. In all their responses, the parents should be told, they can best help their child by being warm and affectionate and, above all, trustworthy.

Action in response to institutional maltreatment may yield evidence of disturbed family relationships. This discovery would return us to the issue and techniques discussed in Chapter Six.

Intervening with Staff. Any staff intervention should distinguish between staff who have been maltreating children and other workers in the facility who must deal with the consequences. Intervention with the maltreating workers should include increasing their awareness of their behaviors and the effect of these behaviors on the children, changing their attitudes, teaching them alternative behaviors, and even removing them from their jobs if no change is observed or if the acts of maltreatment are serious enough to require it. The intervention agent (supervisor or consultant) must confront the maltreating staff member with what was done and clarify the meaning of the child's subsequent reactions. Staff remediation, where feasible, can include role playing, generating ideas about better ways of working with children, providing resource materials, and creating opportunities for contacting other professionals, who can serve as pro-social role models.

The next stage of this intervention should be geared toward the workers' characteristics that, according to previous assessment, have exacerbated the maltreatment. Worker incompetence, inappropriate conditions (overwork, no supervision), unhealthy relationships with administrators, and general stress are all targets for intervention. Workers who are incompetent should be educated about child-rearing practices, handling difficult children, stepping out of confrontations with children, reducing peer abuse, disciplining and controlling children, maintaining warm and stable relationships with children, and promoting competence in children (Campbell-Smith, 1983; Durkin, 1982a; Gil and Baxter, 1979; Hosie, 1979; Krause, 1974; Kunkel, 1983). Beyond these general guidelines for increasing staff competence, workers should be reeducated about the specifics of their task, whether it be working with handicapped children, coping with young children who are away from home, or caring for emotionally disturbed adolescents.

When inappropriate conditions have precipitated the maltreatment, better supervision, more in-service training opportunities, and reallocation of tasks may be needed. Similarly, when the relationship with administrators seems to be fostering maltreatment, staff need more participation in decision making and greater administrator support for their child care activities or for a change in administrative policies. In both cases (inappropriate conditions and relationships with administrators), intervention with the administrators also is needed if the workers' initiatives for change are to have the desired results. When stress seems to be responsible for maltreatment, staff need to create support networks among themselves, find alternative coping mechanisms, and enhance their social lives outside the facility—all as a foundation for altering their practices with the children

(Durkin, 1982a). Workers also can reduce stress and frustration if they recognize that some problems of children are untreatable and avoid futile efforts to deal with these problems (Hirschbach, 1982).

Workers in the facility who are not directly involved in the maltreatment need consultation regarding child maltreatment, since the effects of one case of maltreatment are likely to go beyond the specific worker and the child. They can serve as "peer helpers" for the worker and as trustworthy adults for the maltreated child and for other children. By being consistent, accepting, and interested and by having stable relationships with the children and the worker, they may be able to protect the child from further harm and threat (Thomas, 1982). For example, a psychologically abusive teacher can benefit from learning effective, nonpunitive discipline methods as well as from gaining support from other teachers. A psychologically abusive foster parent is likely to gain from learning to care for and control acting-out children and from developing supportive relationships with other foster parents. A psychologically abusive caseworker is likely to improve by learning to deal with burnout and by gaining support from more experienced child care workers.

Intervening with the Program. When maltreatment occurs in any child care facility, it is an indication that the facility, like the maltreating family, needs help (Hosie, 1979). In this case help may be labeled "systems therapy" (Durkin, 1982a), because it offers a change in organizational practices. As we mentioned earlier, programmatic intervention might be directed toward changing the staff's working conditions or their relationships with supervisors. Further, the goal of such intervention could be to change the overall characteristics of the facility (isolation, size, coordination), conditions in the facility (resources, overcrowding, physical conditions, insufficient staff, staff turnover, rewards and incentives, career development), or organizational procedures (screening, quality of staff, accountability, intervention policies, planning), depending on the findings of the identification and assessment processes.

Scheinfeld (1985) offers an anthropologically oriented model intervening with the organization as a social system. In his approach, which represents a breakthrough in applied anthropology, activities are carried out either "from the bottom up" or "from the top down." In the first case (bottom up), the staff are advised to explain (*through an outside consultant*) which organizational procedures and conditions are problematic and to suggest ways of changing them. In the top-down case, policy changes formulated by administrators, in conjunction with the outside consultant, pull the entire organization toward change. There are advantages and limitations to each approach, and the choice between them should be made specifically for each program (Campbell-Smith, 1983). Criteria for selecting one approach over the other include administrative attitude, staff cohesion, and degree of external coercion (for example, in the wake of disclosure of serious maltreatment).

An outside consultant or the institution's staff or administrators might suggest some of the following avenues for reform: manipulating the size of the units and enhancing coordination among them, encouraging the directors to supplement available resources and physically redevelop the facility, bringing in consultants and supervisors (Gil and Baxter, 1979), developing reward and career mechanisms, improving screening procedures and accountability requirements (Thomas, 1982), and clarifying the intervention plans and staff expectations. In addition, the institution may need to enhance its developmental orientation and its sensitivity to the unique characteristics of its children (Campbell-Smith, 1983; Thomas, 1982), to establish different programs for each age group, to emphasize the children's development of relationship skills, to focus on improving the quality of children-staff relationships (Kunkel, 1983), and to make explicit which control and punishment methods are appropriate to use.

The institution and its staff members are responsible for recruiting and retaining staff who are skillful in working with children and who are aware of and sensitive to the possibility of maltreatment. Thus, directors and staff of a facility where maltreatment has occurred should be encouraged to examine recruitment and retention policies and ensure that the workers have a clear understanding of their responsibilities and the children's rights. The directors should also understand the different contexts of maltreatment and develop internal procedures for reporting and intervention (Gil and Baxter, 1979; Thomas, 1982). Rabb and Rindfleisch's (1985) analysis of reporting indicates that, unless institutional leaders are aggressive in stimulating and reinforcing reporting, the "natural" social processes of institutions will suppress reporting. In addition, there should be clear guidelines covering referrals for treatment outside the facility.

Intervening in Systems of Child and Youth Care. System intervention aims at creating changes in a network of schools, in policies of child welfare systems, or in general processes of foster parenting. Often such intervention has a prevention component, undertaken by professional associations or groups of workers. The system's tendency to maintain itself works against such macro-level changes. Therefore, they are rarely undertaken successfully without long-term commitment and political support. The goals for such an intervention are to dry up the sources of maltreatment, to develop a master program for institutional care that is developmentally oriented, and to clarify referral procedures, release conditions, and follow-up services. More specifically, a system intervention will focus on the following changes: improving the system's efforts to meet children's needs (Campbell-Smith, 1983), improving training and education for workers, emphasizing collaboration between children's social systems, creating mechanisms to relieve workers' stress (Durkin, 1982a), developing procedures and processes to intervene with maltreatment (Gil and Baxter, 1979), clarifying the ideologies and expectations that underlie work with children (Krause, 1974), and developing career paths in child welfare jobs. Thus, an effective interventive and preventive procedure is to facilitate a developmental orientation in all the systems related to the child and to reinforce clear and known standards of working with children (Campbell-Smith, 1983; Thomas, 1982).

A good example of such intervention is the deinstitutionalization movement started in Massachusetts by Jerome Miller (for overview see Miller, 1985). At the time of its inception, documented maltreatment was systematically occurring in large institutions for juvenile delinquents. Policies, programs, and the administrators' and staff's beliefs were responsible for the maltreatment. These institutions were replaced by small, community-based facilities, which were more effective; for example, they discouraged the use of severe incarceration and detention. A similar example comes from Texas, where juridical findings showed that inhumane conditions prevailed in large institutions for children and youth. A court order to the state's Youth Council resulted in the creation of smaller, community-based facilities.

Community Perspectives and Prevention

Maltreatment in out-of-home care is often seen as part of a more pervasive maltreatment, rooted in the society's failure to provide community opportunities for children to develop and grow (Solomons, Abel, and Apley, 1981). Therefore, part of any fundamental intervention aimed at maltreatment in out-of-home care should deal with broader community issues. When the level of intervention is the program or the institution, we talk about linking the institution with the community around it and with the child's home community, using the community as a resource means, letting the children participate in community activities, involving the community in institutional decisions and events, and maintaining the child's involvement in his or her home community.

When the level of intervention is societal or has to do with the system of child and youth care, we talk about communitywide, statewide, or nationwide projects that deal with issues such as public awareness, reporting, development of resources, and training curricula. Thomas (1982) claims that a mandated state agency should undertake projects that have the following features:

1. Increase public awareness and thereby the extent of reporting.
2. Educate families, especially families of institutionalized children, about parents' rights and their responsibility to report anything unusual that happens to their children.
3. Train placement staff to be knowledgeable about abuse and neglect laws and their responsibility to report.
4. Indicate who is responsible for investigating reports of maltreatment in out-of-home care.

5. Teach children about maltreatment, their rights, and the processes of reporting, so that they can make "victim self-reports" when they suspect they are being maltreated.

This can be regarded as a general outline of a community-level intervention and prevention program. It includes the components of public awareness, education of parents and their children, education of staff, and development of procedures to uncover and deal with maltreatment. These components seem to be essential for any large project if it is to have an impact. An example of one such project is the San Francisco Institutional Abuse Project (described in Gil, 1982; Gil and Baxter, 1979). The goals of this project were both interventive and preventive: to increase public awareness of institutional abuse and neglect, to increase reporting, to prevent further abuse and neglect by training staff, and to intervene in cases where institutional abuse and/or neglect was reported. The activities of the project included training, establishing procedures for reporting, and developing community resources. Although the institutions approached by project staff tended to deny the existence of maltreatment, one of the results of the project was increased reporting. Of the 1,005 reports received, 774 were about physical abuse and neglect, whereas the remainder, 231, dealt with sexual abuse. We can only speculate about the role of psychological maltreatment in these facilities.

These examples reveal how crucial reporting is to the process of intervening with and preventing maltreatment in out-of-home care (Gil and Baxter, 1979). More specifically, when making a report, a worker should first of all know when, where, how, why, and by whom a child has been maltreated. Second, the worker should understand which channels of reporting best serve the interests of the child. Is the *child* served better when one reports internally to the director or supervisor or externally to the child protective services (Durkin, 1982b)? Reporting, however, is a much more complicated issue than first appears. Workers who report about a maltreatment that has occurred in the organization where they are employed convey a message to peers and supervisors that the organization is deficient in some respect. How could one let oneself work in such a deficient place? In addition, by reporting, the employees might seem to be opposing the administrators, thereby risking their jobs, especially if the official approach is to keep such occurrences within the organization and as quiet as possible. By reporting, a worker may also seem uncollegial to staff peers. Ideally, of course, the interest of the child *should* transcend all these considerations. In actuality, compromise between circumstantial factors and children's interests is inevitable when the issue is reporting. Rabb and Rindfleisch's (1985) analysis documents that the best interest of children suffers in this process of rationalization.

The problem of reporting is intensified when the organization (for instance, a residential center) is isolated and its practices are removed from public scrutiny and public awareness. This organization may have been treating children well for a long time; once maltreatment is reported there, however, it is likely to be sensationalized by the public media. The organization is then seen negatively and becomes even more isolated. At this point the chances for maltreatment increase, and the process continues cyclically.

Reporting takes place once suspicion of maltreatment has been aroused. It occurs after the fact of maltreatment and in that sense is part of the intervention process. There is a preventive aspect as well, however, since workers, children, and families are alerted to the possibility of maltreatment and its emotional and developmental harm and so become more prepared to take precautions against it, to invest in efforts to prevent it. In other words, the very first step toward prevention is raising public awareness. The issues involved in increasing public awareness are the same for every type of maltreatment, whether its context is an organization or home and family (as we saw in Chapter Seven).

Preventing maltreatment in out-of-home care means creating a social system incompatible with the processes that generate and sustain rejecting, terrorizing, ignoring, isolating, and corrupting. Prevention on the systemic level would then deal with developing policies about the family-child relations when the child is placed, clarifying placement guidelines, creating and maintaining developmentally oriented programs for children, and explicating release conditions and procedures. It includes (1) broad

institutional planning (Mercer, 1982); (2) maintaining an appropriate level of fulfillment of children's physical, emotional,
cognitive, and social needs and closing the gap between the
children's actual and ideal living circumstances (Drotman and
Goldstein, 1977); (3) maintaining standards of training, screening,
and selection of workers as well as of accountability; (4) replacing
large and overcrowded institutions with smaller community-based
ones; (5) increasing the social and professional status of, as well as
career development opportunities for, workers in child and youth
services; (6) lowering the tolerance for objectionable behaviors or
practices in institutions—practices that would be considered
maltreatment if they occurred in the home; (7) setting up developmentally oriented programs, where the children are exposed to
developmentally enriching experiences at each age, encouraged
toward understanding of self and others, helped in relating to
others, taught to communicate effectively, and given appropriate
opportunities to accept responsibility (Campbell-Smith, 1983). In
other words, if we are to prevent maltreatment, we must develop
clear and humane standards for the care and guidance of children
(Thomas, 1982).

Prevention on the organizational, program, or institutional
level should aim at working against the factors that we discussed
in Chapter Eight. In other words, it should aim at (1) improving
the situation of a facility (reduce isolation, improve internal
coordination, eliminate organizational crises, and soften radical
behavioral modification programs); (2) improving conditions in
the facility (improve task allocation among staff, redevelop the
facility, reduce overcrowding, decrease referrals, and improve
success rates); and (3) making organizational procedures appropriate (standardize internal screening procedures, enforce quality
requirements from the staff, emphasize accountability, offer
supervision and/or consultation, clarify internal intervention
policies, and plan the children's stay in the facility). Organizations
where these three factors (overall situation of facility, internal
conditions, and organizational procedures) are judged poor can be
called "organizations at risk for maltreatment," and this label
justifies preventive practices. Beyond what we have mentioned
here, the literature about preventive practices in child welfare

services focuses on adequate and continuous in-service training, proper orientation for new staff, manageable work hours, institutional planning, and clear expectations from staff and children (Mercer, 1982; Drotman and Goldstein, 1977; Thomas, 1982). In short, prevention on the organizational level has to do with creating and maintaining facilities that are conducive to the well-being of children. It is as simple *and* different as that.

Prevention on the staff level is usually accomplished through training and in-service continuing education, as well as supervision or consultation and staff meetings. Its goal is to raise staff members' general competence in working with children and to increase their concern and sensitivity to maltreatment. Components of such training programs should include knowledge of child development and behavior, as well as skills in everyday work with children and their families, other staff members, the organization, and other facilities. Each training program has specific goals, content, and methods; yet they all have the same preventive underlying theme.

In sum, preventing maltreatment in out-of-home care can be addressed on the societal-systemic, organizational-programmatic, and staff-related levels of the phenomenon of maltreatment. In general, prevention efforts should be directed at those factors that place an organization, and therefore its children, at risk for maltreatment.

Conclusion

Psychological maltreatment of children in out-of-home care becomes an issue as overall concern for child maltreatment increases. We now know that the very facilities and services designed to help children are often the site and the vehicle for mistreating them. Actions that would be regarded as maltreatment if performed by parents sometimes are accepted when they are performed by child care workers. These actions by child care workers are tolerated because, as they insist, they are overworked or undersupported or have too many children to care for or because they are performing these actions in the name of treatment. Are we willing to accept this view, or do we contend that these actions

Table 7. Identification, Assessment, Intervention, and Prevention of Maltreatment of Children in Out-of-Home Care.

	Identification	Assessment	Intervention	Prevention
Children and Families	Promoting effects of being different from other children Infants: irritable, resistant, or avoidant; inadequate social responses; anxiety; disturbed behaviors with adults Children: feel unwanted and inferior, negative view of world and people, depressed and withdrawn or overactive and violent, difficulties in relationships, bizarre behavior Adolescents: feel rejected and uncared for, feel worthless, or are convinced that adults will never understand them	Acceptance-Rejection Questionnaire: workers' treatment of children Children's Reports of Parental Behavior Parental Behavior Quesionnaire: children's assessment of workers Maternal Characteristics Scale and Childhood Level of Living Scale Bayley Scales of Infant Development Strange Situation Procedure Tennessee Self-Concept Scale State-Trait Anxiety Inventory Personality Assessment Questionnaire Child Behavior Checklist Child Assessment Schedule	To help child gain back trust in world and people and improve social and interpersonal skills Work with child, parents, worker(s), and/or make a referral Children: play therapy, developmental play, behavioral consulting, social skills training, volunteers, peer helpers, group work Families: should know their rights, guidance and advice, marital counseling, family therapy, parent-child interventions, parenting interventions	
Workers	Incompetent: unaware of children's needs, unrealistic expectations, wrong perception of the development of difficult children Work in inappropriate conditions: overwork, underpay, no career, rare supervision	Competence Test: to assess workers' skills, knowledge, and motivation Task Analysis: to examine components of staff members' everyday work Needs Assessment: to evaluate professional needs and	With workers who maltreated child: increase awareness behaviors and their effects, change attitude, and teach alternative behaviors With all workers: promote competence, improve relationship with administra-	Through training and in-service continuing education Raise staff's competence and awareness of maltreatment Train in: general and specific knowledge of

	and consultation Unhealthy relationships with administrators: workers' needs are neglected, do not participate in decision-making processes, remote from administration Stress: cannot express frustration, burned out Behaviors: physical abuse; neglect, reject, isolate, terrorize, ignore, corrupt; misuse available professional methods; promote conformity and deindividuation; do not appreciate children as persons; sexual misuse	wants of workers Quality of Supervision: to evaluate supervisors' teaching, supporting, and administering functions Burnout Questionnaire: to assess reasons for and extent of workers' burnout	tors, encourage workers to initiate organizational change, train to cope with stress, refresh knowledge and skills	children, specific needed skills, cooperation with other staff and agencies, coping with stress, intervening with maltreatment and preventing it
Program	General situation of the facility: isolated, large, no coordination, chronic crisis Conditions within the facility: minimal resources, need more staff, poor physical conditions, overcrowded, high staff turnover, high referral rate Inappropriate organizational procedures: lack sound screening procedures, no enforcement of quality practice, limited accounta-	Work Environment Scale: to assess the quality of facility as a workplace Treatment Environment Scale: to assess the quality of facility as place to intervene with children	"Systems therapy" Change work conditions of staff and/or their relationship with administrators Change overall facility situation Change conditions within facility Improve organizational procedures Intervene from bottom up or top down; e.g., link facility with community and other agencies, manipulate unit size, bring con-	Improve facility situation Improve conditions within facility Make organizational procedures appropriate Adequate and continuous in-service training Institutional planning Clear expectation from staff and children

Table 7. Identification, Assessment, Intervention, and Prevention of Maltreatment of Children in Out-of-Home Care, Cont'd.

	Identification	Assessment	Intervention	Prevention
	bility, conflicting demands on workers, ambiguous policies, no planning		sultants, develop reward and career mechanisms, clarify planning, redirect the program to be developmentally oriented. Examine policies with regard to workers and children	
Child and Youth Care System	Cannot guarantee safety and developmental opportunities Preplacement: cannot keep children away from poverty, poor education, labeling them as different Placement: vague guidelines, deemphasis on intervening with parents Out-of-home stay: emphasis on achievement rather than personal development, transfer child continuously, not enough assistance to workers Release: no permanency planning, release without follow-up or preparation		To eliminate wide maltreating practices, change policies, develop master programs for institutional care, clarify procedures Improve training programs, emphasize work with the child's social systems, develop procedures and processes to intervene with maltreatment	Develop policies about family-child connection when child is placed, clarify placement guidelines, create developmentally oriented programs, facilitate broad planning, maintain a standard of satisfying children's needs, maintain standards of quality practice

constitute maltreatment no matter who performs them? On the other side, parents are allowed latitude in deviating from community and professional norms of child care when their personal beliefs and preferences, and cultural or life necessity, dictate, whereas the quality of institutional child care is wholly judged only and always by community and professional standards. In addition, agencies or institutions are often expected to provide physical care, supervision, and guidance better than that which families provide (because of the availability of professional, trained staff). Consistent superiority is expected of families only with regard to emotional care (Rabb and Rindfleisch, 1985; Thomas, 1982).

In out-of-home care, staff are often held responsible for maltreatment regardless of the severity of their acts or whether they were intentional or accidental, since their responsibility to protect the child is mandated both by law and by professional ethics (Thomas, 1982). In Table 7 we summarize the major themes that constitute each part of the picture of maltreatment in out-of-home care.

Afterword

It is significant that, at this stage of the development
of child protective services, attention is being focused
nationally on emotional neglect of children.
—*Robert M. Mulford*

Mulford's statement, although it was made more than twenty-five years ago, sounds contemporary. The more things change, the more they remain the same? Yes and no. Mulford wrote in the broad tradition of "child welfare." He was concerned with the general quality of life for children and their families, as one "in the trenches" seeking to understand the problem of emotional deprivation. More recently, in a state-of-the-art discussion, Lourie and Stefano (1978) began their report with this statement: "Mental health professionals have avoided the topic of emotional abuse" (p. 199).

Emotional maltreatment, as everyone who has systematically studied the phenomenon knows, is a frustrating problem because it is so elusive and so very important. Mulford's comment highlights its importance; Lourie and Stefano's, its difficulty. Our goal here has been to shed light on psychological maltreatment and to argue that we must make progress in dealing with it if we are to develop a fuller understanding of child abuse and neglect generally.

Many of us are drawn to the "fever" analogy in explaining the meaning of child abuse and neglect. Typically, we speak of abuse and neglect as indicators of underlying problems in the family, just as a fever indicates infection in the body. We think that the analogy is a good one and that it can be pursued still

further. Most fevers are not intrinsically dangerous. They are
merely indicators, posing no direct threat to the organism. High
fevers, however, particularly among young children, are themselves dangerous. Similarly, most of the physical damage done by
abusive and neglectful parents—although socially distressing,
morally unconscionable, and requiring attention—is not itself a
threat to the long-term health of the child. Only the most extreme
instances of abuse and neglect are life threatening or produce
substantial physical impairment (and most of these injuries affect
very young children). Statistics derived from the American
Humane Association's compilation of report data from states
around the country document this assertion. Despite the fact that
"petty" domestic violence is widespread, fatalities form a very
small proportion of maltreatment cases, and relatively few cases
even require medical attention (the highest concentration being
among infants). Figures like these give rise to the "hard-headed"
assessment that child abuse and neglect are not major medical
problems. Gil (1970, p. 137), for example, concludes that "the
scope of physical abuse of children resulting in serious injury does
not constitute a major social problem," pointing out that other
problems, "such as poverty, racial discrimination, malnutrition,
and inadequate provisions for medical care and education,"
constitute "more widespread and more serious social problems that
undermine the developmental opportunities of many millions of
children in the American society."

The massive increase in reported cases since Gil's study was
undertaken in the late 1960s would certainly enlarge the scope of
the problem identified; nonetheless, the more recent figures
presented in the American Humane Association data still suggest
that serious physical harm is only a relatively small part of the
child maltreatment problem. Does this mean that child maltreatment is a small problem? Clearly, the answer is no. Most professionals and members of the general public almost "instinctively"
recognize that the problem of maltreatment goes well beyond
serious physical harm to children.

Consider, for example, the problem of sexual abuse.
Although physical assault does accompany sexual abuse in
numerous cases, the absence of such assault does little to diminish

the seriousness of the incident. Why? The coercive climate in which most sexual misuse takes place produces an emotional threat to the child. Although our formal statements about child maltreatment focus on physical consequences, most of us recognize that the heart of the matter lies not in the physical but in the emotional domain. This recognition permits us to distinguish between "normal domestic violence" and abuse. There is growing recognition that emotional maltreatment is the central problem with which we are dealing, and in most cases physical injuries are only of secondary concern.

This view is given credence by the available evidence bearing on the "intergenerational transmission hypothesis" concerning child abuse. Many accept as fact the statement that "people who abuse their children were themselves abused." Government pamphlets, public service announcements on television, and conference speakers proclaim this theme. The statement implies that people who abuse their children were physically abused during their own childhood. The evidence, however, is not so clear-cut as these public pronouncements would suggest. As Jayaratne (1977) concludes, and an independent reading of the primary sources will confirm, it is "emotional deprivation," "rejection," and "excessive demands" that generally characterize the childhood of adults who abuse or neglect their children. A close reading of the evidence bearing on the intergenerational transmission principle confirms this conclusion. A statement from the principal "classic" in this field (Steele and Pollack, 1968, p. 100) should suffice for the present purpose: "Without exception in our study group of abusing parents there is a history of having been raised in the same style which they have recreated in the pattern of rearing their own children. Several had experienced severe abuse in the form of physical beatings from either mother or father; a few reported 'never having had a hand laid on them.' All had experienced, however, a sense of intensive, pervasive, continuous demand from their parents."

Although one may question the methodological adequacy of this study and other clinically derived studies, at least this summary focuses attention on the emotional dynamics of the situation. More recent sociologically derived evidence documents

that there is ample domestic violence in the experience of most
children (particularly between siblings) to "teach" it to those who
are inclined to learn and use it. The issue, then, is not simply one
of determining who experiences some form of domestic violence.
The evidence says that most of us do (or did). The task is to
understand the circumstances in which parental behavior is
damaging. Emotional maltreatment—abuse, neglect, or "deprivation"—is at the heart of the matter. Mulford (1958, p. 21) was on
target when he focused on "the parents' failure to encourage the
child's normal development by assurance of love and acceptance."
But what does this mean on a day-to-day basis in parent-child
relations? How is it "operationally defined" as a basis for modern
protective services? This general statement lacks social context, and
this deficiency has been the stumbling block in our efforts. It gave
rise to this book.

What are the child's "rightful" claims on a parent or other
caregiver? In answering this question, we must, as always, employ
a mixture of culture and science, community standards, and
professional expertise. Briefly, we can establish that a child has a
rightful claim (1) to a responsive parent, one who recognizes and
responds positively to socially desirable accomplishments; and (2)
to a parent who does not inflict on the child the parent's own
needs at the expense of the child's. Thus, an emotionally abusive
parent may reject the infant's smiling, the toddler's exploration,
the school child's efforts to make friends, and the adolescent's privacy and autonomy. Such a parent demands that the infant gratify the parent's needs ahead of the child's, that the child take care
of the parent, and that the adolescent comply with the parent's
wishes in all matters (including, perhaps, sexual relations).

In our search for ways to identify and cope with child abuse
and neglect, we have sought to develop specific behavioral and
physical indicators. Though understandable, these efforts have
diverted us from a more comprehensive and valid understanding of
the problem. Emotional maltreatment really is the issue (in almost
all cases). This recognition should lead to a more mature response
to the problem of child abuse and neglect. It may shed new light
on studies documenting the consequences of abuse and neglect.
These studies have thus far shown few significant adverse

consequences associated with *specific* instances of abuse. Rather, they show that certain types of family environments (environments characterized by emotional maltreatment) produce damaged human beings. Thus, child maltreatment is an issue that bridges child welfare and mental health. As noted earlier, if there is a unifying factor in the background of adults who mistreat children, it is pervasive emotional deprivation, the destruction of ego and self-esteem, which leads to a variety of emotional deficits, among them inadequate empathy. Emotional maltreatment conveys developmentally dangerous messages of trauma, of betrayal, of powerlessness, of stigmatization. It is an assault on the psyche, an attack on the self. When it comes to defining emotional maltreatment, the message becomes the meaning.

This brings us to the end of our analysis. As we argued in Chapter One, the concept of child maltreatment does not exist "objectively." Rather, it is an intrinsically social concept, a creature of social conscience and developmental psychology. It depends for its very existence on the efforts of child advocates to find a place for the rights of children in the social realities of community life.

In a sense, then, efforts to conceptualize, define, and operationalize child maltreatment are intrinsically a "movement," a movement with political and ideological dimensions. Child advocacy and child protection are conceptually as well as operationally linked. The very definition of child maltreatment arises out of social change. It *is* social change. This view underlies our approach to psychological maltreatment.

In the 1960s, the physician C. Henry Kempe created the social space for a medicalized approach to child maltreatment emphasizing physical abuse (via the "battered child syndrome"). In the 1970s a feminist-inspired movement extended the rights of children to the sexual domain (through capturing the issue of "child sexual abuse"). Our hope in this book, of course, is that the 1980s and 1990s will be a time for carving out a cultural and political space for "psychological maltreatment" as a concept linked to action on behalf of children.

No long-winded summary is in order here. We have sought to outline the meaning and practical implications of our conception of psychological maltreatment. Rejecting, terrorizing, ignoring, isolating, and corrupting can now come into the language of public and professional discourse. This is essential if efforts to deal with psychological maltreatment are to become an active force in the lives of children. That they will do so is our hope.

Resource A
Assessment Instruments

1. Personality Assessments Used by Psychologists

Following is a brief discussion of some personality assessment techniques that only licensed psychologists are allowed to administer. Their interpretation can be very helpful in assessing psychological maltreatment of children, and we therefore recommend their use, if possible. More detailed descriptions of them can be found in Deinhardt (1983), Megargee (1966), Murstein (1965), and Rabin (1968).

Minnesota Multiphasic Personality Inventory (MMPI). This inventory attempts to measure clinical-psychological characteristics or pathologies, such as hypochondria, depression, conversion hysteria, psychopathy, masculinity/femininity, paranoia, schizophrenia, and social introversion. It has been found to distinguish normal groups from abnormal ones and to differentiate people with emotional and adjustment problems from others.

Rorschach. This instrument (which asks a subject to interpret inkblots) aids in understanding the subject's perceptions of external reality, social interaction patterns, and attitudes toward impulse life. More specifically, it gives information about (1) psychogram—one's access to inner and outer resources in perceiving reality; (2) inner resources and impulse life—the balance between impulse and value system, ability to deal with frustrations, empathic capabilities, and ability to use imagination; (3) organization of affectional needs—one's need for affection, affiliation, and belongingness, the way one handles needs for security, extent of maturity, and lack of control; (4) emotional reactivity to the environment—one's reactions to emotional challenges emerging from the environment and from interpersonal relationships; (5) intellectual manner of approach—the extent and nature of one's efforts to make sense of experiences, to seek relations and to make generalizations, one's need for achievement, and one's level of aspiration.

Thematic Apperception Test. This test attempts to stimulate literary creativity by presenting a picture that suggests some sort of interpersonal situation. It thus seeks to evoke fantasies that will reveal one's covert, or unconscious, complexes. The assumption is that the way one interprets an ambiguous social situation will expose one's personality. Thus, clinical understanding is gained from the subject's response to a stimulus, as well as from that subject's behavior while taking the test.

Draw-a-Person Test. In this test one is asked to draw an unspecified person, a family member, a friend, oneself, or a group of people. The figure(s) in the drawing can be portrayed as doing something or moving but can also be portrayed just as figures. The drawings help to reveal the internal organization of one's personality, as well as any abnormal patterns. They are interpreted according to the relationships among the figures in them, the details that characterize each figure, the story the person tells about the drawing, and the person's behavior while drawing.

2. Instruments for Assessing Psychological Maltreatment

The following instruments, which we described in Chapter Four, can be used by practitioners for assessing psychological maltreatment of children. We list here the sources through which those instruments can be obtained (for complete publication information, see the reference list in this volume).

Family Environment Scale. Appears in the Appendix of Moos (1975) and is described in detail in Moos and Moos (1976). Can be obtained from:

Rudolf H. Moos
Department of Psychiatry
Stanford University
Stanford, CA 94305

Family Adaptability and Cohesion Evaluation Scale.
Described in detail in Olson, Russell, and Sprenkle (1979, 1983).
Can be obtained from:

David H. Olson
Family Social Science
University of Minnesota
290 McNeal Hall
1985 Buford Avenue
St. Paul, MN 55108

Interparental Conflict and Influence Scales. Described in
Schwartz and Zuroff (1979).

Parental Acceptance-Rejection Questionnaire. Described in
Rohner (1980); Rohner and Rohner (1980). Can be obtained from:

Ronald P. Rohner, Director
Center for the Study of Parental Acceptance and Rejection
Box U-158, Room 323, Manchester Hall
University of Connecticut
Storrs, CT 06268

Children's Reports of Parental Behavior Inventory. A
sample of items from this inventory appears in Schaefer (1965a);
also described in Schaefer (1965b). Can be obtained from:

Earl S. Schaefer
Department of Maternal-Child Health
University of North Carolina
Chapel Hill, NC 27514

Bronfenbrenner's Parental Behavior Questionnaire. Described in Devereux, Bronfenbrenner, and Suci (1962) and in
Siegelman (1965). Can be obtained from:

Urie Bronfenbrenner
Department of Human Development and Family Studies
Martha Van Renssaleer Hall
Cornell University
Ithaca, NY 14853

Michigan Screening Profile of Parenting. Described in Helfer, Schneider, and Hoffmeister (1978) and in Schneider (1982). Can be obtained from:

Ray E. Helfer
Department of Human Development
Michigan State University
East Lansing, MI 48824

Maternal Characteristics Scale and Childhood Level of Living Scale. Appear in Polansky, Borgman, and De Saix (1972). Can be obtained from:

Norman A. Polansky
School of Social Work
University of Georgia
Athens, GA 30602

Adult-Adolescent Parenting Inventory. Can be obtained from:

Family Development Associates, Inc.
P.O. Box 94365
Schaumburg, IL 60194

Bayley Scales of Infant Development. Appear in Bayley (1969).

Tennessee Self-Concept Scale. Appears in Fitts (1965). Can be obtained from:

Counselor Recordings and Tests
Box 6184
Acklen Station
Nashville, TN 37212

State-Trait Anxiety Inventory. Appears in Spielberger (1971) and in Spielberger, Gorsuch, and Lushene (1970). Can be obtained from:

C. D. Spielberger
Department of Psychology
University of Southern Florida
4202 Flowler Avenue
Tampa, FL 33620

Personality Assessment Questionnaire. Appears in Rohner, Saavedra, and Granum (1978). Can be obtained from:

Ronald P. Rohner, Director
Center for the Study of Parental Acceptance and Rejection
Box U-158, Room 323, Manchester Hall
University of Connecticut
Storrs, CT 06268

Child Behavior Checklist. Described in Achenbach (1978) and in Achenbach and Edelbrock (1979). Can be obtained from:

T. M. Achenbach
University of Vermont
Burlington, VT 05405

Child Assessment Schedule. Appears in Hodges (1984) and is described in Hodges and others (1982a, 1982b). Can be obtained from:

Kay Kline Hodges
Department of Psychiatry
University of Missouri–Columbia
N 119 Medical Center
Columbia, MO 65212

3. Instruments for Assessing Maltreatment in Out-of-Home Care

The following is a list of sources where instruments for the assessment of maltreatment in out-of-home care can be obtained. These instruments are discussed in Chapter Nine. Other relevant instruments, mentioned in the section headed "Assessing Children's Responses and Worker-Child Relations" in Chapter Nine, appear in the preceding section of this Resource.

Work Environment Scale. Appears in Moos and Insel (1974). Can be obtained from:

Rudolf H. Moos
Department of Psychiatry
Stanford University
Stanford, CA 94305

Ward Atmosphere Scale. Appears in Moos (1974). Can be obtained from Rudolf H. Moos at above address.

Quality of Supervision. Appears in the Appendix of Munson (1983). Can be obtained from:

Carlton Munson
Professional Supervision Institute
1201 Bering Drive, #60
Houston, TX 77057

Burnout Questionnaire. Appears in the Appendix of Munson (1983). Can be obtained from C. Munson at the address above.

Resource B
Key Organizations
and Publications

The organizations listed here can provide information on child abuse/neglect—including, but not limited to, psychological maltreatment. (For resources covering programmed interventions, see the following items in the reference list: American Humane Association, 1980; Bavolek and Comstock, 1985; Eppsteiner, forthcoming; Fischoff, 1986; Goldstein, Keller, and Erne, 1985; Gordon, 1979/80; Payne, 1984; Wells, 1985.)

American Association for
  Protecting Children
Division of American Humane
  Association
P.O. Box 2788
Denver, CO 80201
(303) 695-0811

Child Welfare League of
  America
440 First Street, NW
Washington, DC 20013
(202) 638-CWLA

Clearinghouse on Child Abuse
  and Neglect Information
P.O. Box 1182
Washington, DC 20001
(301) 251-5157

Family Development Resources,
  Inc.
767 Second Avenue
Eau Claire, WI 54703
(715) 833-0904

Family Resource Coalition
230 North Michigan Avenue
  Suite 1625
Chicago, IL 60601
(312) 726-4750

Kidsrights
P.O. Box 851
Mount Dora, FL 32757
(904) 383-6200

Mt. Hope Family Center
685 Mt. Hope Avenue
Rochester, NY 14627
(716) 275-2991

National Committee for
  Prevention of Child Abuse
332 S. Michigan Avenue, Suite
  950
Chicago, IL 60604-4357
(312) 663-3520

National Council on Child
  Abuse and Family Violence
Washington Square
1050 Connecticut Ave., NW,
  Suite 300
Washington, DC 20036
(800) 222-2000

National Family Life
  Education Network
1700 Mission St., Suite 203
P.O. Box 8506
Santa Cruz, CA 95061-8506
(408) 429-9822

Parents Anonymous
National Office
22330 Hawthorne Boulevard
Suite 208
Torrance, CA 90503
(800) 421-0353

Parents United, Inc.
P.O. Box 952
San Jose, CA 95102
(408) 280-5055

Resource C
State Chapters of the
National Committee for
Prevention of Child Abuse (NCPCA)

Alabama

North Alabama Chapter,
  NCPCA
P.O. Box 119
Decatur, AL 35602
(202) 552-1816

Greater Alabama Chapter,
  NCPCA
United Way Building
P.O. Box 2638
Anniston, AL 36202
(205) 237-6097

Alaska

South Central Alaska Chapter,
  NCPCA
Center for Children and Parents
808 "E" St., Suite 200
Anchorage, AK 99501
(907) 276-4994

Fairbanks Chapter, NCPCA
Resource Center for Children
  and Parents
809 College Road
Fairbanks, AK 99701

California

California Chapter, NCPCA
1401 Third St., #13
Sacramento, CA 95814
(916) 448-9135

California Chapter, NCPCA
McLaren Hall
4024 N. Durfee Avenue
El Monte, CA 91732
(818) 575-4362

Colorado

Denver Chapter, NCPCA
Metropolitan Child Protection
  Council
1725 Gaylord Street
Denver, CO 80206
(303) 333-1946

Connecticut

Connecticut Chapter, NCPCA
60 Lorraine Street
Hartford, CT 06105
(203) 236-4868

Delaware

Delaware Chapter, NCPCA
124 "D" Senatorial Drive
  Greenville Pl.
Wilmington, DE 19807
(302) 654-1102

District of Columbia

D.C. Chapter, NCPCA
1690 36th Street, NW
Washington, DC 20007
(202) 965-1900

Florida

Florida Chapter, NCPCA
Florida Committee for
  Prevention of Child Abuse
P.O. Box 1352
Del Ray Beach, FL 33447-1352
(305) 278-8510

Georgia

Georgia Chapter, NCPCA
250 Georgia Ave., SE, Suite 203
Atlanta, GA 30312
(404) 688-0581

Hawaii

Hawaii Chapter, NCPCA
250 Hotel St., Room 300
Honolulu, HI 96813
(808) 524-5600, ext. 218

Idaho

Idaho Chapter, NCPCA
P.O. Box 1866
Coeur d'Alene, ID 83814
(208) 667-3461

Illinois/Iowa

Quad Cities Chapter, NCPCA
525 16th Street
Moline, IL 61265
(309) 764-7017

Indiana

Indiana Chapter, NCPCA
P.O. Box 1186
Lafayette, IN 47902
(317) 742-5046

Iowa

Iowa Chapter, NCPCA
3701½ Douglas Avenue
Des Moines, IA 50310
(515) 281-6327

Kansas

Kansas Chapter, NCPCA
435 S. Kansas, 2nd Floor
Topeka, KS 66603
(913) 354-7738

Kentucky

Kentucky Chapter, NCPCA
4109 Pecunnie Way
Louisville, KY 40218
(502) 491-3310

Louisiana

Southeastern Louisiana
    Chapter, NCPCA
1550 Second St., Apt. 7C
New Orleans, LA 70130
(504) 897-0532

Maine

York County Chapter, NCPCA
York County Child Abuse and
    Neglect Council, Inc.
121 Main Street
Biddeford, ME 04005
(207) 282-6191

Massachusetts

Greater Boston Chapter,
    NCPCA
Massachusetts Committee for
    Children and Youth
14 Beacon Street, #706
Boston, MA 02138
(617) 742-8555

Michigan

Michigan Chapter, NCPCA
116 W. Ottawa St., Suite 601
Lansing, MI 48933-1602
(517) 485-9113

Minnesota

Minnesota Chapter, NCPCA
123 E. Grant St., #1110
Minneapolis, MN 55403
(612) 872-7151

Mississippi

Greater Jackson Chapter,
    NCPCA
2906 N. State, Suite 401
Jackson, MS 39216
(601) 366-0025

Jones County Chapter, NCPCA
P.O. Box 726
Laurel, MS 39441
(601) 649-4060

Missouri

Missouri Chapter, NCPCA
847 S. Pickwick
Springfield, MO 65804
(417) 869-2693 (H)
(417) 836-5000 or 5880 (W)

Nebraska

Nebraska Chapter, NCPCA
6201 Pine Lake Road
Lincoln, NE 68516
(402) 471-7940

Nevada

Northern Nevada Chapter,
  NCPCA
P.O. Box 6274
Washoe County District
Health Department
Reno, NV 89513
(702) 785-4290

Southern Nevada Chapter,
  NCPCA
606 S. Ninth Street
Las Vegas, NV 89101
(702) 384-0713

New Hampshire

New Hampshire Chapter,
  NCPCA
P.O. Box 607
Concord, NH 03301
(603) 225-5441

New Jersey

New Jersey Chapter, NCPCA
17 Academy St., Suite 709
Newark, NJ 07102
(201) 643-3710

New York

New York Chapter, NCPCA
151 Chestnut Street
Albany, NY 12210
(518) 463-1896

North Carolina

North Carolina Chapter,
  NCPCA
321 Ashe Avenue
Raleigh, NC 27606
(919) 733-6895

Ohio

Central Ohio Chapter, NCPCA
League Against Child Abuse
360 S. Third Street
Columbus, OH 43215
(614) 464-1500

Oregon

Oregon Chapter, NCPCA
232-W N.E. Lincoln
Hillsboro, OR 97123
(503) 640-3446

Rhode Island

Rhode Island Chapter, NCPCA
160 S. Main Street
Woonsocket, RI 02895
(401) 766-0900

South Carolina

Midlands Chapter, NCPCA
1800 Main St., Suite 2C
Columbia, SC 29201
(803) 733-5430

Piedmont Chapter, NCPCA
411 Wembley Drive
Greenville, SC 29607
(803) 288-5629

South Dakota

Rapid City Chapter, NCPCA
Children Protection Council of
   Rapid City
P.O. Box 2507
Rapid City, SD 57707
(605) 348-7250 (W)
(605) 787-5620 (H)

Tennessee

Middle Tennessee Chapter,
   NCPCA
5701 Knob Road
Nashville, TN 37209
(615) 352-3010

Texas

El Paso Chapter, NCPCA
P.O. Box 13489
El Paso, TX 79912
(915) 779-7311

Houston Chapter, NCPCA
P.O. Box 1562
Houston, TX 77251
(713) 222-3141

Houston Chapter, NCPCA
12714 Skynoll Lane
Houston, TX 77082
(713) 497-5598

Laredo Chapter, NCPCA
P.O. Box 2579
Laredo, TX 78040
(512) 722-5174

South Plains Chapter, NCPCA
Texas Tech. Univ. Health
   Sciences Center
School of Medicine
Lubbock, TX 79403
(806) 743-2310

San Antonio Chapter, NCPCA
1101 W. Woodlawn
San Antonio, TX 78201
(512) 732-1051

Utah

Utah Chapter, NCPCA
P.O. Box 349
385 24th Street
Ogden, UT 84401
(801) 621-8270

Vermont

Chittendon County Chapter,
   NCPCA
Council for Children and
   Families
1110 Pine Street
Burlington, VT 05401
(802) 863-1327

Virginia

Virginia Chapter, NCPCA
205 W. Franklin Street
Richmond, VA 23220
(804) 780-3909

Washington

King County/Seattle Chapter,
  NCPCA
1211 E. Adler
Seattle, WA 98122
(206) 343-2590

Clark County Chapter, NCPCA
Office of the Attorney General
500 W. 8th Street, Suite 55
Vancouver, WA 98660
(206) 696-6471

West Virginia

Southern West Virginia
  Chapter, NCPCA
P.O. Box 2611
Charleston, WV 25329
(304) 344-5437

Wisconsin

Wisconsin Chapter, NCPCA
1045 E. Dayton St., Room 202D
Madison, WI 53703
(608) 256-3374

References

Aber, J. L., and Zigler, E. "Developmental Considerations in the Definition of Child Maltreatment." In R. Rizley and D. Cicchetti (eds.), *Developmental Perspectives on Child Maltreatment.* New Directions for Child Development, no. 11. San Francisco: Jossey-Bass, 1981.

Achenbach, T. M. "The Child Behavior Profiles. I: Boys Aged 6–11." *Journal of Consulting and Clinical Psychology,* 1978, *46,* 478–488.

Achenbach, T. M., and Edelbrock, C. S. "The Child Behavior Profiles. II: Boys Aged 12–16 and Girls Aged 6–11 and 12–16." *Journal of Consulting and Clinical Psychology,* 1979, *47,* 223–233.

Ackerman, N. W. *Treating the Troubled Family.* New York: Basic Books, 1966.

Agathonos, H. "Institutional Child Abuse in Greece: Some Preliminary Findings." *Child Abuse and Neglect,* 1983, *7* (1), 71–74.

Ahkisson, C. C., and others. "A Working Model for Mental Health Evaluation." *American Journal of Orthopsychiatry,* 1974, *44* (5), 741–753.

Ainsworth, M. D. S., and Bell, S. M. "Mother-Infant Interaction and the Development of Competence." In K. J. Connolly and J. Bruner (eds.), *The Growth of Competence.* Orlando, Fla.: Academic Press, 1974.

Ainsworth, M. D. S., Blehar, M. C., Waters, E., and Wall, S. *Patterns of Attachment.* Hillsdale, N.J.: Erlbaum, 1978.

Alexander, H., and Kempe, R. S. "The Role of Lay Therapist in

Long-Term Treatment." *Child Abuse and Neglect,* 1982, *6,* 329–334.

Alfaro, J. "Impediments to Mandated Reporting of Suspected Child Abuse and Neglect in New York City." Paper presented to the Seventh National Conference on Child Abuse and Neglect, Chicago, Nov. 1985.

Alinsky, S. D. *Rules for Radicals: A Pragmatic Primer for Realistic Radicals.* New York: Random House, 1972.

Alton, I. R. "Nutrition Services for Pregnant Adolescents in a Public High School." *Journal of the American Dietetic Association,* 1979, *74,* 667–669.

American Humane Association. *Helping in Child Protective Services: A Casework Handbook.* Denver: American Association for Protecting Children, American Humane Association, 1980.

Anderson, C. "A Community Health Nursing Role in Child Abuse/Neglect Intervention." *Child Abuse and Neglect,* 1980, *4,* 33–38.

Anderson, J. *Social Work Methods and Processes.* Belmont, Calif.: Wadsworth, 1981.

Arch, S. D. "Older Adults as Home Visitors Modeling Parenting for Troubled Families." *Child Welfare,* 1978, *57,* 601–605.

Austin, M. J., and others. *Evaluating Your Agency's Programs.* Beverly Hills, Calif.: Sage, 1983.

Balla, D. A., and Zigler, E. "Preinstitutional Social Deprivation, Responsiveness to Social Reinforcement, and IQ Change in Institutionalized Retarded Individuals: A 6 Year Follow-Up Study." *American Journal of Mental Deficiency,* 1975, *80,* 228–230.

Barrera, M., and Balls, P. "Assessing Social Support as a Prevention Resource: An Illustrative Study." *Prevention in Human Services,* 1983, *2* (4), 59–74.

Bateson, G. *Steps to an Ecology of Mind.* New York: Chandler, 1972.

Bavolek, S., and Comstock, C. *The Nurturing Program.* Eau Claire, Wis.: Family Development Resources, 1985.

Bavolek, S. J., Kline, D. F., McLaughlin, J. A., and Publicover, P. R. *The Development of the Adolescent Parenting Inventory (API): Identification of High Risk Adolescents Prior to Parent-*

hood. Logan: Department of Special Education, Utah State University, 1979.

Bayley, N. *Manual for the Bayley Scales of Infant Development.* New York: Psychological Corporation, 1969.

Bell, R. A., Sundel, M., Aponte, J. F., and Murrel, S. A. *Needs Assessment in Health and Human Services.* Louisville: Louisville National Conference, 1976.

Belsky, J. "Child Maltreatment: An Ecological Integration." *American Psychologist,* 1980, *35,* 320–335.

Belsky, J. "The Determinants of Parenting: A Process Model." *Child Development,* 1984, *55,* 83–96.

Belsky, J., Gilstrap, B., and Rovine, M. "Stability and Change in Mother-Infant and Father-Infant Interaction in a Family Setting: 1 to 3 to 9 Months." *Child Development,* 1984, *55,* 692–705.

Belsky, J., and Vondra, J. "Characteristics, Consequences, and Determinants of Parenting." In L. L'Abate (ed.), *Handbook of Family Psychology and Therapy.* Vol. 1. Homewood, Ill.: Dow-Jones-Irwin, 1985.

Belsky, J., and Vondra, J. "Child Maltreatment: Prevalence, Consequences, Causes and Interventions." In D. Crowell, I. Evans, and C. O. Donell (eds.), *Childhood Aggression and Violence: Sources of Influence, Prevention and Control.* New York: Plenum, forthcoming.

Biddle, W. W., and Biddle, L. J. *The Community Development Process: The Rediscovery of Local Initiative.* New York: Holt, Rinehart & Winston, 1965.

Bishop, E. R. "The Art of Home Visiting." In N. B. Ebeling and D. A. Hill (eds.), *Child Abuse and Neglect.* Littleton, Mass.: John Wright, 1983.

Blumer, H. *Symbolic Interactionism: Perspective and Method.* Englewood Cliffs, N.J.: Prentice-Hall, 1969.

Bolton, F. G., Laner, R. H., and Gai, D. S. "For Better or Worse? Foster Parents and Foster Children in an Officially Reported Child Maltreatment Population." *Children and Youth Services Review,* 1981, *3,* 37–53.

Boszormenyi-Nagy, I., and Framo, J. L. (eds.). *Intensive Family Therapy.* New York: Harper & Row, 1965.

Boszormenyi-Nagy, I., and Spark, G. *Invisible Loyalties: Reciproc-*

ity in Intergenerational Family Therapy. New York: Harper & Row, 1973.

Bowlby, J. *Attachment and Loss.* Vol. 2: *Separation: Anxiety and Anger.* New York: Basic Books, 1973.

Brager, G., and Specht, H. *Community Organizing.* New York: Columbia University Press, 1973.

Brazelton, T. B. "Joint Regulation of Neonate-Parent Behavior." In E. Z. Tronick (ed.), *Social Interchange in Infancy: Affect, Cognition, and Communication.* Baltimore: University Park Press, 1982.

Breton, M. "Resocialization of Abusive Parents." *Social Work,* 1981, *26* (2), 119–122.

Broderick, C. B., and Smith, J. "The General Systems Approach to the Family." In W. Burr, R. Hill, F. Nye, and I. Reiss (eds.), *Contemporary Theories About the Family.* Vol. 2. New York: Free Press, 1979.

Bronfenbrenner, U. *The Ecology of Human Development: Experiments by Nature and Design.* Cambridge, Mass.: Harvard University Press, 1979.

Bronfenbrenner, U., Moen, P., and Garbarino, J. "Families and Communities." In R. Parke (ed.), *Review of Child Development Research.* Vol. 7. Chicago: University of Chicago Press, 1984.

Bronson, W. "Early Antecedents of Emotional Expressiveness and Reactivity Control." *Child Development,* 1966, *37,* 793–810.

Brown, S. E. "Social Class, Child Maltreatment and Delinquent Behavior." *Criminology,* 1984, *22,* 259–278.

Brown, S. E., Whitehead, K. R., and Braswell, M. C. "Child Maltreatment: An Empirical Examination of Selected Conventional Hypotheses." *Youth and Society,* 1981, *13,* 77–90.

Bullard, D. M., Glaser, H. H., Hagarty, M. C., and Pivchik, E. C. "Failure to Thrive in the 'Neglected' Child." *American Journal of Orthopsychiatry,* 1967, *37* (1), 680–690.

Burgdorff, K. *Recognition and Reporting of Child Maltreatment: Findings from the National Study of the Incidence and Severity of Child Abuse and Neglect.* Washington, D.C.: National Center on Child Abuse and Neglect, 1980.

Burgess, R. L., and Richardson, R. A. "Coercive Interpersonal Contingencies as a Determinant of Child Abuse: Implications for Treatment and Prevention." In R. F. Dangel and R. A. Polster (eds.), *Behavioral Parent Training: Issues in Research and Practice.* New York: Guilford Publications, 1984.

Caffo, E., Guaraldi, G. P., Magnani, G., and Tassi, R. "Prevention of Child Abuse and Neglect Through Early Diagnosis of Disturbances in the Mother-Child Relationship in Italy." *Child Abuse and Neglect,* 1982, *6* (4), 453–463.

Campbell-Smith, M. "The School: Liberator or Censurer?" *Child Abuse and Neglect,* 1983, *7* (1), 329–337.

Cataldo, C. Z. *Infant and Toddlers Programs: A Guide to Very Early Childhood Education.* Reading, Mass.: Addison-Wesley, 1983.

Chase, N. F. *A Child Is Being Beaten: Violence Against Children, an American Tragedy.* New York: Holt, Rinehart and Winston, 1975.

Cohen, S., and McKay, G. "Social Support, Stress, and the Buffering Hypothesis: An Empirical Review." In A. Baum, J. E. Singer, and S. E. Taylor (eds.), *Handbook of Psychology and Health.* Vol. 4. Hillsdale, N.J.: Erlbaum, 1984.

Commonwealth of Pennsylvania, Department of Public Welfare, Child Protective Services. *Social Services Manual,* Section 2-23-41. Hillsdale, N.J.: Erlbaum, 1976.

Coopersmith, S. *The Antecedents of Self-Esteem.* New York: W. H. Freeman, 1967.

Copans, S., and others. "The Stress of Treating Child Abuse." *Children Today,* 1979, *8* (1), 22–27.

Corson, J. *Child Abuse and Neglect: The Problem and Its Management.* Washington, D.C.: U.S. Department of Education, 1975.

Corson, J. "A Survey of the States' Statutes: Do They Include 'Emotional Abuse' in Their Definitions of Child Abuse and/or Neglect?" Paper presented at International Conference on the Psychological Abuse of Children and Youth, Indianapolis, 1983.

Cox, F. M., Erlich, J. L., Rothman, J., and Tropman, J. E. (eds.). *Strategies of Community Organization: A Book of Readings.* (3rd ed.) Itasca, Ill.: Peacock, 1979.

Dawson, P., Robinson, J., and Johnson, C. "Informal Social Support as an Intervention, in Zero to Three." *Bulletin of the National Center for Clinical Infant Programs*, 1982, *3* (2), 3–7.

Dean, D. "Emotional Abuse of Children." *Children Today*, 1979, *8* (4), 18–20.

Deci, E. L. *Intrinsic Motivation*. New York: Plenum, 1975.

DeCourey, P., and DeCourey, J. *A Silent Tragedy*. Sherman Oaks, Calif.: Alfred Publishing, 1973.

Deinhardt, C. L. *Personality Assessment and Psychological Interpretation*. Springfield, Ill.: Thomas, 1983.

Densen-Gerber, J., and Hutchinson, S. F. "Sexual and Commercial Exploitation of Children: Legislative Responses and Treatment Challenges." *Child Abuse and Neglect*, 1979, *3*, 61–66.

Devereux, E. C., Bronfenbrenner, U., and Suci, G. J. "Patterns of Parent Behavior in the U.S.A. and the Federal Republic of Germany: A Cross National Comparison." *International Social Science Journal*, 1962, *14*, 488–506.

Dougherty, N. "The Holding Environment: Breaking the Cycle of Abuse." *Social Casework*, 1983, *64* (5), 283–290.

Drotman, P. D., and Goldstein, M. S. "Viewpoint: Institutions Are Abusive." *Human Ecology Forum*, 1977, *8* (1), 2–3.

Durkin, R. "Institutional Child Abuse from a Family Systems Perspective: A Working Paper." *Child and Youth Services*, 1982a, *4* (1–2), 15–22.

Durkin, R. "No One Will Thank You: First Thoughts on Reporting Institutional Abuse." *Child and Youth Services*, 1982b, *4* (1–2), 109–113.

Egeland, B., and Erickson, M. "Deprivation of Attachment." In M. Brassard, R. Germain, and S. Hart (eds.), *The Psychological Maltreatment of Children and Youth*. Elmsford, N.Y.: Pergamon Press, 1986.

Egeland, B., Sroufe, A., and Erickson, M. "The Developmental Consequence of Different Patterns of Maltreatment." *Child Abuse and Neglect*, 1983, *7*, 459–469.

Elder, G. H. *Children of the Great Depression*. Chicago: University of Chicago Press, 1974.

Elmer, E. *Children in Jeopardy: A Study of Abused Minors and*

Their Families. Pittsburgh: University of Pittsburgh Press, 1967.

Emery, R. E. "Interparental Conflict and the Children of Discord and Divorce." *Psychological Bulletin,* 1982, *92* (2), 310–330.

Eppsteiner, F. *Simplified Parent Training.* Rochester, N.Y.: Mt. Hope Family Center, forthcoming.

Erikson, E. *Childhood and Society.* New York: Norton, 1963.

Eron, L. D. "Relationship of TV Viewing Habits and Aggressive Behavior in Children." *Journal of Abnormal and Social Psychology,* 1963, *64,* 193–196.

Etzioni, A. *Complex Organizations: A Sociological Reader.* New York: Holt, Rinehart & Winston, 1961.

Etzioni, A. *A Comparative Analysis of Complex Organizations: On Power, Involvement, and Their Correlates.* (2nd ed.) New York: Free Press, 1975.

Faller, K. C. "Resources for Intervention." In K. C. Faller (ed.), *Social Work with Abused and Neglected Children.* New York: Free Press, 1981.

Fine, M. J. "The Parent Education Movement: An Introduction." In M. J. Fine (ed.), *Handbook on Parent Education.* New York: Academic Press, 1980.

Finkelhor, D. *Sexually Victimized Children.* New York: Free Press, 1979.

Finkelhor, D. *Child Sexual Abuse.* New York: Free Press, 1984.

Fischoff, A. *Birth to Three: A Self-Help Network for New Parents.* Eugene, Ore.: Castalia Publishing, Parent Education Division, 1986.

Fitts, W. H. *Manual: Tennessee Self-Concept Scale.* Nashville: Counselor Recording and Tests, 1965.

Fontana, V. J. *Somewhere a Child is Crying: Maltreatment— Causes and Prevention.* New York: Macmillan, 1973.

Fortin, P. J., and Reed, S. R. "Diagnosing and Responding to Emotional Abuse Within the Helping System." *Child Abuse and Neglect,* 1984, *8* (1), 117–119.

Fraiberg, S. *Clinical Studies in Infant Mental Health.* New York: Basic Books, 1980.

Freudenberger, H. J. "Burnout: Occupational Hazard of the Child Care Worker." *Child Care Quarterly,* 1977, *6,* 90–99.

Fried, S., and Holt, P. "Parent Education: One Strategy for the Prevention of Child Abuse." In M. J. Fine (ed.), *Handbook on Parent Education.* Orlando, Fla.: Academic Press, 1980.

Friedman, D. H., and Friedman, S. "Day Care as a Setting for Interventions in Family Systems." *Social Casework,* 1982, *63* (5), 291-295.

Friedman, D., Sale, J., and Weinstein, U. *Child Care and the Family.* Chicago: National Committee for Prevention of Child Abuse, 1984.

Friedman, R. M. *Therapeutic Foster Homes in Florida: A Mid-1982 Status Report.* Tampa: Florida Mental Health Institute, University of South Florida, 1983.

Furrh, P. E. "Emancipation: The Supervised Apartment Living Approach." *Child Welfare,* 1983, *61* (1), 54-61.

Gaines, R., Sandgrund, A., Green, A. H., and Power, E. "Etiological Factors in Child Maltreatment: A Multivariate Study of Abusing, Neglecting and Normal Mothers." *Journal of Abnormal Psychology,* 1978, *87,* 531-540.

Gamble, T., and Zigler, E. "The Effects of Infant Day-Care." *The Network,* 1985, *6* (4), 4ff.

Garbarino, J. "A Preliminary Study of Some Ecological Correlates of Child Abuse: The Impact of Socioeconomic Stress on Mothers." *Child Development,* 1976, *47,* 178-185.

Garbarino, J. "Latchkey Children." *Vital Issues,* 1980, *30* (3), 1-4.

Garbarino, J. "Child Welfare and the Economic Crisis." *Child Welfare,* 1984, *63* (1), 3-15.

Garbarino, J. "How Do Children Respond to Sexual Abuse Prevention? A Preliminary Study of the Spiderman Comic Book." Unpublished manuscript, 1985.

Garbarino, J., and Associates. *Children and Families in the Social Environment.* Hawthorne, N.Y.: Aldine, 1982.

Garbarino, J., and Associates. *Adolescent Development: An Ecological Perspective.* Westerville, Ohio: Merrill, 1985.

Garbarino, J., and Crouter, A. C. "Defining the Community Context of Parent-Child Relations." *Child Development,* 1978, *49,* 604-616.

Garbarino, J., and Ebata, A. "On the Significance of Ethnic and

Cultural Differences in Child Maltreatment." *Journal of Marriage and the Family,* 1983, *45,* 773-783.

Garbarino, J., and Gilliam, G. *Understanding Abusive Families.* Lexington, Mass.: Lexington Books, 1980.

Garbarino, J., Schellenbach, C., Sebes, J. and Associates. *Troubled Youth, Troubled Families.* Hawthorne, N.Y.: Aldine, 1986.

Garbarino, J., and Sherman, D. "High-Risk Neighborhoods and High-Risk Families: The Human Ecology of Child Maltreatment." *Child Development,* 1980, *51,* 188-198.

Garbarino, J., and Vondra, J. "Psychological Maltreatment: Issues and Perspectives." In M. Brassard, R. Germain, and S. Hart (eds.), *The Psychological Maltreatment of Children and Youth.* Elmsford, N.Y.: Pergamon Press, 1986.

Gardner, L. I. "Deprivation Dwarfism." *Scientific American,* 1972, *227* (1), 76-82.

Garmezy, N. "Resilience to the Development of Psychological Disorders." Colloquium presented at Pennsylvania State University, April 1983.

Germain, C. "Ecology and Social Work." In C. Germain (ed.), *Social Work Practice: People and Environments.* New York: Columbia University Press, 1979.

Gil, D. G. *Violence Against Children: Physical Child Abuse in the United States.* Cambridge, Mass.: Harvard University Press, 1970.

Gil, D. G. "Unraveling Child Abuse." *American Journal of Orthopsychiatry,* 1975, *45* (3), 346-356.

Gil, D. G. "Child Abuse: Levels of Manifestations, Causal Dimensions, and Primary Prevention." *Victimology,* 1977, *2* (2), 186-194.

Gil, E. "Institutional Abuse of Children in Out-of-Home Care." *Child and Youth Services,* 1982, *4* (1-2), 7-13.

Gil, E., and Baxter, K. "Abuse of Children in Institutions." *Child Abuse and Neglect,* 1979, *3* (3-4), 693-698.

Glampson, A., Scott, T., and Thomas, D. N. *A Guide to the Assessment of Community Needs and Resources.* London: National Institute for Social Work, 1977.

Goffman, E. *The Presentation of Self in Everyday Life.* New York: Doubleday, 1959.

Goldstein, A. P., Keller, H., and Erne, D. *Changing the Abusive Parent.* Champaigne, Ill.: Research Press, 1985.

Goldstein, J., Freud, A., and Solnit, A. J. *Beyond the Best Interests of the Child.* New York: Free Press, 1973.

Goldstein, J., Freud, A., and Solnit, A. J. *Before the Best Interests of the Child.* New York: Free Press, 1979.

Gordon, M. "Child Maltreatment: An Overview of Current Approaches." *Journal of Family Law,* 1979/80, *18,* 115–145.

Gottlieb, B. H. "Preventive Interventions Involving Social Networks and Social Support." In B. H. Gottlieb (ed.), *Social Network and Social Support.* Beverly Hills, Calif.: Sage, 1981.

Gray, J., Cutler, C., Dean, J., and Kempe, C. H. "Prediction and Prevention of Child Abuse and Neglect." *Journal of Social Issues,* 1979, *35,* 127–139.

Greene, B. L. (ed.). *The Psychotherapies of Marital Disharmony.* New York: Free Press, 1965.

Grosser, C. F. *New Directions in Community Organization: From Enabling to Advocacy.* New York: Praeger, 1976.

Guerney, L. "Filial Therapy Program." In D. L. Olson (ed.), *Treating Relationships.* Lake Mills, Iowa: Graphic Publishing, 1976.

Guerney, L. "Introduction to Filial Therapy: Training Parents as Therapists." In P. Z. Keller and L. G. Ritt (eds.), *Innovations in Clinical Practice: A Sourcebook.* Vol. 3. Sarasota, Fla.: Professional Resource Exchange, 1983.

Gumaer, J. *Counseling and Therapy for Children.* New York: Free Press, 1984.

Gurman, A. S. "Contemporary Marital Therapies: A Critique and Comparative Analysis of Psychoanalytic, Behavioral and Systems Theory Approaches." In T. J. Paolino and B. S. McGrady (eds.), *Marriage and Marital Therapy.* New York: Brunner/Mazel, 1978.

Haley, J. *Problem-Solving Therapy: New Strategies for Effective Family Therapy.* San Francisco: Jossey-Bass, 1976.

Hargreaves, W. A., Attkisson, C. C., Siegel, L. M., and McIntyre, M. H. *Needs Assessment and Planning.* San Francisco: National Institute of Mental Health, 1974.

Hart, S. "Mental Health Neglect." Position paper. Office for Study of the Psychological Rights of the Child, Indiana University, Indianapolis, 1985.

Harter, S., and Zigler, E. "The Assessment of Effectance Motivation in Normal and Retarded Children." *Developmental Psychology*, 1974, *10*, 169–180.

Haynes, C. F., Cutler, C., Gray, J., and Kempe, R. S. "Hospitalized Cases of Nonorganic Failure to Thrive: The Scope of the Problem and Short-Term Lay Health Visitor Intervention." *Child Abuse and Neglect*, 1984, *8*, 229–242.

Helfer, R. E., and Kempe, C. H. (eds.). *The Battered Child.* (2nd ed.) Chicago: University of Chicago Press, 1968.

Helfer, R. E., and Kempe, C. H. (eds.). *The Battered Child.* (3rd ed.) Chicago: University of Chicago Press, 1980.

Helfer, R. E., Schneider, C. J., and Hoffmeister, J. K. *Report on Research Using the Michigan Screening Profile of Parenting (MSPP): A 12-Year Study to Develop and Test a Predictive Questionnaire.* Washington, D.C.: Office of Child Development, Department of Education, 1978.

Hermalin, J. A., and Weirich, T. W. "Prevention Research in Field Settings: A Guide for Practitioners." *Prevention in Human Services*, 1983, *2* (3), 31–48.

Herrenkohl, R. C., and Herrenkohl, E. C. "Some Antecedents and Developmental Consequences of Child Maltreatment." In R. Rizley and D. Cicchetti (eds.), *Developmental Perspectives on Child Maltreatment.* New Directions for Child Development, no. 11. San Francisco: Jossey-Bass, 1981.

Herrenkohl, R. C., Herrenkohl, E. C., and Egolf, B. P. "Circumstances Surrounding the Occurrence of Child Maltreatment." *Journal of Consulting and Clinical Psychology*, 1983, *51*, 424–431.

Hetherington, E. M. "Children and Divorce." In R. Henderson (ed.), *Parent-Child Interaction: Theory, Research, and Prospects.* Orlando, Fla.: Academic Press, 1981.

Hetherington, E. M. "Stress and Coping in Children and Families." In A.-B. Doyle, D. Gold, and D. Moskowitz (eds.), *Children in Families Under Stress.* New Directions for Child Development, no. 24. San Francisco: Jossey-Bass, 1984.

Hetherington, E. M., Cox, M., and Cox, R. "The Aftermath of Divorce." In J. Stevens and M. Mathews (eds.), *Mother-Child, Father-Child Relationships*. Washington, D.C.: National Association for the Education of Young Children, 1977.

Hirschbach, E. "Children Beyond Reach?" *Child and Youth Services*, 1982, *4* (1-2), 99–107.

Hodges, K. K. "The Child Assessment Schedule." Unpublished manuscript, University of Missouri, 1984.

Hodges, K. K., and others. "The Child Assessment Schedule (CAS) Diagnostic Interview: A Report on Reliability and Validity." *Journal of American Academy of Child Psychiatry*, 1982a, *21*, 468–473.

Hodges, K. K., and others. "The Development of a Child Assessment Schedule for Research and Clinical Use." *Journal of Abnormal Child Psychology*, 1982b, *10*, 173–189.

Hops, H. "Social-Skills Training for Socially Withdrawn/Isolate Children." In P. Karoly and J. J. Stefren (eds.), *Improving Children's Competence: Advances in Child Behavioral Analysis and Therapy*. Vol. 1. Lexington, Mass.: Lexington Books, 1982.

Hosie, K. "Violence in Community Home Schools." *Child Abuse and Neglect*, 1979, *3* (1), 81–87.

Howze, D. C., and Kotch, J. B. "Disentangling Life Events, Stress, and Social Support: Implications for the Primary Prevention of Child Abuse and Neglect." *Child Abuse and Neglect*, 1984, *8* (4), 401–409.

Hyman, I. *Psychological Abuse in the Schools*. Philadelphia: National Center for the Study of Corporal Punishment and Alternatives in the Schools, 1985.

Jacoby, S. "Emotional Child Abuse: The Invisible Plague." *Reader's Digest*, Feb. 1985, pp. 86–90.

Jayaratne, S. "Child Abusers as Parents and Children: A Review." *Social Work*, 1977, *22*, 5–9.

Jenewicz, W. J. "A Protective Posture Toward Emotional Neglect and Abuse." *Child Welfare*, 1983, *62*, 243–252.

Justice, B., and Justice, R. *The Abusing Family*. New York: Human Sciences Press, 1976.

Kadushin, A. *Supervision in Social Work*. New York: Columbia University Press, 1976.

Kadushin, A. *Child Welfare Services*. (3rd ed.) New York: Macmillan, 1980.

Kadushin, A., and Martin, J. A. *Child Abuse: An Interactional Event*. New York: Columbia University Press, 1981.

Kahn, A. J. *Theory and Practice of Social Planning*. New York: Russell Sage Foundation, 1969.

Kantor, D., and Lehr, W. *Inside the Family: Toward a Theory of Family Process*. San Francisco: Jossey-Bass, 1975.

Kaus, C. R., and Garbarino, J. "Sexuality and Intimacy in Adolescence." In J. Garbarino (ed.), *Adolescent Development: An Ecological Perspective*. Westerville, Ohio: Merrill, 1985.

Kaye, K. *The Mental and Social Life of Babies: How Parents Create Persons*. Chicago: University of Chicago Press, 1982.

Kempe, C. H. "Approaches to Preventing Child Abuse." *American Journal of Diseases of Children*, 1976, *130*, 941–947.

Kempe, C. H. "Prediction and Prevention." In V. J. Fontana (ed.), *Child Abuse: The Developing Child*. London: Openbooks Original, 1978.

Kempe, C. H., and Helfer, R. E. *The Battered Child*. (3rd ed.) Chicago: University of Chicago Press, 1980.

Kinney, J. M., Madsen, B., Fleming, T., and Haapala, D. A. "Homebuilders: Keeping Families Together." *Journal of Consulting and Clinical Psychology*, 1977, *45* (4), 667–673.

Knoff, H. (ed.). *The Psychological Assessment of Child and Adolescent Personality*. New York: Guilford Publications, 1986.

Krause, K. "Authoritarianism, Dogmatism, and Coercion in Child Care Institutions: A Study of Staff Attitudes." *Child Welfare*, 1974, *53* (1), 23–30.

Krugman, R. D., and Krugman, M. K. "Emotional Abuse in the Classroom." *American Journal of Diseases of Children*, 1984, *138*, 284–286.

Kunkel, B. E. "The Alienation Response of Children Abused in Out-of-Home Placement." *Child Abuse and Neglect*, 1983, *7* (4), 479–484.

Lally, J. R. "Three Views of Child Neglect: Expanding Visions of Preventive Intervention." *Child Abuse and Neglect*, 1984, *8*, 243–254.

Lally, J., and Honig, A. S. "Education of Infants and Toddlers from Low-Income and Low-Education Background: Support for the Family's Role and Identity." In B. Z. Friedlander, C. M. Sterritt, and G. E. Kirk (eds.), *Exceptional Infant*. Vol. 3. New York: Brunner/Mazel, 1975.

Lemke, S., and Moos, R. H. "The Supra-Personal Environment of Sheltered Care Settings." *Journal of Gerontology*, 1981, *36*, 233–243.

Liberman, R. P. "Behavioral Approaches to Family and Couple Therapy." *American Journal of Orthopsychiatry*, 1970, *40*, 106–118.

Lieber, L. L., and Baker, J. M. "Parents Anonymous—Self-Help Treatment for Child Abusing Parents: A Review and an Evaluation." *Child Abuse and Neglect*, 1977, *1* (1), 133–148.

Light, R. "Abused and Neglected Children in America: A Study of Alternative Policies." *Harvard Educational Review*, 1973, *43*, 556–598.

Lonnborg, B., Fischbach, M., and Bickerstaff, M. J. *Youth Helping Youth: A Directed Group Experience for Abused Adolescents*. Boys Town, Neb.: Boys Town Center, 1981.

Lourie, I., and Stefano, L. "On Defining Emotional Abuse." In *Proceedings of the Second Annual National Conference on Child Abuse and Neglect*. Washington, D.C.: U.S. Government Printing Office, 1978.

McCandless, B. R. *Children: Behavior and Development*. (2nd ed.) New York: Holt, Rinehart & Winston, 1967.

MacCarthy, D. "Recognition of Signs of Emotional Deprivation: A Form of Child Abuse." *Child Abuse and Neglect*, 1979, *3*, 423–428.

McCoy, R., and Koocher, G. P. "Needed: A Public Policy for Psychotropic Drug Use with Children." In G. P. Koocher (ed.), *Children's Rights and the Mental Health Professions*. New York: Wiley, 1976.

McDonnell, P., and Associates. *Children at Risk: Decision Criteria for Removal and/or Return Home*. Chapel Hill, N.C., and Chicago: National Child Welfare Leadership Center and Taylor Institute, 1985.

McKnew, D. H., and others. "Offspring of Patients with Affective Disorders." *British Journal of Psychiatry*, 1979, *134*, 148–152.

McSweeny, A. J., Fremouw, W. J., and Hawkins, R. P. (eds.). *Practical Program Evaluation in Youth Treatment*. Springfield, Ill.: Thomas, 1982.

Maddus, G. F., Scriven, M., and Stufflebeam, D. L. (eds.). *Evaluation Models: Viewpoints on Educational and Human Services Evaluation*. Boston: Kluwer-Nijhoff, 1983.

Maluccio, A. N. *Promoting Competence in Clients: A New/Old Approach to Social Work Practice*. New York: Free Press, 1981.

Manis, J. G., and Meltzer, B. N. *Symbolic Interaction: A Reader in Social Psychology*. (3rd ed.) Newton, Mass.: Allyn & Bacon, 1978.

Maslach, C. "Burned Out." *Human Behavior*, 1976, *5*, 16–22.

Maslach, C., and Jackson, S. E. "The Measurement of Experienced Burnout." *Journal of Occupational Behavior*, 1981, *2*, 99–113.

Mauzerall, H. A. "Emancipation from Foster Care: The Independent Living Project." *Child Welfare*, 1983, *61* (1), 46–53.

Mayhanks, S., and Bryce, M. *Home-Based Services for Children and Families*. Springfield, Ill.: Thomas, 1979.

Mayhall, P. D., and Norgard, K. E. *Child Abuse and Neglect: Sharing Responsibility*. New York: Wiley, 1983.

Megargee, E. L. (ed.). *Research in Clinical Assessment*. New York: Harper & Row, 1966.

Meier, R., Guttmann, E., and Eisikovitz, Z. "Measuring Ecology in Social Work Supervision: The Relationship Between Work and Treatment Environments and the Quality of Supervision in Israeli Public Welfare Agencies." *Journal of Sociology and Social Welfare*, 1984, *11* (2), 327–365.

Mercer, M. "Closing the Barn Door: The Prevention of Institutional Abuse Through Standards." *Child and Youth Services*, 1982, *4* (1–2), 127–132.

Miller, J. G. "Some Thoughts on Reform." Paper presented at a study group on "Rethinking Child Welfare: International Perspectives," Hubert H. Humphrey Institute of Public Affairs, University of Minnesota, Spring Hill, 1985.

Minuchin, S. *Families and Family Therapy*. Cambridge, Mass.: Harvard University Press, 1974.

Moos, R. H. *Evaluating Treatment Environments: A Social Ecology Approach.* New York: Wiley, 1974.

Moos, R. H. *Evaluating Correctional and Community Settings.* New York: Wiley, 1975.

Moos, R. H., and Insel, P. *Work Environment Scale: Preliminary Manual.* Palo Alto, Calif.: Consulting Psychologists Press, 1974.

Moos, R. H., and Moos, B. S. "A Typology of Family Social Environments." *Family Process,* 1976, *15,* 357–371.

Moos, R. H., and Otto, J. "The Community-Oriented Programs Environmental Scale: A Methodology for the Facilitation and Evaluation of Social Change." *Community Mental Health Journal,* 1972, *8,* 28–37.

Morris, R., and Binstock, R. H. *Feasible Planning for Social Change.* New York: Columbia University Press, 1966.

Mulford, R. "Emotional Neglect of Children." *Child Welfare,* 1958, *37,* 19–24.

Munson, C. E. *An Introduction to Clinical Social Work Supervision.* New York: Haworth Press, 1983.

Murstein, B. L. (ed.). *Handbook of Projective Techniques.* New York: Basic Books, 1965.

Nagi, S. Z. *Child Maltreatment in the United States: A Challenge to Social Institutions.* New York: Columbia University Press, 1977.

National Center on Child Abuse and Neglect. *Interdisciplinary Glossary on Child Abuse and Neglect.* Washington, D.C.: U.S. Department of Education, 1978.

Neill, A. S. *Summerhill.* New York: Hart, 1960.

Neuber, K. A., and Associates. *Needs Assessment: A Model for Community Planning.* Beverly Hills, Calif.: Sage, 1980.

Nichols, M. *Family Therapy: Concepts and Methods.* New York: Gardner Press, 1984.

Nicholson, M., and Schneider, C. *The Family Center.* Grant No. 90-C-73. Washington, D.C.: U.S. Department of Education, 1978.

Ohlsen, M. *Group Counseling.* (2nd ed.) New York: Holt, Rinehart & Winston, 1977.

Olds, D. L., Henderson, C. R., Chamberlin, R., and Tatelbaum, R. "The Prevention of Child Abuse and Neglect: A Randomized

Trial of Nurse Home Visitation." Unpublished manuscript, 1984.

O'Leary, K. D., and Wilson, G. T. *Behavior Therapy: Application and Outcome.* Englewood Cliffs, N.J.: Prentice-Hall, 1975.

Olson, D. H., Portner, J., and Bell, R. *Family Adaptability and Cohesion Scales (FACES II).* St. Paul: University of Minnesota, 1982.

Olson, D. H., Russell, C. S., and Sprenkle, D. H. "Circumplex Model of Marital and Family Systems. VI: Theoretical Update." *Family Process,* 1983, *22,* 69–83.

Olson, D. H., Sprenkle, D. H., and Russell, C. S. "Circumplex Model of Marital and Family Systems. I: Cohesion and Adaptability Dimensions, Family Types, and Clinical Applications." *Family Process,* 1979, *18,* 3–28.

Osborne, Y. "A Retrospective Study of Self-Identified Victims of Psychological Child Abuse." Unpublished manuscript, Louisiana State University, Baton Rouge, 1985.

Oswin, M. "The Neglect of Children in Long-Stay Hospitals." *Child Abuse and Neglect,* 1979, *3* (1), 89–92.

Patterson, G. R., and Thompson, M. G. G. "Emotional Child Abuse and Neglect: An Exercise in Definition." In R. Volpe, M. Breton, and J. Mitton (eds.), *The Maltreatment of the School-Aged Child.* Lexington, Mass.: Heath, 1980.

Patton, M. Q. *Qualitative Evaluation Methods.* Beverly Hills, Calif.: Sage, 1980.

Paulson, J. S. "Covert and Overt Forms of Maltreatment in the Preschools." *Child Abuse and Neglect,* 1983, 7 (1), 45–54.

Paulus, P., Cox, V., McCain, G., and Chandler, J. "Some Effects of Crowding in a Prison Environment." *Journal of Applied Social Psychology,* 1975, *5* (1), 86–91.

Payne, C. (ed.). *Programs to Strengthen Families: A Resource Guide.* Chicago: Family Resource Coalition, 1984.

Perlman, R., and Gurin, A. *Community Organization and Social Planning.* New York: Wiley and Council on Social Work Education, 1972.

Polansky, N. A., Borgman, R. D., and De Saix, C. *Roots of Futility.* San Francisco: Jossey-Bass, 1972.

Polansky, N., Chalmers, M., Buttenweiser, E., and Williams, D. "The Isolation of the Neglectful Family." *American Journal of Orthopsychiatry*, 1979, *49*, 149-152.

Polansky, N., Chalmers, M., Buttenweiser, E., and Williams, D. *Damaged Parents*. Chicago: University of Chicago Press, 1981.

Polansky, N. A., De Saix, C., and Sharlin, S. *Child Neglect: Understanding and Reaching the Parent*. New York: Child Welfare League of America, 1972.

Polansky, N., and Gaudin, J. *Treatment of Families Exhibiting Violence Toward Children*. Bethlehem, Pa.: Center for Social Research, Lehigh University, 1976.

Polansky, N., and Gaudin, J. "Preventing Child Abuse Through Public Awareness Activities." Working Paper no. 019. Chicago: National Committee for Prevention of Child Abuse, 1983.

Polansky, N. A., and Pollane, L. "Measuring Adequacy of Child Caring: Further Developments." *Child Welfare*, 1975, *54*, 354-359.

Potok, C. *The Chosen*. Greenwich, Conn.: Fawcett, 1967.

Powell, G. F., Brasel, J. A., and Blizzard, R. M. "Emotional Deprivation and Growth Retardation Simulating Idiopathic Hypopituitarism." *New England Journal of Medicine*, 1967, *276* (23), 1271-1278.

Price, G. "Factors Influencing Reciprocity in Early Mother-Infant Interaction." Paper presented at biennial meeting of the Society for Research in Child Development, New Orleans, March 1977.

Provence, S. A., and Lipton, R. C. *Infants in Institutions: A Comparison of Their Development with Family-Reared Infants During the First Year of Life*. New York: International Universities Press, 1962.

Rabb, J., and Rindfleisch, N. "A Study to Define and Assess Severity of Institutional Abuse/Neglect." *Child Abuse and Neglect*, 1985, *9* (2), 285-294.

Rabin, A. L. (ed.). *Projective Techniques in Personality Assessment: A Modern Introduction*. New York: Springer, 1968.

Reid, J. B., Patterson, G. R., and Loeber, R. "The Abused Child: Victim, Instigator, or Innocent Bystander?" In D. J. Bernstein (ed.), *Response Structure and Organization*. Lincoln: University of Nebraska Press, 1982.

Reppuci, N. D., and Sanders, J. T. "History, Action and Change." *American Journal of Community Psychology,* 1977, *5,* 399–412.

Rindfleisch, N. "Identification, Management and Prevention of Child Abuse in Residential Facilities." Unpublished manuscript, College of Social Work, Ohio State University.

Rindfleisch, N., and Rabb, J. "How Much of a Problem Is Resident Mistreatment in Child Welfare Institutions?" *Child Abuse and Neglect,* 1984, *8* (1), 33–40.

Rohner, R. *They Love Me, They Love Me Not.* New Haven, Conn.: Human Relations Area Files Press, 1975.

Rohner, R. P. "Worldwide Tests of Parental Acceptance-Rejection Theory: An Overview." *Behavior Science Research,* 1980, *15,* 1–21.

Rohner, R. P., and Rohner, E. C. "Antecedents and Consequences of Parental Rejection: A Theory of Emotional Abuse." *Child Abuse and Neglect,* 1980, *1* (3), 189–198.

Rohner, R. P., Saavedra, J. M., and Granum, E. O. *Development and Validation of the Personality Assessment Questionnaire: Test Manual.* Ann Arbor, Mich.: ERIC Clearinghouse on Counseling and Personnel Services, 1978.

Rossi, P. H., and Freeman, H. E. *Evaluation: A Systematic Approach.* (2nd ed.) Beverly Hills, Calif.: Sage, 1982.

Rothman, J. "Three Models of Community Organization Practice." In F. M. Cox, J. L. Erlich, J. Rothman, and J. E. Tropman (eds.), *Strategies of Community Organization: A Book of Readings.* (3rd ed.) Itasca, Ill.: Peacock, 1979.

Russ, M. G. *Community Organization: Theory, Principles, and Action.* (2nd ed.) New York: Harper & Row, 1967.

Rutter, M. "Parent-Child Separation: Psychological Effects on the Children." *Journal of Child Psychology and Psychiatry,* 1971, *12,* 233–260.

Sager, C. J. "Couples Therapy and Marriage Contracts." In A. S. Gurman and D. P. Kniskern (eds.), *Handbook of Family Therapy.* New York: Brunner/Mazel, 1981.

Sagi, A., and others. "Security of Infant-Mother, -Father, and -Metapelet Attachments Among Kibbutz-Reared Israeli Children." In I. Bretherton and E. Waters (eds.), *Growing Points in*

268

References

Attachment Theory and Research. Chicago: Society for Research in Child Development, 1984.

Sanders, R., and Welsh, R. "The 'Bug in the Ear.'" Paper presented at annual meeting of the Western Psychological Association, Denver, 1965.

Santostefano, S. G. *A Biodevelopmental Approach to Clinical Child Psychology, Cognitive Controls, and Cognitive Control Therapy.* New York: Wiley, 1978.

Satir, V. *Conjoint Family Therapy.* Palo Alto, Calif.: Science and Behavior Books, 1967.

Savells, J. "Child Abuse in Residential Institutions and Community Programs for Intervention and Prevention." *Child Abuse and Neglect,* 1983, *7* (4), 473-475.

Schaefer, E. S. "Children's Reports of Parental Behavior: An Inventory." *Child Development,* 1965a, *36* (2), 413-424.

Schaefer, E. S. "A Configurational Analysis of Children's Reports of Parent Behavior." *Journal of Consulting Psychology,* 1965b, *29* (6), 552-557.

Scheinfeld, D. "A Research Proposal to Study the Social and Cultural Determinants of the Feelings of Anger and Hostility Experienced Toward Patients by the Staff of Child and Adolescent Psychiatric Wards." Unpublished manuscript, Erikson Institute, Chicago, 1985.

Schmitt, B. "The Prevention of Child Abuse and Neglect: A Review of the Literature with Recommendations for Application." *Child Abuse and Neglect,* 1980, *4,* 171-177.

Schneider, C. J. "The Michigan Screening Profile of Parenting." In R. H. Starr (ed.), *Child Abuse Prediction: Policy Implications.* Cambridge, Mass.: Ballinger, 1982.

Schwartz, J. C., and Zuroff, D. C. "Family Structure and Depression in Female College Students: Effects of Parental Conflict, Decision Making Power, and Inconsistency of Love." *Journal of Abnormal Psychology,* 1979, *88,* 398-406.

Seligman, M. E. P. *Helplessness: On Depression, Development, and Death.* New York: W. H. Freeman, 1975.

Seligman, M. E. P., Maier, S. F., and Solomon, R. L. "Unpredictable and Uncontrollable Aversive Events." In F. R. Brush (ed.),

Aversive Conditioning and Learning. Orlando, Fla.: Academic Press, 1971.

Shaughnessy, M. F. "Institutional Child Abuse." *Children and Youth Services Review,* 1984, *6* (4), 311–318.

Siegelman, M. "Evaluation of Bronfenbrenner's Questionnaire for Children Concerning Parental Behavior." *Child Development,* 1965, *36* (1), 164–174.

Simpson, R. L. "Behavior Modification and Child Management." In M. J. Fine (ed.), *Handbook on Parent Education.* Orlando, Fla.: Academic Press, 1980.

Solomons, G., Abel, C. M., and Apley, S. "A Community Development Approach to the Prevention of Institutional and Societal Maltreatment." *Child Abuse and Neglect,* 1981, *5* (2), 135–140.

Soumenkoff, G., and others. "A Coordinated Attempt for Prevention of Child Abuse at the Antenatal Case Level." *Child Abuse and Neglect,* 1982, *6* (1), 87–94.

Spielberger, C. D. "Trait-State Anxiety and Motor Behavior." *Journal of Motor Behavior,* 1971, *3,* 265–279.

Spielberger, C. D., Gorsuch, R. L., and Lushene, R. E. *The State-Trait Anxiety Inventory.* Palo Alto, Calif.: Consulting Psychologists Press, 1970.

Spitz, R. A. "Hospitalism: An Inquiry into the Genesis of Psychiatric Conditions in Early Childhood." *Psychoanalytic Study of the Child,* 1945, *1,* 53–74.

Spitz, R. A. "Hospitalism: A Follow-Up Report." *Psychoanalytic Study of the Child,* 1946, *2,* 113–117.

Spitz, R. A., and Cobliner, W. G. *The First Year of Life: A Psychoanalytic Study of Normal and Deviant Development of Object Relations.* New York: International Universities Press, 1965.

Spitzer, R. L., Endicott, J., Fleiss, J. L., and Cohen, J. "The Psychiatric Status Schedule." *Archives of General Psychology,* 1970, *23,* 41–55.

Sroufe, L. A. "Infant-Caregiver Attachment and Patterns of Adaptation in Preschool: The Roots of Maladaptation and Competence." In M. Perlmutter (ed.), *Development and Policy Concerning Children with Special Needs.* Minnesota Symposia on Child Psychology. Vol. 16. Hillsdale, N.J.: Erlbaum, 1983.

Starr, R. H. "A Research-Based Approach to the Prediction of Child Abuse." In R. H. Starr (ed.), *Child Abuse Prediction: Policy Implications.* Cambridge, Mass.: Ballinger, 1982.

Steele, B. F. "Parental Abuse of Infants and Small Children." In E. J. Anthony and T. Benedeck (eds.), *Parenthood: Its Psychology and Psychopathology.* Boston: Little, Brown, 1970.

Steele, B., and Pollack, C. B. "A Psychiatric Study of Parents Who Abuse Infants and Small Children." In R. E. Helfer and C. H. Kempe (eds.), *The Battered Child.* (2nd ed.) Chicago: University of Chicago Press, 1968.

Stocking, S., and Arezzo, D. *Helping Friendless Children: A Guide for Teachers and Parents.* Boys Town, Neb.: Boys Town Center for the Study of Youth Development, 1979.

Sugar, M. (ed.). *Adolescent Parenthood.* Jamaica, N.Y.: SP Medical and Scientific Books, 1984.

Suransky, V. *The Erosion of Childhood.* Chicago: University of Chicago Press, 1982.

Sweet, J. J., and Resick, R. A. "The Maltreatment of Children: A Review of Theories and Research." *Journal of Social Issues,* 1979, *35,* 40–59.

Thomas, G. "The Responsibility of Residential Placements for Children's Rights to Development." *Child and Youth Services,* 1982, *4* (1–2), 23–45.

Thursz, D. "Social Action as a Professional Responsibility." *Social Work,* 1966, *11* (3), 12–21.

Trankina, F. J. "Clinical Issues and Techniques in Working with Hispanic Children and Their Families." In G. J. Powell (ed.), *The Psychosocial Development of Minority Group Children.* New York: Brunner/Mazel, 1983.

Tulkin, S., and Covitz, F. "Mother-Infant Interactions and Intellectual Functioning at Age Six." Paper presented at biennial meeting of the Society for Research in Child Development, Denver, April 1975.

Turner, J. H. *The Structure of Sociological Theory.* (3rd ed.) Homewood, Ill.: Dorsey Press, 1982.

United Way of America. *Needs Assessment: The State of the Art.* Alexandria, Va.: United Way of America, 1982.

Wachs, T. "Utilization of a Piagetian Approach in the Investigation of Early Experience Effects: A Research Strategy and Some Illustrative Data." *Merrill-Palmer Quarterly,* 1976, *22,* 11–30.

Walker, L. "Intervention by Criminal Justice Agencies: Spouse Abuse." Paper prepared for "Working Meeting on Family Violence as a Criminal Justice Problem," National Institute of Justice, Washington, D.C., Oct. 25–27, 1984.

Wallerstein, J. S., and Kelly, J. B. "The Effects of Parental Divorce: Experiences of the Preschool Child." *Journal of the American Academy of Child Psychiatry,* 1975, *14,* 600–616.

Wandesman, A. "Getting Together and Getting Things Done." *Psychology Today,* 1985, *19* (11), 64–71.

Warren, R. L. *Truth, Love, and Social Change.* Skokie, Ill.: Rand McNally, 1971.

Warren, R. L. *The Community in America.* (3rd ed.) Skokie, Ill.: Rand McNally, 1978.

Watkins, H. D., and Bradbard, M. R. "Child Maltreatment: An Overview with Suggestions for Intervention and Research." *Family Relations,* 1982, *31,* 323–333.

Weissbourd, B. "History of the Family Support Movement." In S. Kagan and others (eds.), *Family Support.* New Haven, Conn.: Yale University Press, forthcoming.

Wells, S. J. *How to Make Decisions in Child Protective Services Intake and Investigation.* Chicago: American Bar Association, 1985.

Welsh, R. "A Highly Efficient Method of Parental Counseling: A Mechanical Third Ear." Unpublished paper, Rocky Mountain Psychological Association, Denver, 1966.

West, D. J. *Present Conduct and Future Delinquency.* First Report of the Cambridge Study in Delinquent Development. New York: International Universities Press, 1969.

West, D. J. *Who Becomes Delinquent?* Second Report of the Cambridge Study in Delinquent Development. London: Heinemann Educational Books, 1973.

Whiting, L. "Defining Emotional Neglect." *Children Today,* 1976, *5,* 2–5.

Whittaker, J. K. *Social Treatment: An Approach to Interpersonal Helping.* Hawthorne, N.Y.: Aldine, 1974.

Whittaker, J. K. "Social Support Networks in Child Welfare." In J. K. Whittaker, J. Garbarino, and Associates, *Social Support Networks in Formal Helping in the Human Services*. Hawthorne, N.Y.: Aldine, 1983.

Whittaker, J. K. "The Role of Residential Institutions." In J. Garbarino, P. Brookhauser, and K. Authies (eds.), *Special Children, Special Needs: Protecting Handicapped Children from Abuse and Neglect*. Hawthorne, N.Y.: Aldine, forthcoming.

Whittaker, J. K., Garbarino, J., and Associates. *Social Support Networks in the Human Services*. Hawthorne, N.Y.: Aldine, 1983.

Wohlwill, J. F., and Van Vliet, W. (eds.). *Habitats for Children*. Hillsdale, N.J.: Erlbaum, 1986.

Wood, P. E. "Residential Treatment for Families of Maltreated Children." *Child Welfare*, 1981, *60* (2), 105–108.

Wooden, K. *Weeping in the Playtime of Others: America's Incarcerated Children*. New York: McGraw-Hill, 1976.

Young, L. *Wednesday's Children: A Study of Child Neglect and Abuse*. New York: McGraw-Hill, 1964.

Ziefert, M., and Faller, K. "The Interdisciplinary Team and the Community." In K. Faller (ed.), *Social Work with Abused and Neglected Children*. New York: Free Press, 1981.

Zuckerman, E. *Child Welfare*. New York: Free Press, 1983.

Name Index

Subject Index